Also by Stephen Longstreet

THE BOY
IN
THE MODEL-T

A JOURNEY IN THE JUST GONE PAST

BY *Stephen Longstreet*

WITH LINE DRAWINGS BY THE AUTHOR

SIMON AND SCHUSTER · NEW YORK · 1956

LIBRARY OF CONGRESS CATALOG CARD NUMBER: 56-6665
MANUFACTURED IN THE UNITED STATES OF AMERICA
BY KINGSPORT PRESS, INC., KINGSPORT, TENN.

To a good friend
and the best of editors
HENRY SIMON

"That is the land of lost content,
I see it shining plain.
The happy highways where I went
And cannot come again. . . ."
              —A. E. HOUSMAN
        (From Gramp's notebooks)

CONTENTS

THE BOY IN THE MODEL-T

GRAMP WHEN I KNEW HIM

We all once had a girl and her name is Nostalgia.
  —ERNEST HEMINGWAY

A WORD BEFORE

I HAVE NEVER CHANGED MY IDEA THAT MY MOTHER AND my grandfather, when I knew them, were two of the greatest living Americans. They spawned no atomic discoveries or new revelations, but danced well and knew they would not live forever. Their lives had never fitted into the expected American success story, and I have often wondered what they would have thought of a play I wrote about them called *High Button Shoes.* It ran almost three years on Broadway when music and dancing were added to it. Road companies and summer productions of the play still wander around the nation, and there are versions of it in England, Sweden and other parts of the world. I never saw *High Button Shoes* on Broadway. I had little faith in the play the night it opened and was on my way back to California, to write a motion picture: *The Jolson Story.* Perhaps the true reason I didn't stay for the cheering and the press notices was the fact that Gramp was lost in the Philadelphia tryouts of the play. No actor vital enough could be found to play the part the way I had written it, and so George Abbott, the director (always a quick man to cut and stitch), removed the part of Gramp and gave his lines to a balding comic from burlesque, who suddenly, to his own surprise, had the biggest part in the show. Mamma remained in the play and a vile little boy called Stevie, and my father and my aunt. But without Gramp it didn't seem like the family.

I had no intention of writing more of the family, but my good friend Earle MacAusland, publisher and editor of *Gourmet* magazine, who had published some personal family history by me before, asked for new texts.

It was an aunt—owner of an old trunk—who found an aged sketchbook of mine dated 1919, Gramp's notebooks, and a chocolate box (Sherry's Hard Centers) full of Mamma's letters; all helped bring back to me one of the most fascinating events of my life, a trip Gramp and Mamma and I took in 1919 and 1920, crossing and recrossing the United States by car in the early tin age of the automobile, before the de luxe service station, the super highways and freeways were even dreamed of. Gasoline was still pumped by hand (when you could get it) and road maps were a mockery of the truth: closer to the globes of the Middle Ages with their sea monsters and mermaids than the actual facts of life. The motel, the balloon tire, the V-8 engine, air conditioning, electric iceboxes, wax paper, radio, TV, practical windshield wipers, nylon, cellophane, puncture-proof tires, rest rooms with flush plumbing, and traffic-control lights were either not yet invented or not in popular use. We didn't miss any of all this; we just did the best with what we had. Gossip columns, talking motion pictures, Superman, World War II, tape recording, and jet planes were also undreamed of.

I have invented nothing in this book, and if I have looked more often on the bright side than on the dark patches of mood and weather we often ran into, remember I was only twelve years old then, and even with the kind of total recalling that some writers are cursed with, a child would mostly remember the images and voices that pleased, amused, or entertained him. My recall does have holes in it you could throw a Model-T Ford through, but I have jumped over these lapses without trying to fill in details. I have used Mamma's letters and Gramp's notebooks (which never really got beyond listing foods and road details and cursing out nature, cheap whisky, and dishonest natives). But Gramp has helped to get onto paper some details that then didn't impress me. My own sketchbook, drawn and written in a callow lead pencil, is a dismal pound or two of once damp sheets, holding nothing that posterity would care to see again. The drawings I made on the trip, drawn in a faulty and dim pencil line, are, if I had continued in that direction, something that would have labèled me by now as Grandpa Moses. The text and the drawings are a re-creation from memory of a past I once inhabited. The character called Stevie is perhaps someone I once was but can no longer fully understand or know.

I've tried to present Mamma and Gramp as they were, with all their virtues, naturally, but I have glossed over none of their offbeat facets of character that make them what they were, and not somebody else. I may have toned down Gramp's language; for as a man who fought the Civil War with Grant in the Wilderness, and knew Mark Twain, he could produce profanity in a way to delight any artist of words and sound. Both Mamma and Gramp have passed from this earth. Both of them believed with Henry James that this was the only world we are sure to have, and if we don't make our life what we want it to be in this world, in what world are we sure of living? I was too young, of course, to know very much about their ideas of immortality, godheads, history, the future of mankind, and the hope of salvation. I can report some of their ideas on the human race, society, food, morality, codes of ethics, the proper way to ice wine, wear diamonds, cure a hang-over, and their respect of humanity for its efforts rather than its crusades. They were, as we all are, weighted down by the dreadful burden of time, but they preferred to float pleasantly on tradition if they could. They knew mankind at its worst and liked most of it for its liveliness, humor and courage in trying to face logic and truth on such a short journey. There was a serious side to them that I am sure I never fully got to know—their laments, sorrows, their struggle to survive as they were and wanted to be rather than conform.

Mamma and Gramp never conformed much. What passed for success in those days never interested them. Gramp used to say, out of his vast knowledge and reading, "A proper man is one who has built a house, planted a tree and begotten a child." And Mamma would say, "Little pitchers," and point at me. But of course I was used to Gramp by then, and wonder now why it took me years to understand what he meant by saying, "One tries hard to be a philosopher but cheerfulness keeps breaking in." He was not always a cheerful man, but the glum moments of his life didn't last long. He was packed as full of curiosity as an egg and never stopped to brush up his dignity unless he wanted to impress people, which he did at times, being human and given to looking down at half-wits and popular minds and too much respectability.

Mamma had a loyalty to Gramp and the family that wasn't always earned; to her our geese were *always* swans, I fear. Her letters showed great talent, and her ear for dialogue was perfect, and I have used much of her words here, often without giving her full credit. She would, in her rage, stamp her tiny foot (well shod) and shout, "Devil take them all but me." But she trusted people more than Gramp did, for she hadn't lived as long. Gramp had a cynic's eye, a stoic mouth (always holding up a good cigar); he viewed the world ironically, suspecting, I was sure, that even in heaven there must be a hell. Heaven was to him like his friend Mark Twain's idea of classical music: better than it sounded.

He lived in an era when men were wittier, took more time to create their leisure, and the world wasn't in such a hurry to make history. He and Mamma must be seen in the picture frame in which they lived, and not in the too-swift focus of our own baffling race beyond the sound barrier. Neither can they be evaluated as the average citizens of their world. They baffled their own family as much as they worried some of the people they met on this trip. For they lacked a real interest in popular success. Gramp would growl and say, "Damn it, to bother about popular success is like asking a man just hung if he has a headache."

I cannot talk here in great detail of the subtleties, shades of evaluations, absolute truths, the complexities of things in their lives. I was young and fairly innocent, and I accepted Gramp's judgment: "The world is going to hell in a hack." I still feel it is and that it always will, and that the ride is often more interesting than the bumps.

It may seem that the people we met on the trip are often very odd and amusing. They certainly are not the accepted characters of normal travel books. I think one reason for this is that one remembers best the people who excite or interest one. It was a livelier, freer world in those days. I have seen many simple freedoms pass. I have watched fears enter our national and personal lives. Today we no longer stand where I stood as a boy; the weather in our streets is wilder and the sun shines as brightly but gives no heat; men who have given away some of their freedom don't as often any more stand on their own hind legs and howl in pleasure. Here I have written of other, and perhaps more colored, times. I have tried to find no message, no symbol. Like Gramp, a book of this sort should stand at an angle to the ideas of society and not want to defend its position.

I agree fully with V. S. Pritchett: "The meaning of life? One day that will be revealed to us—probably on a Thursday."

STEPHEN LONGSTREET

Elm Drive
California

WHEN I WAS VERY YOUNG

PICTURE OF THE FAMILY

SPIRALING BACKWARD INTO TIME THE BOY I ONCE WAS comes with a bump to a certain part of my life when I was thickly inbedded in family. And buried there were adventures as real as the beautiful bones of prehistoric monsters that men dig up—a few years when I was very close to my grandfather and when he and my mother and I went on a wonderful journey.

My mother and father were living in New Brunswick, New Jersey, a town that had big ideas and less hope of fulfilling them than any town or city I was to see as a child. My father was like the town, but my mother was to me then a seething vital force, like those acids I played with in the barn, pent up in a glass tube that I mixed and stirred, looking for one item that would blow the mixture up. My mother never found that exploding agent, but I did go head over heels, backward, out of the barn one day —to have glass fragments picked out of my hair for two days.

The town of New Brunswick—and I can see its bright streets in my memory as I write—like most American towns, had many strange examples of architecture, but I doubt that there was anything like my father's house: the house of the small bourgeois, the family home diffused in the glare of much sun.

It stood on a rise—a rise that I have heard had once been a windy farm hill and a grove of elm and poplar trees—but now it was a street and the clanging trolley cars bounced past the door every twenty minutes; and from Polack Point the soot of factories and the whistle of the mills were always in the air. But it was an odd little house, surrounded on all sides by shoddily built rows of clapboard real-estate bargains with their unwholesomely fading façades.

My father had bought the house because he liked the garden and the old tired peach and apple orchard and the great oaks winging over the small, yellow house. My father was like that: a fool over nature—and my mother would tell him so very often with her usual irreverence. Too often.

It was a solid little house, the foundation built of great field-stones and the two top stories of reclaimed brick covered with yellow clapboards. There was a low attic smelling of mice and plaster, and three chimneys of old rose, weather-aged brick— most of which had been cemented up, for open fireplaces used too much wood and coal and gave no heat.

My father told everyone it had once been an old colonial farmhouse—I believed him for years. But my mother would snort, "Nonsense!" with a deprecating gesture and then expand on the word. Then my father would go up to the attic where he did his cabinetmaking and stay there until my mother had talked herself out. Once he stayed up there three days, but that was during a crisis when my mother was at the peak of one of her explosive tumults.

My father came of a long line of outdoor people who theoretically despised wealth. Cattle dealers and lumbermen and farmers. His father had gone into railroads and broken the spell. My father hated cities as all men must hate the city that has taken them in when their fields have failed and given them a corner to lie in and bread in return for freedom.

He had led a wonderful youth. He had been a timber merchant—cutting trees of the forests and trimming away the branches. He was a good storyteller, and his version of great dank woods with dead leaves piled into heaps by the centuries and left there (so that he could be the first human being to wipe his feet on them) were very good. He told me many tales of wolves under ink-and-silver skies—and always the trees.

Then he had traded horses and cows and always he had hoped to buy, someday, a wooded corner of land with just enough soil to plant some rows of corn and vegetables, to keep alive and happy. He felt secure, armored, impregnable to the attack of the cities. But a log jam caught him and broke his leg and he limped slightly from then on.

My father was not a tall man. He was short, and made to appear shorter because of his heavy legs and his huge, muscled arms. He was handsome, with crisp brown curling hair worn over one eye in a fringe, and even his great hinge of a nose could not spoil his looks. Small teeth in a small mouth added to his attraction. And as a child I remembered his sensual explosion of laughter. When I was old enough to understand him the best part of him was gone.

My mother had had an interesting life before she married my father, but I have never been able to check the facts. She had been—I often heard—the wild tomboy daughter of a very respectable family who had been sent away from home at sixteen, having been discovered wildly in love with someone her family could never approve of. She had then become the governess to a Baltimore family, and during the Spanish-American War one of the sons, a hero in full uniform, had tried to climb her balcony, to kiss her good night, and had fallen off the trellis and broken his leg. She went on to New York, where she tried earning a living working in shops, but gave it up as not very exciting. She became a model, posing for, among other things, certain heads of the Gibson period; but most of her work did not ever become that famous. Some very fine large photographs of her in costume existed when I was a boy. They were then already turning yellow and were covered with fine cotton nets to keep off the flies at one of the farms my father was working at the time.

Mamma was one of the beauties of her time, but as she grew older she began to fear a lonely life. She was several years older than my father (we never did find out her birthday or her age), and she had him helpless and defenseless in a matter of a few days. She frightened my father by her drive and boldness, and a ,week before the wedding (Gramp being out of the country), he called on her and said he had decided to call off the marriage. She cried on his shoulder, and several of her friends took my father aside and told him the wedding invitations had already been printed and that it would be a waste of money. They gave my father a few drinks, and so they were married as called for on the printed date.

The couple went away to New York City for a honeymoon. My father hated the grinding horsecars and the thunder of elevated trains and the rush of people all going to foul places in a hurry. He sat sullen in sodden apathy in his hotel room.

He thought of the earth seeded and ready for spring and the bursting green earth seasons. . . .

But if my father didn't like New York, he liked New Brunswick less when he got back. The gabble of the streets made him shiver. The couple set up temporary quarters while my father went around looking for a farm. He wanted to take up the thick fabric of his desires.

The soil was calling him again, and now that he had a wife he wanted to feel the loam of fertile fields and measure the length of a tree with an ax. Half articulate, sweating with hope, he tried to make Mamma understand.

My father had saved enough to buy a good farm and with

his strong shoulders and sturdy body he dreamed of filled barns and cackling chickens and a writhing grape arbor over the back door. He never lost this vision—even later when he was head over heels in debt and was pointed out as one of the biggest holders of second-rate real estate in town (when there wasn't enough bread on the table, he could walk into any of the banks and get fifty- or sixty-thousand-dollar loans to buy more shaggy, rotting street-front property) he still talked of the farm. He consumed himself—eating his own meat in bitter futility in town.

He was a simple man who got simpler as he grew older. I felt it as a child. There was something solid and firm about him, something calm and even about his outlook on life—an out-, look he fumbled and faltered with. I never remember him saying a brilliant thing or gloating over the hopes of ever being wealthy in the sense of having real cash in the bank. His mind never worked in that way. He loved the land and I came to know the lost burial of his hopes on his face. He loved children, and at times he admired the wonder that was his wife's mind; but he knew what he wanted and had lost—a farm and fields and old trees and the scent of hay and the buzz of bees and the good earth like a night beast drinking in the rain.

He was surprised, just after the marriage, that Mamma had never protested his hunt for a farm. He would return at evening with bags of soil and samples of crops and eat his meal with noises that my mother could never cure him of. Then he would light his pipe and grunt it into burning clearly and he would look into the fire and say, "Saw some nice land today. . . ."

My father always started that way. I wasn't born then—but in later years I often heard that opening gun of a lost campaign. My mother would pucker up her small mouth and say, "Land—land. Can you eat it, cook it, put it into your mouth? A big grown man acting like a child with a bucket of dirt on the front steps!"

"Now, Sari, you know you can't eat land—but land can feed you."

"Fiddle-dee-dee."

"It's a good farm. . . ."

And then my mother would flood the room with her talk. Not directly protesting—just talking around the project, nibbling away any encouragement he may have gotten, driving his plans into a corner and taking them apart not by logic but a flood of words. She was very beautiful and my father grew to love her very much. And she—although I couldn't swear—at that time she, too, must have been in the first flush of the experience and must have felt a glow of pleasure in the sturdy handsome man with brown curly hair and small teeth and big nose. She was of turbulent blood, and the pulsing conduits of her body flushed her cheeks all her life.

The land hunt terminated one day when my mother said she was going to have a baby and *she* wasn't going to have it in the wilderness. Besides which, they were eating into their nest egg and my father had better get back to money-making before his wife and child starved to death and they had to get charity to support them. My mother was always very dramatic at such times. I have often witnessed her performances when my father wanted to break away and do something he had set his heart on. Her emotions were always nakedly projected and her words flowed with a steady pace.

"Go ahead—go ahead—walk in cow over your boot tops. But my children are going to get educated and are going to be somebody. Not a farmer—not a clumsy land dealer. Do what you want. I can take care of them. I'll scrub floors. I'll wash windows. Don't think I'll not. I've got no pride—not a thumbful. Let the town talk. I'll get a bucket and a brush and scrub floors for my children. I'm thin and frail but while there is still an ounce of strength in my feeble arms, they'll *not* want for anything. I don't mind scrubbing floors—*not* for my children!"

My father knew he was licked. When my mother's daydreams reached the floor-scrubbing stage he would light his pipe and pick up a walnut or oak dowel and rub it with sandpaper and say, "Now, Sari, don't chew so." He always called her talking "chewing the wind." "Don't chew. I was only thinking out loud."

"Well, I must say—a fine way to talk to a wife! *Chew*, do I?"

"Do what you want. I've got a highboy to finish."

And my mother would do what she wanted. That time she went out alone and roamed the streets and found the yellow house and made my father think he wanted it. It was old but well built—not that she ever knew anything about construction—and it was near the business section, on Prospect Street, and she wanted to be a mistress of a house and tie my father to the town, put his hopes into a state of spiritual refrigeration.

I was born in the great depression of 1907, in New York City. My mother, who had many amazing and amusing habits, did not believe in doctors at births, and so I was brought or aided into the world by a midwife. I was the second child, the first having died soon after birth, my mother always claimed by their loving it too much and knowing too little about raising it. Certainly at the age of a few weeks, I myself, while my mother was away and while my father was preparing the meal (he did most of the cooking as Mamma was a miserable though daring cook), was dropped face first on the surface of the hot coal stove. I bear no scar or memory of the event and have never feared fire.

When I was two weeks old my mother and father moved back to New Brunswick, New Jersey. My father did not protest too much. He never protested too much against anything life did to him. We moved into the house. He admired the old trees on the plot, the back stretch of garden and the old decaying peach and apple orchard. He sniffed at the outhouse, felt the old silvered wood of the tool and vegetable shed and let my mother lead him to Jake Fry's law office on French Street, where he turned over his cash for a title to the property. Naked insurrection did not rise in him. Painfully he scratched his name.

So the dream of land faded from my father's eyes—for a while, anyway. He moved his lathe and his saws and glue pot and shiny steel tools into half of the barn behind the house. He turned over the soil and tested it and nodded that it was good and planted it with tomatoes and corn and lettuce and turnips and potatoes. It wasn't much but it was something.

And when times got hard, we moved in with my grandfather in New York City till Papa got together his nerve to go back to our New Brunswick house to try again. We did this a dozen times while I was growing up. I still don't know how we managed to hold on to that house.

I was one of those children who got along fine with himself, and it was just as well. My mother wasn't very expert with children. My father loved children with a gripping love tenderly expressed by his brown eyes and his soft kind mouth.

I remember first the goodness of sunshine and the great pleasure of soil and grass and my bare feet in them, wet with dew, and a luxurious buttery gluttony for life. But it was all emotion and I don't carry over my images beyond the swaying of the great oak that I lay under as an infant, and the hiss of wind among its leaves and dimly, far away, the tingle of the trolley bell. And the fear, the black-and-indigo of summer storm sounds.

I was four when images came and stayed and etched themselves in my limp memory. I was pulling three little strawberry boxes tied together with string and I was howling like a train at a crossing. Already, like Gramp, I had a yeastily stirring yearning for distant places.

One day I was eight. . . .

It was a fine sunny day, the heated tar street in front of the house gave off scent and heat haze. My grandfather drove up in a buggy, the little paint pony digging his newly shod feet into the soft tar pavement, snorting inarticulate sounds through his big yellow teeth.

"Hello, Stevie," Gramp said, taking his pipe from his mouth and patting the flank of his pony. "Hot enough to fry a lawyer alive."

"Hello, Gramp," I said with awe and respect. For many years

I was to confuse Gramp with God. His white dramatic mustache, his loud voice, the icy-blue eyes, and great knotted brown hands were to me signs of force and power. He had all his own teeth—big and yellow like kernels of corn. He was beginning to bend a little with the years and he had taken to hiding his left hand, from which the small finger was missing. He had lost it in action at Cold Harbor—and the more he thought about the people he had saved the Union for, the less proud he was of his war wounds. His eyebrows, stiff and thick, surrounded his eyes like heraldic lions. I overheard relatives call him a lusty, whisky-drinking old lecher.

"Come for a ride, Stevie."

"Mom said stay in the yard."

"Come on, hop in and I'll buy you an ice-cream cone to hide your face up to the ears."

My grandfather opened the gate and I hurried across the brick walk, watching the paint-colored pony kick at flies with his little cruel hoofs.

Gramp lifted me up and I smelled good whisky and old tobacco and soap and clean linen. I sat on the buggy seat very frightened and very proud. I had never been that high over the street before. I was cantilevered over the cobblestones and felt anything but brave.

My mother came walking up the street on tiny heeled shoes, waving a small handkerchief in her pretty warm face.

"Where is the child going?"

"I'm taking him downtown."

My mother stopped and smiled. I can see her as she was then, as I really saw her for the first time and remembered her. Tiny, with red-gold hair worn in a wave and back to a bun, an abbreviated nose—very pert, very small—beautiful gray eyes and a darting glance and a rosebud mouth, her well-built body swaying, delicate wrists and ankles in motion.

"He hasn't been well. Delicate throat."

Gramp got into the buggy and took up the reins. "He'll live."

"Don't upset his stomach," Mamma said to the stonily im-
passive back. "It's very tender."

"Giddup!"

There never was anything the matter with my throat and
stomach. But it gave my mother an excuse to take me over to
Aunt Netta while she wandered over the town looking for bargains in corner lots, lumber or a scheme for a concert hall.

"Wait."

"What's up?" asked Gramp, relighting his pipe, pulling in the
waltzing paint pony.

My mother danced back on her small feet and waved her
arms over her head. Behind her the shade trees looked drowsy
in their green leaves.

"I'm buying that stand of oak near Western Brook. I'll have
it cut and stacked for drying and make a fortune in it. Oak is
scarce and boards are sky high."

"That oak is no good—full of rot and mildew. You're a damn
fool, Sari."

"Now, Father, I know lumber and I know cutting and this
stand should get me at least a hundred thousand feet of prime
board. . . ."

"Lucky if it cuts half that. Well, it's your money—or rather,
Henry's. Go on, Roger!"

Roger was the paint pony. Gramp flicked the shaggy back
with a flip of the whip and we went down the street swiftly,
Gramp looking at me from under a pale, decisive eyebrow.

I heard my mother talking. When we were halfway down the
street I turned and looked back. She was standing in the middle
of the street and shouting at us something about "a steam saw
and carload timber lots," that untrammeled expression still in
her face.

We turned a corner and the paint pony went along swiftly.

"You got yourself a mother. . . ." The big aquiline nose was
wrinkled in thought.

"Yes, Gramp."

"A hellcat for fair and a demon for money in the bargain."

"Is Roger a boy horse?"

"Huh? He's a gelding."

"Is that a boy or girl horse?"

"It doesn't make much difference as far as Roger is concerned."

"We going to the woods today, Gramp?"

My grandfather turned a blue eye on me, and with his mutilated hand pressed down the burning tobacco in his briar pipe. I could feel an inexplicable surge fill him with anger.

"Court today. Goddamn lawyers are feasting on my ribs and pulling the lean meat off my bones. Giddup, Roger!"

Roger felt the old man's anger and stopped playing and swaying and got down to pulling.

When I was twelve we moved in with Gramp in New York City again. This time I felt we would stay for good. We almost did.

The house of my grandfather, which to me was once more permanent than the Roman Empire, has long since been pulled down. It was a narrow, wedding-cake, Italian Renaissance building, supposed to have been designed by Stanford White during one of his more respectable periods. My grandfather had bought it cheap in a run-down condition from the heirs of a Chicago meat-packer who had built it for a lady to whom he was not married. The house stood on lower Fifth Avenue, near Washington Square, and my grandfather scraped the black paint off the brass handrails, got the white marble steps close to their original color, put in modern plumbing (modern for its period), and wired the place for electric lights. In the back were stables, a small patch of dog-worried garden, and a clothesline on which I tried to hang myself daily with the idea I was playing muscle-building games.

Mark Twain lived near Gramp's house; they were old friends from the West and they used to meet outside the house and light their stogies and go haunt the dark dignified bar of the

Lafayette. I was three years old when Mark Twain died, so I have no memory of him, but I do have a dim memory of Gramp's polishing his special formal top hat on his coat sleeve and sadly announcing, "Sam's dead. I've got to go help plant him." If I am wrong, that is if I only heard Gramp tell this, I must have created in my own mind the hat-polishing image from the many times Gramp told the story.

My mother told me that once when I was a baby in my pram, and Gramp was walking by the side of the nurse pushing me under the trees of Washington Square, Mark Twain met them, made some remarks on my appearance (now forgotten), and wheeled me himself for two blocks. It is a small thing, and perhaps the closest I shall ever come to greatness in writing.

The house on Fifth Avenue was the shelter of Gramp's six sons and their families. My father had failed again in the New Jersey wilds. We were living on the fourth floor of Gramp's house. It was a narrow four-story building, but deep, and over a dozen people lived in it from time to time. As one branch of the family prospered, there was always some branch limping badly and coming home to Fifth Avenue for food, shelter, and repair.

I liked Gramp's house; it smelled of furniture polish and good whisky, rotting wild-game heads, silver polish, lilac bath powder used by the daughters-in-law, the wool clothes and urine of the young fry in various states of being housebroken. And always the fine odors of good cooking coming up from the cellar kitchen.

Gramp had bought the old and good, but tired, name of a Wall Street firm that dealt in railroad bonds. Most of his sons worked for him from time to time. He trusted them in nothing; perhaps he was right. Gramp had been a railroad engineer and had built thousands of miles of railroad all over the world. He had made and lost several fortunes, or so the family legend said. He had had three wives and suffered, or so *he* claimed, in several prolonged and amazing love affairs.

And one day Gramp came home with an automobile. For

years I was ashamed to admit he had bought it secondhand. He was well off in those days, but he had a fetish about buying anything new. "Why pay for paint and polish? A good, well-broken-in thing is best. Shows it can stand the strain and has been worked into a comfortable object of use."

His great bearskin coat, black as coal, he had bought from a circus man stranded by the IOI Ranch Show. His canes he found in small dusty shops that had windows full of aging, sun-faded fiddles, field glasses, and collections of old lodge buttons on red velvet trays. His books, and he had a great many, were old sets of chipped leather which had already had many readers, and he added to their wear and tear. Balzac he devoured and he would read him aloud to me for hours. Dickens he damned for his plots but enjoyed for his talk. So when there was talk that the family could really use a motorcar and turn the stable into a garage, Gramp said neither no nor yes. And when we did get our first motorcar, it had been well used. That was why it was always in need of repair during the long trip we made in it. And that is why what is to follow may sound like the saga of a Stone Age repairman. When I first saw the car it shone with the splendor of what I supposed Roman high life must have glittered with; I was taking my ideas of the world in those days from Gramp's big set of Gibbon's *Decline and Fall*. Gramp used to shout I was an early reader "and a late riser!"

AT HOME

1.

*Genealogy is an account of one's
descent from an ancestor who
did not particularly care to trace
his own.*

—AMBROSE BIERCE
(From Gramp's notebooks)

THE GASOLINE CAR

IT WAS IN 1919 THAT GRAMP BOUGHT THE CAR. MR.
Woodrow Wilson had just ended wars forever, and Gramp came
home to lower Fifth Avenue one spring day and banged his cane
against the bronze Chinese gong in the hallway. "I've done it. I
bought a motorcar!"

"They explode," said Mamma, coming down the teak staircase in her best hat, me at her tiny heels.

"Just had my first lesson. Destroyed a tree and part of a
garden wall, but I tell you this is the age of speed. Did twenty-
two miles an hour."

Uncle Willie was living with us then; he was between colleges.
"Why don't you get a Stutz Bearcat; they're really something."

Gramp scowled. "Nobody is going to get me to lay down on
my back to drive a car." The Bearcat was a low car.

Mamma asked, "Did it cost much?"

Gramp grinned and beat me playfully on the rear with the flat of his gold cigar case. "I've sold the horses, sold the carriage. We travel in style from now on."

"Not I," said Mamma, who was watching her grammar that day.

Gramp winked at me. "I'm going to California by car, Stevie. I'm taking you; room for one more and the baggage. You always wanted to visit relatives in St. Louie, Sari."

Mamma perked up and smiled her best smile. "Can't we go by train?"

Uncle Willie said, "As well go by covered wagon! It's a new age, Sari, a new world."

"Didn't we just whip the damn Germans, save the French and English, bury the Czar? It's the twentieth century, gal," Gramp said.

I said, "One nine, one nine, nineteen-nineteen."

Mamma gave in with grace; she had a new fur coat—a gift from Gramp—and she wanted to test it on the eyes of the relatives in St. Louie (we never said St. Louis—always St. Louie). She said, "It sounds reasonable."

The next morning there was the sound of braying in front of the house and I ran out onto Fifth Avenue, buttoning as I went, and there in front of the white marble stepping stone labeled LONGSTREET was a shiny, square motorcar. It was black and solid looking and stood like a barn. Behind the wheel sat a man wrapped in a brown linen duster, with a cap on backward, and huge goggles strapped across a big nose. A cigar smoldered and spat fire, and the figure pumped the hand horn, and the mooing sound came out of iron lips and filled the street. The Ford car of the period was a product to dazzle the eye and numb the mind of a twelve-year-old boy. (It also did things to the rear of man-and-boy anatomy, I found out.)

Gramp (the driver was Gramp in his motoring costume) shouted, "How does it look, Stevie? How does it sound?"

"Nice and loud, Gramp," I said with respect.

"Jump in and we'll try the neighborhood fences."

I climbed in, and cars were high in those days. ("On a clear day, Stevie, you can see Sandy Hook from up here.") I sat down by Gramp's side and he let down the brake, did something with a gas lever (no foot feed in those cars), did a short tap dance on some piano levers set on the car boards, and the car shook, gasped and moaned, and began to smoke. Then we moved, moved quickly, eating up the street at fifteen miles an hour, twenty, and when we hit Mr. Montgomery's Sanitary Fresh Mountain Ice wagon we were doing thirty, but the brakes gripped at last. (It cost us ten dollars for the ice, and five dollars to repaint the car's fender.)

Gramp limped a little at dinner that night, and I had a black eye where I had hit the dashboard, but no one noticed it because Gramp was in a growling mood. The sons and the daughters-in-law and the small fry not too damp to eat in the children's room all sat and waited for Gramp to thank God for the roast beef, the clear soup, the baked whitefish, the stewed meatballs in sweet-and-sour sauce, the watercress salad and the spiced peaches, the apple pie as big as a wagon wheel, and the heavy cups of very black coffee. It was an ordinary meal for a family at home *without* company. Real eating called for the Spode china, the handmade silver service, the soup tureen of rare Ming, filet mignon Clemenceau, oysters, and Crêpes Suzette Longstreet (Gramp's way of burning sugar in the sauce). Gramp called it "living high off the hog."

Gramp looked up and rubbed his hurt leg. "I'm leaving for California in two weeks. On the way I'm inspecting my copper holdings in Butte. I'm taking Sari and Stevie. No one is to do any business until I get back, and, Henry, get me a thousand dollars in ten-dollar bills from the firm for the trip."

Papa sighed. "Now, Father, you know things are bad, a postwar depression."

"Get it, Henry," said Gramp. "And, Willie, I want six bottles of good brandy."

"Papa, you know America has given up drinking. It's against the law."

"That's right," I said, for I inspected *The New York Times* every morning and wondered why they didn't run comic strips.

"Bootleggers. You wouldn't buy from them, Gramp," Mamma said.

"Wouldn't I?" (Gramp became the first scofflaw in our family.)

The Ford behaved very well. It had to be wound up like a clock to start. Papa usually cranked her while Gramp shouted orders and gripped the steering wheel. Once started, Papa usually flew backward a few feet. The car started in jerks or leaps, like an eager rabbit. Gramp sat way over the wheel, wearing his driving cap backward. (He was an admirer of Barney Oldsfield, the great racing driver, and dressed like him.)

I was on the shakedown trip made around Central Park the night before we started across the plains of New Jersey. There were no traffic lights in those days, and the police all knew Gramp (and carried his gift cigars close to their hearts just over their long underwear). We found out that the car didn't like to steer left.

We didn't damage Central Park much, but we did change a spark plug. Gramp was to become an expert repairman. He carried wrenches, screw drivers, and pliers in his fountain-pen pockets, and the big pockets in the back of his pants were full of short lengths of wire, carter pins, steel nuts, and bits of wire. Repair services were not well organized at that time, so the driver had to know the secrets of his car.

Papa and Uncle Willie loaded the car that night, and we named her "Emma" after a departed cook who always got overheated when we had company and used to put her head in the icebox to cool off.

I had a feeling that both Gramp and Mamma, emotional freebooters, were escaping domestic confinement. Neither was very happy at home. I was, of course, unaware at the time we left on the trip just how desperate both of them were, and how, both being romantics, this escape by motorcar was really a hope for a fast clutching at life before it passed them by. I got clues to their dilemma as the trip progressed, and before it was over I was aware (as much as a boy can be aware) of the problems of an adult world.

Gramp used to grin and pull my ear. "Your mother has a string of troubles longer than a poor widow's clothesline."

Both Mamma and Gramp presented a veneer of hard-boiled joy to organized society, and both were educated to the knocks of the world and had early learned to dodge them or, better still, use them as props. Children very early (and this was just before Freud really became overpopular here) become keenly aware of the prowlers into their society and of the illnesses of the adult world they live in.

I hardly slept the night before we started for California. I was in one of my moods of unreality in which I spent most of my very young childhood.

I stood, I remember, at dawn at the window, feeling sad; the streets were full of falling leaves, the rain would come soon, gray and wet, and bring the sky down to my head level and the dirty color of all things would be seen through a wind that would shout like some sick thing in its sleep (I was recovering from some mysterious fever). The doors and windows were shut tight, but it would not be enough. The wind would come in drafts and the air would be cold inside the houses. "You're alone," I said. The wind would lift up the rugs, the tin roofs would roar like stage thunder, slates would fall, and the neglected house plants across the way would wave yellow arms, their feet in pots of clay as hard as stone. The mice I always heard in Gramp's walls would crouch together among the droppings and stale odors. (Being a kid is no fun while the rest of the house still sleeps. Children know that they are cut off from the tall living world, that they live in a different climate. . . .)

Then the sun came up, and I laughed and shouted. Down-stairs people stirred, everything was alive and real again.

We had a big breakfast, everyone present. Papa pale, but controlled. The car was ready out front. The bootleg whisky went on the floor boards; over this went Mamma's trunks and Gramp's bags and mine. On the running board (dear departed running boards) were clamped a folding steel camp stove, a small icebox, and three steel cans marked: *Water, Gas* and *Oil*. There was also a folding tent and an oil lamp—a red railroad oil light in case the headlights failed us. We put up the canvas top, a "one-man top" it was called as it took one man for *each* corner. It was made of heavy black canvas on oak frames set into steel elbows and held down by tanned leather belts. The top took as much trouble to furl as the sails of a prize racing yacht. But at last we were ready. Gramp at the wheel, a gleam in his goggles, the usual cigar held by its neck in his strong teeth. Me at his side, seated on a sack of onions—Gramp was going to camp and eat out a lot. In the back on the buffalo robes and luggage Mamma sat, small but game, her second best hat on her best hair-do, waving weakly to the family on the red stone steps of the house. Papa sniffed back a tear.

"Henry!" Gramp shouted.

Papa took the car crank and Gramp figured on the spark and gas levers and nodded. Papa spun the car crank. Nothing. Papa spun again, the car howled, the body shook, and Papa landed five feet away, but on his feet holding his arm tenderly to his chest as if it were of great value. Everybody shouted "Good-by!" Mamma turned a shade lighter and greener and waved back, the car jack-rabbited down the block and then went on, headed for the downtown ferry station. Behind us a feeble cheer rang out, and I turned and thumbed my little nose at my little cousins. It was ten o'clock and (an old journal of Gramp's gives me the date) April 18, 1919.

Steering only right, unless we couldn't help it, we made the ferry station and got on board the boat behind a pair of big brewery horses. "A good omen," Gramp said. Mamma had a little *"mal de mare,"* as she called it in high-school French, but Gramp held her head while I held a horse, and we landed in New Jersey. We headed south, past Newark, the slaughterhouses smelling. We went past Elizabeth and past our summer place in New Brunswick, which Gramp saluted by tooting twice and running over a large dog, who got up, dusted himself and bit one of our tires.

"Where," asked Mamma, "are we heading for?"

"I'm hungry," I said.

Gramp grinned. "All stomach. We're heading for the Red Lion Inn, near Trenton. Great place."

"Trenton?" said Mamma as if she were saying a dirty word. "Isn't that the place they have the electric chair?"

I was sorry we didn't stop in New Brunswick so I could show the car to the kids in the town and brag of how far we were going. I remembered how Mamma used to play ball with me on the sidewalk in front of our house and how all the children sang out:

> *I asked my mother for fifteen cents*
> *To see the elephant jump the fence;*
> *He jumped so high,*
> *He reached the sky,*
> *And never came back till the Fourth of July.*

We went on and lost Trenton a few times and met some cows that may have been amazed at Gramp's command of language. At last we saw a low brown barn of a place and outside it a big red sign with a golden lion rampant on it and the letters: YE OLDE RED LION INN.

We drove up, Emma snorting in tired glee, her front end steaming. We stopped and Mamma said she had to "collect herself." Gramp leaped down and hammered on the big oak door until it opened and a large old man with one low eyelid came out and shook his head.

"Hain't opened for the season yet."

"Kimmil, my daughter-in-law and grandson, Sari and Stevie."

"Pleased to meet up with you. Come in and I'll roust out the cook and get some food out of the spring house."

The Red Lion was very interesting inside if you liked elk horns, wolf skins, wagon wheels, old guns, cobblestone fireplaces, pictures of old circuses, Civil War people, and dead fish with glass eyes in cases. Americana was already a fad.

First Mr. Kimmil (Major Kimmil, Bull Run, Gettysburg, *and* Cold Harbor with Gramp) brought up two bottles of wine.

"Never mind that French stuff," he said. "The last of the real good Rheingau wines. Spatlese, and here look at *this*, Captain."

Gramp nodded. "Beerenauslese—it can't be!—and the vintage year, 1907."

"Yep, the real McCoy, from Rudensheim."

Gramp saluted, opened the bottle and poured. He was very tired. I had two drops in a big glass of water. By this time two colored boys had set a table, and a chicken broth with rice was steaming and we attacked it. Except for eating a pepper gherkin which I shouldn't have and Mamma getting a caraway seed stuck between her beautiful little teeth, the dinner went well, finished off with an Austrian *Gebäck* pastry that Mr. Kimmil had taught the colored boys to make.

There wasn't much use trying to stay awake after eating, and Mamma and I retired into our room, the one with the stuffed wildcat (with real teeth) on the wall, and downstairs we could hear Gramp and Mr. Kimmil over the Munich *Bier* refighting Little Round Top and talking about how the dead piled up in the peach orchard so long ago. I had heard it a dozen times and still was thrilled by it.

Morning came cold and too early, and Mamma washed us both in bottled mineral water and I remember we all had breakfast. When we were finished and Gramp and Mr. Kimmil had exchanged a last round of brandies, we went out and had relays of colored boys work on the cranking of the car into life. It took twenty minutes and only worked after Gramp jacked up a back wheel (an early starting trick of the Model-T days), and we were off. Mr. Kimmil stood waving and weaving and the colored boys took turns shining up the silver dollar Gramp had given them.

We drove in the direction of Philadelphia, and Mamma moaned and kept her feet on two hot bricks wrapped in a blanket. I had out my air rifle and banged away at fence posts and Bull Durham posters: a sign, by the way, of a well-hung bull stallion that was the pride of any farmer who could get it on his barn wall. Gramp sang, in the remains of a flawed voice, but loud:

"Did you ever hear tell of Sweet Bessie from Pike
Who crossed the wild prairies with her lover Ike?
Out on the prairie one bright starry night
They broke out the whisky and Bessie got tight.
She sang and she shouted and danced o'er the plain
And showed her bare ass to the wagon train. . . ."

"Gramp!" said Mamma. "Little pitchers."

"Why did she, Gramp?" I asked.

"Let's find the Delaware River," said Gramp, scowling at Mamma. "If Washington could, so can we."

"What does it look like?" I asked.

"Like water, acres of it."

We found the river at last and a ferry to carry us across, and on the other side was Philadelphia, all right, but the car had a flat tire. We were no place near those signs reading *Free Air* (a novelty just then), so Gramp got out the hand pump and we both took turns putting air into the tire; but it was no use so we got out iron ham bones and husked the tire off the wheel (no demountable rims on this car; the iron ham bones were the only tools for this work). We found a Philadelphia nail in the inner tube. Gramp patched it and pressed it tight from a smelly

tube of rubber repair parts and we got it on and pumped full
and Gramp was so mad he decided to head right for Gettysburg and see the old battlefield.

The day turned fine and yellow and green and Mamma was
only car sick twice and only cried once. I got stung by a bee
and had to sit one-sided, but after a good lunch finished off with
apple pie and cheese and local cider we drove on. Mamma no
longer objected to Gramp's old army songs.

We got to Gettysburg late in the afternoon and stopped the
car on a high ridge. Gramp—limping slightly—got out and
shouldered his cane like a gun and looked across at another
ridge. He was grim-faced, and I think was sniffing back a tear.

"Here I was on the ridge here, looking down and across. Fifty
thousand butternut rebels hell-for-leather, firing, firing; down
there are the peach orchards. And Meade rides up and he says,
'Who the devil is in those goddamned peach orchards?' . . .
'Rebels,' I say. . . . 'Git 'em out,' he yells. . . . 'Yes, sir,' I
say, and I wave my sword—captain I was then—and I started
running and the boys dismounted and started running after me,
and it's bayonets in the peach orchard and the second day at
Gettysburg. . . ." He sat down and wiped his face and cried
unashamed.

"Were you brave, Gramp?"

"We were *all* brave. On *both* sides, even across there. I know
every foot of this battlefield."

An old man with a cap labeled *Guide* came up to us. Gramp
waved him off. "Don't need a guide. Fought on this Yankee
ridge myself."

The guide ate a corner off a square of eating chaw. "You
musta fought a damn funny battle, mister. This is the rebel
ridge. The Union one is over *there*."

Gramp recovered his spirits and laughed, slapped the guide
on the back, smiled, and handed him a cigar. "I mean it was
Union after we took it. Well, let's move on and find lodgings
for the night."

I never did find out if Gramp had mistaken the ridges, and Mamma said I wasn't to ask Gramp about it again as old soldiers have a way of fading away into dreamlike states and not always remembering the full facts.

Gramp didn't talk about the Civil War for a week. He was an emotional man and proud of his war record, and I think he remembered his powerful youth in the war and resented the old man he had become. We both worked over the map in his journal and figured we only had a few more thousand miles to California. The map had marked on it in Gramp's handwriting the words: "Booneville, bought a genuine signature of George Washington for ten dollars." A year later a professor told me it was the rarest of all Washington signatures, "being the only one signed to a sheet of paper bearing a 1903 watermark."

Gramp was a man who lived fully and in great excitement over what pleased him in his old age and colored his world. That he was human, mortal, and could be mistaken first began to stain my thinking on this trip. He had roared through my babyhood, a red face and bloodshot eyes over my crib, and he had been a giant who tossed me into the air and said, "Hell, you can't hurt them at this age, bones like rubber. They don't become human until six."

But in time on the trip, he was reduced to his six feet three, and his faults and his rages made him enjoyable and amusing. I was to find out that as he grew wilder on the trip, Mamma, the dainty one, was to become wiser and cooler, and in command of many situations that would have wrecked lesser travelers. I remember how pleased I was to find them as human as I was.

MAMMA'S 1919 HAT

2.

GO WEST, OLD MAN

GRAMP WAS A VERY OLD MAN. I WAS THEN UNAWARE OF this. He seemed like the center of the universe to me and solid as an oak tree, like the tree my pony once ran me into and which almost cracked my skull. He was not fully a happy man all the time, for he hated old age, and as he felt his strength and his powers ebb away he cursed louder and drank more. But at the time I was unaware of the losing battle he was fighting with the inevitable.

It was spring all the time that first part of our trip. Spring when it was summer and spring when it was fall; I was young and Gramp was old and Mamma was very car sick. I remember it as spring, and there were always blowouts and no gas and un-paved highways and insects in the fields over the cooking Gramp did when we couldn't find a good place to eat.

"Hell, boy, I'd rather singe my own food than swallow the stable stews of some of these black holes called hotels."

"My shoes are all muddy," Mamma would say, looking at her high button shoes.

The Model-T Ford was ugly but game, and it pushed mud and ate brook water and snorted and shouted like a "bull in fly time," to quote Gramp from his old journal.

We passed Lancaster and Hagerstown and were boiling down the Potomac toward Washington. I was sitting at Gramp's side, and Mamma sat in the back on the bearskin and buffalo robes, the camp stove, *and* on her dignity.

"Did Washington really toss a silver dollar across the Potomac?" I asked.

"Yes," said Gramp, setting fire to his cigar. "Today you can throw it twice as far because the dollar is worth half as much." (Which proves that jokes of this kind are not very new.)

"Gramp," said Mamma in her baby-talk voice, "I think I'm dying."

"You need some food stuck on your pretty ribs, Sari," said Gramp. "Some pig side, some good beer, a mess of fried fish and some potatoes boiled in sour milk."

Mamma always liked to be called pretty (even if she was really beautiful). "How far to Washington?"

Gramp shook his head. "Who knows? These signposts don't mean a thing they say. You'd think they were still trying to fool the rebel scouts."

The car snorted, shook, suddenly exploded into a tall column of steam, a gun went off (it seemed) in the engine, and we rattled slowly to a stop. Gramp cursed, got out and lifted his driving jacket, exposing the wrenches and lengths of wires and other inner plumbing of the car he carried in his back pockets.

"What is it, Gramp?" I asked brightly.

Gramp cursed as he burned a finger on the hot motor. "We can't fix this. Let's find a blacksmith!"

We had lunch at the Ramdon Rifle Range, which, while golf was already a popular pastime, was one of those places where the embassy people came out from Washington to hit clay birds and drink the cocktail of the period out of coffee cups. A country speak-easy, I suspected later.

A large Italian with a proud stomach let us into the dining room.

"You are de member?" he asked Gramp, who looked like a Negro minstrel end man, car grease and soot on his face and hands.

"Just became one." Gramp pointed to Mamma. "Will you show the countess the ladies' room? She's in delicate condition."

The Italian washed his hands with phantom soap and bowed.

"De countess, her condition, oh, yes, of course de countess."

Mamma was used to Gramp's social habits and tricks, but she did need the privacy and the comforts of retirement, and she followed a fat finger pointing to an oak door marked *Powder Room.*

It was early speak-easy décor. It had a raftered ceiling, fake grape leaves and glass grapes, lots of booths with little checked tablecloths, and a smell of beer over everything.

Gramp said, "We are in a hurry to get to Washington, so just give us the best. The countess will join us in good time. You do serve food here, I suppose?"

The Italian set two raffia-covered Chianti bottles on the table and said, "De best Italian cuisine. Grind my own *polenta*, import the *pomidoro;* I don't use de local tomato pulp and the *pasta*—" he beat his belly with his fist— "I eat here myself."

Gramp winked at me, looked at the waiter, and said, "Give me *antipasto*, just the pickled mushrooms, the anchovy fillets, artichokes, and pepper and fennel with the cold veal, and a white Falerno, or a strong Torre Guilia."

The Italian looked at the grapes on the ceiling, then at Gramp, and wiped his face. "I lie to you. To a man who knows all *this*, I can not keep up the lie. I have, however, the Lucca olive oil, I will try a *risotto alla Milanese* for you."

"With the saffron?" Gramp asked, winking at me again. He was in a mean mood.

The Italian lowered his head as if kicked. "Look, I am a liar. This is just a dump, a dive, I sell bad wine, needled beer. I will not fool you or the countess, I have not even a *fritto misto* or a *gnocchi*, not even a shred of Gorgonzola or Pecorino. The best I can do is give you mine own lunch I am cooking out back, *ravioli en di pollo.*"

Gramp said it would do if the wine were not too bad, and when the poor man was gone Gramp turned to me and said, "Let this be a lesson to you. Never talk big or fancy. Never use big words you can't back up. Or somebody will eat your lunch. Anyway, this will be something for my journal."

I never forgot that poor waiter and how badly beaten down he was and how good his lunch was.

The sad Italian suffered as we ate his lunch and said he was sorry he had to be such a liar as he had to make a living and the police had to be paid off. He was happy to serve the countess, and serve us all, and did we mind if he sort of spread it around that the countess had been to his place.

Gramp said, "Not at all. Let's have the bill."

But he wouldn't take any money, I remember, and he said to Mamma, "I hope it is a boy—a real big boy."

Mamma said, "What?"

I said, "Your interesting condition."

The blacksmith found us on the porch and said there wasn't much the matter with the car. "Nuttin' at all."

"I know that," said Gramp. "I can put that car together blindfolded."

The native nodded. "You must have. You forgot to connect the end spark plug to the wire. Two dollars."

We got to Washington—I was thrilled at the sight of it—in one of those hot wet evenings that Washington is famous for. We stayed at a big hotel whose name I no longer remember.

(It may have been the Willard—Gramp loved it because he had stayed there during the Civil War.) It had big whirling fans in the ceiling, and chains attached to the fans once led off to a small steam engine that had been built in 1842.

Mamma was tired, so after a dinner of the expected Southern-fried chicken and hot biscuits and the canned fruit and having the bread crumbs brushed off your tablecloth into your lap by a colored man with a silver crumb scraper, Mamma went up to bed and Gramp and I went for a walk. The city was warm and dark and the heavy stone buildings were hidden in the dusk as we walked toward the White House. Gramp and I stood against the railing and peered in. He looked tired and grim. Then he said something that today still gives me the creeps.

"We fought the war, saved the Union. Grant saved the Union, never forget it, boy, and then later we had to save the Union from President Grant. Keep the generals out of the White House. It's a lesson we have to learn every two or three generations, keep the generals out of the White House. Grant was a fine man but a failure in politics. Washington was a fine country village in the Civil War days, Stevie. The streets smelling of the best horses, troops marching, and on the old chain bridge across the river, they used to pull up the planks at night so no one could cross over or get out of the city. A dirty, brave human war."

He stopped to light his cigar. "Life had a flavor then, Stevie. You were for the Union or against the Union, and *all* the women were beautiful. They still are, thank God for these old eyes, but they had a sway and a way, but you'll learn about that later for yourself. We marched down this street when Abe Lincoln lay dead in there in a big black coffin, and the drums were muffled and the horses had black ribbons on their bridles. It was a sad day and the people stood around and cried on the sidewalks. A big country was born that night. A bunch of farmers and city slickers and factory hands knew they were burying a great man and that they were growing up. Goddamn it, you listening, boy? I want you to remember all this."

"I'm listening, Gramp. Was it a hard war?"

"They are always hard wars if you're in there in the battle. Maybe not for some fat people, and Washington was full of fat cats in clover. But out there in Virginia mud, the fever and smoked bacon and the ground horse corn and the wormy hard-tack, it was hard. We all looked like smoked hams after the war and it took us years to get back to sleeping in beds and using forks and getting over chewing tobacco. Your grandmother never liked that habit and spent her last ten years painting forget-me-nots and roses on tin spittoons for me. She was a regular Corot of the cuspidors."

"Were you a brave soldier?"

"Hell, they didn't come no braver. I ate the army food, fired horse pistols made by contractors who never heard of steel, and I rode in the wilderness with Grant at twenty-four and my beard was black and long." He stopped and took my hand with shaking fingers. "I was young, Stevie, young as a courting rooster and the juices in me were alive. Come on, it's time an old man was in bed snoring through a few remaining teeth. . . ."

Gramp's pity for himself and his wild youth happened about twice a year and we always expected it. And waited till he got over it. The next morning I found him in the hotel bar and he was already red in the face and touching bourbon. I respectfully stood aside and waited, knowing the old man always got out of his depressive periods with the aid of good whisky. He saw me and grinned, his head shaking a bit, his grip on his glass not too steady.

"Great day, huh?"

"Yes, Gramp. Can I have a drink?"

"Set one up for my grandson," Gramp said to the barman. "A slug of lemonade with a jigger of sugar . . . and don't spare the lemons, the kid can take it."

I was let down. "Can I smell your breath, Gramp?"

Gramp nodded and I inhaled good bourbon and sipped my lemonade.

"We're taking your mother to the Hungarian Embassy for lunch. Be sure she dresses to the nines and is curried and combed. A nice filly, Sari. Too good for your father. Poor Henry, he's a clod and will always be one. . . . He didn't get any of my red blood, just my baby blue eyes." Gramp laughed and ordered another drink. He was recovering fast.

I went up to our rooms and gave Mamma her marching orders, and she said, "He's drunk!"

"He's high," I admitted, expressing myself in one of Uncle Willie's phrases. "He was very sad last night."

"The Hungarian Embassy? Are you sure we are invited?"

"*Yo istenim*," I said, "*muderul bessailnee?*"

Mamma went pale. "Where did you learn that?"

"From Gramp. It's Hungarian; he learned it when he was building a railroad in Europe. He also taught me how to swear. *Ta nem yo bulund.* . . ."

"Stevie, has he been letting you smell his breath?"

"Just a whiff."

Mamma cried a bit and said I would end up a drunkard like my Uncle Roc. But she dressed very well and did up her face (she was one of the first respectable married women to use lipstick). And being Mamma, began to enjoy the idea of having lunch at the Hungarian Embassy. (I learned that it was the old Austro-Hungarian Embassy, but Gramp didn't like the Austrians and so left them out.)

I remember the Embassy. It was just after the war and it wasn't really open yet, but some people, I think, were getting ready to open it up. It was a grand place, so full of china and pictures and gold doorknobs that it seemed to sink at least a foot extra into the ground. According to Gramp's journal we were guests at lunch of Count Sandor Ladislaus Miklos Harvath; "a genuine sixteen-jewel Hungarian" was what Gramp called him. There were several other guests at a long table and the footmen did not have their knee pants and white wigs on, but it was very fancy. Gramp was still *high* and getting *higher*.

There was Danubian carp and Lake Balston fogas imported
on ice via steamship from the Old World. I must admit I don't
know if these Magyars had any Tokay that day but there was a
strudel, I know, because I got a little ill from overeating. I remember eating and looking up into Gramp's face in our taxi
going back to the hotel, and saying, "We gotta save the Union
from President Grant. . . ."

"You bet," said Gramp. "We gotta lick 'em once and for all."

"Men are beasts," said Mamma, rubbing my aching brow.
"Baby Boy, are you very sick?"

I had the king of all bellyaches that night, and Gramp fell
asleep after feeding me slugs of castor oil and orange juice, and
it was a few days before we could travel. Gramp said his "old
war wounds" were troubling him, and I wondered why he wore
an ice pack on his head because he had no old war scars there.
I lived on milk and crackers, and Gramp and I refought the
last days before Richmond in 1865 in great detail.

Mamma came to my room in a new hat, with feathers on it,
and Gramp said we were ready to move west. "Washington is
certainly no place for civilized people. The pace is killing."

"And the whisky expensive," Mamma said crisply. (She
could be very cruel—"a true female," Gramp would call her.)

"That hurts, Sari," Gramp said, going up behind Mamma
and putting his arms around her. "But I'll tell you what I'll do.
You neglect to write home *all* the details of our visit here and
I'll pay for that hat. . . ."

"How do you like it?" asked Mamma. "It's an Irene Castle
model."

"On toast with hard-boiled eggs," said Gramp, "I'd like it."

Mamma said he was still high but she smiled at the idea of his
paying for the hat. We all made our peace and I tested out my
new stomach on a steak at lunch. It held firm.

The Ford was in front of the hotel, and as Gramp tried to get
behind the wheel Mamma shook her head and pushed him
aside.

"I'm driving, Gramp; you're still a little, well, *full* of war-wound medicine."

Gramp couldn't make a scene in front of the hotel and I could see his head was still aching, so he moved over and Mamma got us under way with a series of jerks and jumps, and somehow we got out of town and headed west. Gramp suddenly came alive and said, "Sari, where did you learn to drive?"

"I didn't. I've just been watching you. I wasn't going to trust my life and the life of my innocent child to your Roman orgies and sprees."

Mamma suspected Rome of all vices.

Gramp looked mad, got out a cigar, set it alight and refused to speak for fifty miles, until we had to get out and change a tire. Mamma walked me down the road and out of ear range as he cursed.

"I'm glad we're out of Washington, Baby Boy. It's a town I wouldn't care to live in. Promise me you'll never be in politics even if it means being President of the United States."

I promised. Several times I was tempted, but I never gave in. A boy's promise to his mother is pretty sacred.

I LIKE THE COUNTRY

3

Judge, judge, tell the judge
Mamma has a baby.
It's a boy, full of joy,
Papa's going crazy.
Wrap it up in tissue paper,
Send it down the elevator.
How many pounds did it weigh?
One, two, three. . . .
(In my handwriting in Gramp's
notebooks)

WHEN I WAS A TURTLE

A MAN NAMED DRIS, SON OF ONE OF GRAMP'S OLD PART-
ners, invited us to visit his camp in the Blue Ridge Mountains.
Mamma said, "No thank you," and we parked her and the car
at a hotel. We tossed our packs into a buggy and went singing
up to Dris's house. We slept that night under the great porch
on cots. But about eleven o'clock when I was ready to turn in
Gramp suggested we crawl out on the kitchen roof and sleep
on the low-pitched roof. I felt it was a foolish idea, but Gramp
had his way and soon we lay on the roof, arms folded behind our
heads, staring up at a moon low enough to bite.

Gramp tossed aside his blankets and sat up. His big body was a dark flat shape in the moonlight.

"Steve, people go mad under a moon—go walking along the roof ridge and nothing can make them fall."

"You feel mad, Gramp?"

He stood up. "I don't know. I don't think so. Let's see."

"Well, if you walk the roof ridge, Gramp, you walk it alone."

Gramp was looking up at the moon. He held his arms up toward it and began slowly to climb up the high house roof. I saw him above, standing balanced on the roof ridge. Then something rolled away toward the low side of the house. It wasn't much of a drop into the hedges. Gramp wouldn't be hurt. I yawned and dozed off. I never had any moon madness. I was, I suppose, crazy in lots of other ways.

Dris's hill place had a dawn that was cold and smelled of honeysuckle vine and it bit into the bone when the first rays of the sun came walking across the hills. Dris, big, brown, handsome, threw open the windows and routed Gramp and me from the roof with a howl of wild jubilance.

"Rise and shine! Rise and let's eat!"

This morning the mist was crawling along the fields trying to scare the cattle. And everything was seen as if through a veil from our humid morning roof bedroom.

Gramp got up first and he dragged me to the yard pump and doused me and I howled while he dug into my ears with a rough husk towel and polished my neck red while I yelped on. The water was ice cold. The hound dogs barked and blew their great rubbery cheeks in glee and bounced off our chests. We beat them off with our fists and went in to breakfast through the clucking, addlepated hens.

The camp cook had griddle cakes and sides of lean bacon ready and he grinned and begged us to tuck in as "Mr. Dris he drove a fast pace in the hills." Gramp sat at the head of the rough table stuffing some foul tobacco into a huge pipe. "Can't keep a cigar going on a trail."

The brown pack horse was already at the door and I had but time to pull apart my fetlock, which I had dipped into the maple sugar, when the dogs began to howl and Dris kicked out at them and brought them to heel. Gramp was in checked flannels and high leather shoes and an old sweater full of holes, and his faded yellow cotton hat was strung with feathered fishing flies.

"Great day, boy."

Dris pulled the diamond hitch tight on the supply packs until the horse grunted; then he looked Gramp and myself over and inspected our shoes and patted me across the rump and handed me the draw line and I started the pack horse along the trails. The dogs, all except a liver-spotted hound, Major, who was to come with us, were locked howling in the house. Roses and nasturtiums grew along the path. The horse was no trouble at all.

The sun was still cold. By noon we were beyond the range of the valley smoke and the last hint of a chimney against the sky. Splendid ranges soared above us in the sun, dewy fields dampened us. Gramp said, "Don't get your ass wet."

We walked into the afternoon, the horse having a fine time tearing, with his ragged teeth, at the green boughs that were stupid enough to dare the open paths of the trail. The going was hard—turning from packed clay to shale and from that to a carpet of pine needles and old red oak leaves. We passed men hewing tan bark. The way was rising all the time and the trees grew taller and the wind was wilder. The dog, Major, sniffed the pungent blossoms and sneezed.

The lakes were silver and the birch matched them tone for tone, but later in the day the water turned darker and the sky held a steady cobalt blanket between a few cotton clouds. Gramp gathered some flagroot and sweet fern. "Good for gripe, bloat and insect bites."

Dusk came suddenly but Dris was ready for it. We were soon against a great outjutting castle of a rock and our tent was up and the coffeepot bubbling and sending brown odors into the fast darkening air. A hedge of hemlock broke the wind on our back.

Dris said, "Like it?"

I said, "I sure do."

"Dan'l Boone came this way."

Gramp said, "Those were real times."

Dris took his rod and came back from the lake with a hatful of leaping fish, and Gramp had the fire roaring itself out into a bed of embers and soon the fish were dipped in crackerdust and jacketed in bacon and frying. We ate them with beans and hot bread freshly made in a closed pot, sitting among ginseng and yellow violets that Gramp pointed out, educating me. The coffee was too hot and I swallowed it until tears came, and then we all leaned over and wiped out the frying pan and had more coffee. Dris and Gramp lit their pipes and the night sounds and the night moths closed in. We sat, three dark shapes and a dog, against a darker night-rock and night-wood, and all we did was digest and look into the fire, and then we went down to the lake to wash. It was a fine night. "A primordial vapor haunts the lakes," Gramp said, snapping his suspenders. "That's poetry, Stevie. Poor poetry."

I hunted big roots and logs and banked the fire, and Dris had laid the blankets over fresh cut pine branches, and slowly we sank back and with arms folded behind our heads looked at the stars brushing the treetops. Across the lake a loon sounded. And something crushed its way through the woods and we heard the picketed pack horse chewing grass, tearing with his broken teeth at the earth and pulling nourishment into himself. Then the dog came back from a tour, mouth open, tongue out, laughing about something he had scented near the dead patch of lightning-struck trees. Then I yawned.

Dris said, "Nice sound that horse makes."

Gramp grunted, yawned and turned on his side. "I hope you drove the horse stake in deep."

I awoke once to find Gramp pulling the blanket closer around me and the fog drifting in over the lake. The moon was bigger than it would ever be. The dog sniffed the ashes near the dying fire and I was asleep again—asleep until the morning wind made seaside sounds in the birch leaves. I sat up yawning, spit, and looked about me. The piny air tickled my throat. I wondered what Mamma was doing.

"Get up, you damn loafer," Gramp said.

Gramp was skinning a rabbit, and the bread baking in the closed pot was the most wonderful thing I had ever smelled. Far out on the lake Dris was fishing from the rubber folding boat. He shouted something and waved and it took a long time for his voice to reach us. Higher, I saw coarse mountain pasture, a world remote, rock, clouds.

I said, "Do I brush teeth up here?"

I closed my eyes and lay back on the blankets and wriggled my toes for joy and it was not until the dog came over and ran his cold nose over me that I got up, mother-naked, and went down to the lake to bathe, stretching and yawning and groaning. I dried myself on grass.

Gramp roared. "Get your duds on, and eat."

We did not stay at the lower lakes. We gathered our stuff and banged the load onto the pack horse until his knees shook, but we drew in the ropes, his eyes rolled, and then we went higher. The going was rough, the trail less marked among laurel and rhododendron.

Dris said, "Watch for Indian arrowheads."

I have never seen such trees. They were Dris's trees, and he was fighting to keep them out of the lumbering saws' greedy steel teeth. They were ropy, aged trees, and the moss was on them like the coating of age on a mud turtle's shell. It took me almost a full minute to walk around some of them through the clinging underbrush. They filled the sky and made a darkness, a green-blue underworld like a sea bottom, for us to walk through. In some places we broke away from the trail, and there we found ten feet of dead leaves and vegetable matter and old

limbs and seed pods that had been piling up, Gramp said, for
five and six hundred "and maybe more" years. Ours were the
first feet to cut into this mold, to break the surface of this
piled-up wealth of fungus, festering mold and fertile soil. I was
impressed that trees that had never seen man before sheltered
us, and earth that had not seen the sun in almost a thousand
years of tree-made darkness formed our beds. Gramp got bitten by a wasp. The dog lifted his leg at a porcupine.

The big trees passed and we were on the backbone of the
world where Gramp said only rocks had families and the little
twisted, warped versions of trees were, I decided, out of fairy
tales, evil fairy tales. (I hated fairy tales, and Mamma bought
me all on the market.)

But that, too, was soon passed, and we crossed the ridge by a
tumbling iron-rock trail. Waterfalls met us and spume from
columns of water wet us to the skin. Below were the fat golden
hills, the haze of distance.

At noon we all stripped nude and lay on pale red rocks and let
the sun dry us, and Gramp told us tales out of his youth.

"All true, Stevie," he said.

"It doesn't matter. I like them."

"Hell, it does to me."

I fingered a scar on his ribs that he claimed an evil day had
brought to his body.

"The whole damn year was unlucky."

He was a giant grown old, a perfect machine running down,
and the strength was still in the hard calves and in the stony
biceps, but the flesh of the belly was beginning to sag and the
pucker around the throat crisscrossed like a road map. The
proud mustache was white. It was sad to see a man's body betray him, to see the steady, dreadful tearing down of tissue and
form that would be completed only when the grave took over
the one you love. I was young then and callous, and not full of
kindly instincts, as I hope I am now, and so perhaps I did not
think too much of old age that day. I was as yet self-conscious
in my nudity.

"Stevie, expose the body, air the mind, and keep your bowels open."

Dris was a man of perfect muscled design and when he yawned and kicked the ground with his hard heels, the body muscles rippled. I didn't pay too much attention to myself. I was at the age of string-bean thinness. The adolescent pride in faint body hair was already there, however.

But a chill breeze drove off the sun, and so we dressed and dug the horse's face out of a greengage bush, whistled for the dog, pulled him away from the bad taste of a tree marked by polecats, and went on. We passed many poplars.

That night we camped on a sand bar alongside a rushing stream. In the eddy it was calm and the sand bar was bone-white in the moonlight. Fish leaped and turned over in the air all around us, and the dog treed something and did not let it rest until dawn. Then he lay down and snored in the sand until Gramp kicked him and he yelped. The sky of morning was one golden disk of light. The sand bar and the stream and green edges of the world were merged into one eye-blinking glare. And closer, I remembered Gramp's lessons: it became wild grape and savin, walnut, spruce.

"Know the names, boy, and you'll love nature."

I swam a long time in the lime-green water, and Dris came and ducked me and I choked and swallowed muddy bottom water, but I got away at last.

"When I'm bigger I'll come back and duck you."

Dris grinned. "It's a date, shrimp."

We made permanent camp against the friendly back of an old tree that could no longer stand erect, and Dris built up a platform of stones and covered part of it with elm and pine branches. And I set up the tent. Gramp and Dris plastered up a stone pit for cooking and sent the horse up a close valley and fenced in the opening with saplings so he could eat, as Dris pointed out to me crimson sorrel and crowfoot blossoms in safety.

We hunted that morning, I very proud of a stinking little

kicking devil of a gun that left a red badge of pain on my shoulder. Deer were out of season, but Dris got one at the edge of a clearing, deep in goldenrod and spiked germander.

The deer stood there, his wet eyes looking at me and his black mouth twitching a handful of greens. Then he turned and leaped over a log. I wanted to cry out, "Let the bastard go! Don't kill him!" Dris shaped the gun against his shoulder and flame blasted out of it and the deer turned in mid-air and stood still in space for a moment. I could see the hillside under his belly and his face was hurt and the big eyes were bigger. Then he made a gasping sound. He crashed over on his face and lay there twitching and his hard little heels kicked at the soil. He dunged and rolled over. Dris fired again. The slug sank into a shoulder of flesh and tissue and bone and fur and then the deer no longer cared, and Dris pulled his hunting knife across the taut throat and the hiss and escape of red life ended what was a deer and all we had was good meat to eat. I began to shake.

Gramp said roughly, "Don't be ashamed of being a meat-eater. Look at what you eat before it's food. It will make you humble."

We ate a great deal of it, and Dris staked out the pelt and we hung haunches high in a tree. And that night I felt less sorry for the deer. I had eaten too much.

The next morning there was a mist rolling like a gray rug on the earth. Later the sun would tear it away and we would go down to the lake. It was very cold. Cold enough, Gramp said, to hurt the private anatomy of brass monkeys. But it was fine, too, to float around and lash out with chilled arms until I could feel the blood pounding through my chest, journeying to warm my toes and my shivering body. I wished I had a bigger set of muscles. I felt childish, immature and shy.

Dris was the best developed. A tall, wide young man with a barrel chest and long, brown limbs. Gramp and I would float in the water watching him swim away out into the middle of the lake and back again, his head flashing like Chinese lacquer in the wet morning, the long hair flicked back on a laughing head. Then we came out of the water naked and stood in the sun drying out by the shadbushes and harebells. I sketched us all on a paper bag.

Gramp was all bone and muscle, with a slack belly and a brown, white-haired chest and long limbs that showed almost in outline what a fine figure he had once been and still was in a way. Dris was filling out, the sepia buttons on his paps were hard and round, and the water ran off his smooth hide into the hardness of his belly and down his legs. He was a man and I envied him his powers. But I was growing and could chin myself four times on the limb of the pine tree that grew with crazy pride over the lake.

Gramp said, "Don't knock any damn teeth out."

Dris fished and I gathered wood and dug a peony bush for Mamma. Gramp stirred secrets in a pot and we ate. Gramp had a few bottles of beer cooling on strings in a spring bottom and the two men drank them down and belched gas up through their noses.

Then we had no more tinned milk. Dris fixed dough and baking soda and wound it around sticks and toasted it. Soon we were down to coffee and potatoes and a side of bacon, and so we hunted small animals and skinned them and salted and peppered them and ate them with relish. The dog grew wilder. I tore a hole in my knee.

"Now you've got a war wound," Gramp said.

Our hair grew, and Dris and Gramp had beards and I had, I thought, a mild fuzz on my upper lip. We lived off the land and it was fine. Dris would brood over his fishing lines. And once I ducked him deep in a spiral of phosphorescence during a night swim.

"You've got mean blood in that boy," he told Gramp.

"Yep, my side of the family."

We moved high on the ridge and were beside a chortling stream. The fire was low; rabbits came to stare at us but we were too full of a hot day's bathing and hunting and fishing to bother them. The last of the coffee bubbled in the pot, tossing the lid like a chatter of wild teeth.

Gramp said from behind his pipe, "A pulsing feline silence broods over the wilderness."

"More poetry?" I asked.

Gramp was carving a cane out of a knob-rooted bit of hickory. Dris came toward the coffeepot, lifted it off the fire with his old hat, and poured it into our tin cups until the pot was empty. There was no sugar left. We looked at each other and smiled. I knew that tomorrow we would break camp, find the hobbled horse grazing below somewhere, and head back. But I only heard Gramp tell me about nature.

I was rubbing Gramp's stiff arm while he talked, the light gilding the solid planes of his face. . . .

And I can remember word for word what he said that night, and years later I used it to end a novel. He began slowly:

"In the body of the female of the great deep-sea turtle, Stevie, the future of the horny turtle race is kept safe in the twenty to forty thousand eggs that the plastron shell of her green body holds together. The deep-sea turtle is our lesson for tonight. She lays four or five hundred of these eggs a year, and so the smallest egg is not to be laid for almost a century. In the body of the giant deep-sea turtle a slow steady pregnancy of fifty to a hundred years goes on—you know all about birth by now. In the hard shell the future turtle generations lie waiting to spawn. Like the genes waiting in you, boy, don't forget it.

"In the night the creeping turtle comes out on the sand and digs by some subtle reasoning of nature a hole, and lays her yearly deposit of eggs, lays them toward the continuance of the race of deep-sea turtles. She covers them with sand and goes back to the sea, leaving the future to take care of itself. Those eggs that the sun warms into turtles on the lonely shore. You paying attention?"

"I am."

"The first young turtle breaks out of the egg and comes out

into the light of day. Clumsily the small bit of spunk waddles out of the nest, followed by brothers and sisters. In single file they make for the shallows of sea wreck and kelp. Here wait hungry fish who have tasted young turtle before and have real hunger and no mercy. Of the two or three hundred little turtles that leave the nest, not more than ten or twenty reach the reefs leading to the open sea. The rest are gone from life into the bellies of the fishes; they have lived a short time and served their purpose: holding and delaying the hungry turtle-gulpers so that ten or twelve brothers and sisters can reach the reef."

"It seems cruel, Gramp."

"Nature is not cruel or kind. Just indifferent."

"What happens then?"

"Once through the breakers, where half the remaining turtles are lost to gobbling bass or spotted eels, the few survivors plunge into the swirling sea where bigger fish wait. One or two little fellas may escape to their destiny, to life; and from their own inner organs will the race of deep-sea turtles go on living all over the face of the earth."

"That's good."

"Someday, perhaps, the sea teeth will be too many, Stevie, and no young turtle will be able to struggle through into life. And in a couple of turtle generations or so, the sea will be empty of plastron shell. No more big sea turtles.

"That it hasn't happened so far in the natural history of the world is no sign that it can't happen. And not just to turtles. Good night."

I lay a long time feeling sorry for all living things. Then I slept until the sun hit my eyes. We came down from the mountains that day. Mamma was waiting for us on the hotel steps, looking amused, beautiful and very stylish. She hugged me to her and said, "I wouldn't know my Baby Boy, so brown and lean. What's happened to you?"

"He's growing up," Gramp said. "How's the car running?"

"I ruined a tire and bought a new one. I think they changed the motor fat."

"Oil," said Gramp, and he looked back over his shoulder at the Blue Ridges dancing in the distance. He said to Mamma, "A man could get to like it. If I had another life I'd be a woods-and-mountain bum."

Mamma told us all the hotel gossip and made me take a scalding shower. But I refused to let her in to scrub my back; I had grown much less dependent on her in the mountains.

As we went on I began to understand Gramp better. What had at first been amusing in my grandfather, what made him unlike other people, began to come clear to me. I saw why he was such a reader of Thoreau. I used to listen to him read and suddenly, even to me, a boy with no reason to have any wider outlook, it began to make a reason for my grandfather's outlook on life. He would read to us: " 'If a man does not keep pace with his companions, perhaps it is because he hears a different drummer. Let him step to the music which he hears, however measured or far away.' That make sense to you?"

It took a little thinking, but I soon agreed with it. And Gramp no longer seemed so much God's angry man.

MAMMA INVADES RICHMOND

4.

He saith among the trumpets,
Ha, Ha! and he smelleth the bat-
tle afar off, the thunder of the
captains and the shouting. . . .
—KING JAMES BIBLE
(From Gramp's notebooks)

GRAMP TAKES RICHMOND

IN HIS PRIME MY GRANDFATHER HAD BEEN SIX FEET four inches tall, but as he admitted, "I'm down to six feet three. As you grow older the soft padding between the bones of your spine shrinks, and you lose an inch or so." His hair had mostly gone too; he was completely bald, a heroically polished skull but for a long fringe of white hair worn like a shaggy halo around his brown head. His skin was tanned like a good book leather, and his great curved nose led a life of its own, like a hawk's bone beak. Under it he cultivated an upsweeping mustache, the kind no longer seen on earth. It proudly thrust forth two curved white spikes in Texas longhorn style and he was always twisting it; the ends were dangerous spikes of mustache wax. Under this white bush lived almost always a live cigar,

stogie, cheroot—whatever dark rolled tobacco was at hand—
a glowing coal continually fanned by nostrils expelling smoke.

He walked a little bent over sometimes, but when angry he
would arch his back like a tomcat and his eyes, iron blue and
still shiny, would almost pop like ripe plums from his head.
He was very strong, even in old age. But his paunch was heavy,
and he favored his right leg, which had been shattered at
Chancellorsville and badly set by military doctors—"hoss
doctors, that is."

He moved quickly, he danced well, he skipped like a child
along the walks on a good day. He used a gold-headed cane like
a sword and banged it near heads he disliked.

Diseases of old age attacked him and he fought back howling,
scattering pills and lifting his fist to the skies to damn whatever
power had so cursed him and Job. Gout could often cripple him,
but his drinking had as yet not cowed his kidneys. Rich sauces
had been put on a list of forbidden foods to give up, and he
didn't. Often after a big feast he would beat his chest and groan,
and hot water and lemon would be sent up for his gall bladder,
"a weak organ in the family." He promised that if he were ever
cut for gallstones he would make each daughter-in-law a set of
gold-mounted earrings with the results.

His eyes were good, but for reading small print he secretly
wore narrow gold-rimmed glasses. He hated to be caught with
them on. He read a lot, thick fat books: Gibbon, Pepys, the
Greek stoics, Chekhov, Tolstoy, Balzac, Mark Twain. Except
for Mark Twain he disliked all modern novelists and enjoyed
best Fielding, Defoe, Smollett. When Proust was published in
France, he read every word of it. He was a true stoic, tainted
by romanticism, and he followed no organized godhead. He
once told a bishop, "God had good intentions but must have
died young." The bishop said, "You must admit, sir, Jesus was
a gentleman." He always carried a copy of the Old Testament,
King James Version, and would read it out loud, banging with
his fist to capture the beauty of its wonderful rhythm and the

power of its images. "That's it, Stevie, the great books of the great Jews. Everything you need to know is there. Everything has been said there better than any place before or after. The world is all there, all its laments, passions, joys, hopes, morals, and vices. What a letdown to read the New Testament after this grand old thunder and fire. Read it for style, Stevie, and for wisdom, and for the secrets of the human mind and human meanness. We're a sad lot, boy, but we're lively as a frog in a frying pan, begetting and begetting and warring and warring. A great book; pass an old man a drink."

He didn't grow old gracefully; he raged and he carried on like a man of forty. He was always in love, always involved with women. When gripped by love he would glow, flush, smile, and recite poetry; but out of love he would curse the female and bury his head in his hands. "Keep away from the sex, Stevie, remember an old man's advice. Women aren't worth the effort and the love we waste on them. They exist only in perfection in our inner vision. We don't fall in love with a real woman as she is, but with the illusion of our heart and desire that we have built up. They're nothing but inferior males; less muscle, flabby, growing their hair and fingernails long. Their minds are shallow, their morals no wider than a diamond bracelet. They will betray you for a whim, and cheat you for a lark. Better to go to the dogs than to women."

And yet the next week he would get a close shave, scent himself all over, and go prancing off, carrying a package of hothouse fruit and a dozen roses, his cigar burning like Antony for Cleopatra.

His fires smoldered for a long time. And even as a very old man they never went out, but remained banked and ready to burst into flame. He never forgave Henry James saying: "I love France as I never loved woman."

Mamma understood the old man; Mamma understood a great deal. Her own tragic fate was never to understand herself fully. She was only five feet two inches tall, bronze-red hair with a wave in it to freeze a true artist to his tracks. Her features were classic, except for a slight mocking tilt to her perfect nose. Small-mouthed, with tiny white teeth. Her head, an oval on a long neck, had a grace that is still to be seen in the best paintings of Sargent or in some of the drawings by Charles Dana Gibson. She had real hips and tiny feet that often danced in rage as well as joy. Her hunger for life drove her, but unlike Gramp, she could not flout too often the morals and manners of her time. She remained, after her gay youth, boxed in, under tension, a spring wound up too tight and ready to let go at all times. In an age when women were not yet supposed to think in public or speak out of turn, she defied convention until her marriage and broke out of the domestic reservation whenever she could. She disdained all sports except horseback riding. She never was a proper hostess, but often an interesting one. She mixed her society, and all her life I remember her as hunting some final satisfaction in life that never came to her. I think, in her old age, when almost everything around her had turned to dust, her hopes and her plans unrealized, she began to understand that the best part of life was the seeking, the looking, the pleasure of hunting for it, and that maybe she had had the best of it. Then she cultivated a pride that at first sight aped humility.

She was not like Gramp, given to brooding, to depressive moods. She had the ability always to land gracefully on her feet. She was skillful in extracting the most from everything that happened to her. And she always looked forward to tomorrow. She wrote good letters with witty phrases, but she did not read much, not even the daily newspaper; I do not think she was aware of much of contemporary history, or cared anything about it. Her interest in governments, literature, art (except opera in the social sense) was small. Churches for her were places built to burn incense in; music was invented for the dance. Life later never defeated her, but it battered her. The auto trip with Gramp was her last glorious escape, a final free fling, a nose-thumbing at her destiny. I think she knew this. To me she will always be a great man.

Mamma was getting a little wind-blown and a little weather-stained on our trip. In 1919 the modern comfort station had not yet reached its peak of perfection, and Mamma had to recover herself in shabby hotels, inns only remotely out of Dickens, and converted stables that were already turning cobblers' benches, hog buckets, wagon wheels and the oil lamps of the hired hand into "genuine rare collector's items of early Americana."

Gramp was driving as we crossed over into Virginia, and the red mud roads bumped us and the dust of small towns covered us. His old journals read: "Alexandria, Charlottesville, Roanoke, *and* the James River. Here the natives say God's Country becomes God's Own Country. The extremes of beatitude and bestiality."

It was warm, it was sunny, and Gramp held the steering wheel like death's other brother, and pulled the gas lever down until we hit a neck-breaking thirty miles an hour. Suddenly there was a blur of color in front of us, then a scattering of gay feathers, a loud lamenting crow of despair, and Gramp pulled up as a large shattered rooster staggered into a mad little dance, fell over on his back, his tattered stern feathers at half-mast.

Gramp walked over and picked the creature up by its now limp neck and looked it over in admiration.

"Two of these roosters used to lick a mule in the old days with U. S. Grant."

"Now Gramp," said Mamma, "put it down before you start looking for a bullfight."

Gramp said, "Not in Virginia."

"Can I have the feathers for an Indian hat?" I asked.

A large red-nosed man with a shotgun appeared from behind some apple trees and nodded politely to Gramp. He was chewing tobacco slowly.

"Passin' through?" he asked casually.

"Yes," said Gramp. "This hen just committed suicide."

"Nothin' to live for," said the fat man. "Ain't a hen, it's a rooster. In the prime of life it was too."

"We all have to go. A rooster?"

"Ought to know," said the man. "Raised 'em from an aig."

"A what?"

"Aig. Ham and aigs, bacon and aigs. What do you think that critter is worth?"

"No idea," said Gramp, lowering his victim and taking out his cigar case and offering one to the fat man.

"Aigs from his harem, why I got people standin' in line to buy."

I looked at Gramp and looked at the shotgun, and somehow that scene has never left me. I remember every shadow, every sun-heated detail: Mamma stiff in the car, Gramp lighting the two cigars, the late departed harem boss resting like a dead English king on the ground. I even remember the deep fat-backed voice of the shotgun owner as he puffed his cigar alive.

"Wouldn't take a hundred dollars for that rooster."

Gramp said sternly, "Wouldn't give you a hundred. Wouldn't give you ten dollars. Give you five. In gold."

The fat man looked at his smoldering cigar end and said, "Pretty good ropes you smoke, Cunn'el. Five it is and two more cigars—damn good cheroots. Pardon me, Madame."

The gold changed hands. In those days there was still gold coin in the nation, and Gramp wore a big money belt with lots of big old-fashioned green bills and some clinking gold coins around his big stomach. Gramp sadly rebuttoned his belt.

The man with the shotgun said, "I'll give him a nice burial, Cunn'el. Only fittin', he was a real Don Jewonnee, rather futt than eat. Pardon me, Madame."

Gramp picked up the victim and shook his head. "I'll just take *my* bird along with me. He broke his neck banging into the front end of the car. A good clean way to go. No suffering."

The fat man unloaded his shotgun and pushed his two extra

cigars into the barrels. "It's your rooster, Cunn'el. Nice to have met up with you."

He walked off among the apple trees singing "The Bonnie Blue Flag." Mamma said in her crisp small voice, used only at those moments when life became much too big for her, "I am *not* traveling with that cadaver."

"Now, Sari," said Gramp, slinging the body on board. "It's a long way to Richmond yet, and we'll have to camp out soon and I'm going to show you how to cook a hen U.S. Army style, in the field, better than anything they ever had at Delmonico's or Rector's."

"Camp out?"

"Nothing between us and Richmond but Yankee-haters, squatters, and empty fields. Let's go."

We got the car going and drove along into the tall shadows of afternoon, Mamma sitting grimly in the back seat, not moving or glancing at the brightly colored little body on the floor boards. Gramp and I looked at the road ahead not wanting to hit any of the straying cows, for as Gramp explained, "I don't want to pay for any Holstein or Jersey. Besides, I can't butcher a whole cow, haven't the saws and knives and chopping blocks."

"Men are monsters," said Mamma.

"*Homo homini lupus*," said Gramp in his best Latin. "Man is a wolf after fellow men," he translated freely for me.

I was struggling with school Latin and thanked him.

Mamma got more wind-blown and said she was going "to cat" if Gramp didn't change the subject. Around dusk we came to a huge field with forests on either side, and Gramp pulled up beside a small, swift stream and we made camp for the night. The three of us put up the one-man car top. Mamma would sleep in the back seat, and Gramp and I put up what was known as a pup tent. "Called a pup tent, Stevie," he told me, "because no self-respecting pup would sleep in it, only damn-fool people."

Mamma refused to pluck the feathers off the rooster, so Gramp built up a nice fire between some stones, got out the big iron pot, heated water, and stuffed the rooster in, feathers and all, and then pulled out the feathers, cleaned the pot, and set more water to boiling. Like a great doctor performing his favorite operation, he dissected the rooster, inspecting it and its anatomy with professional interest until Mamma said, "Gramp, it's not a patient. I'm getting real ill. I don't think I'll eat any of it."

"Nonsense," said Gramp. "I'm going to make a boiled soup and dinner General Custer style. We have any spices or onions, cloves, carrots, cabbage, or pepper, cinnamon, saffron? And some potatoes, a can of peas—and we still have beef left over from last night. No beef? Then smoked ham and the rest of the bacon."

"*What* are you making?" Mamma asked, looking ready to cry.

"Army boiled dinner. Toss all that stuff into the pot. No leeks, have we? Well, we'll do without. We also cut in some blood sausages. Well, we'll use the rest of the frankfurters. . . ."

"Can I stir?" I asked.

"Cooking this is an art, cooking chicken is an art. In China they make *Ti mai Kai*, chicken with nut and barley. In the East Indies they shred it into *Ajam Abon-Abon*. With noodles and eggs it's called *Aki Tsuki* in Japan." (All this worthless information is in Gramp's notebooks of the trip. There are a lot of quotations from books, and on food; I'll use some of them.)

"The water's boiling, Gramp," I said.

"The soup, *not* the water." He added the sections of rooster and stirred. "As a sambal they eat it with spicy red peppers. In Haiti they cook it in a batter called *Marinade de Poulet;* it's not true they leave on the feathers. Now, with ham and rice in Equatorial Africa——"

"I feel ill," said Mamma, sitting down on a large stone. "Real ill."

Gramp said, "You need milk, udder-fresh milk. Stevie, you get the tin bucket and we'll go to the farmhouse up the road and get some milk for Sari. Just keep it stirring, Sari, till we get back. Work will take your mind off your illness."

Mamma said, "Are there any bears in these parts?"

"Nope, we ate them all when the Civil War was on. Ate crow, too. Crow isn't bad; tastes like spring friers if you get them and put them on a rifle ramrod *and*—— All right, Sari, I'll stop talking. Just stir that boiled dinner."

Gramp and I went up the road and left Mamma weeping and retching and stirring. Thinking back, I can see how cruel we were to her, and how brave she was, but at the time I was only interested in finding out what udder milk was. I knew "mother's milk" was gin; Gramp's cook had told me that.

The farmer sold us a gallon of milk for a dime, and he let me try my hand at milking, but it wasn't a very well-trained hand and the cow tried to mash the top of my head in with a kick. The cow was much more a Yankee-hater than Jeff Davis, and I looked, I suppose, like young innocent Yankee meat to her.

When we got back to camp Mamma was asleep by the fire, wrapped in a blanket, the iron stirring spoon still gripped in her little hands like a protective weapon.

Gramp got out our tin camping plates, and he ladled up sections of rooster and the boiled dinner and woke Mamma. She opened her eyes and said, "I dreamed I was dead and was laid out in the big front room at home. I could smell the good candles. It was fine to be home, and now you woke me up and we're in the wilderness."

"Morbid, morbid," said Gramp, handing her a bowl of rooster stew. "Here, Sari, clap yourself around this. Stevie, here's a man's share for you. Let's all start together. You're in for a treat."

I took a section of rooster in my mouth and chewed. I chewed a long time and wondered why I was so tired. I looked at Mamma and she too was chewing. Gramp had his head down, then looked up and smiled. "Needs a little more flame."

Mamma said, "All hell-fire is what it needs," and began to weep. Gramp said it would be all right, and we got more wood and cooked the rooster again, but it seemed to grow tougher with the heat. After a while we just sat holding our aching jaws and feeling very hungry now, sipping milk. The pot on the fire bubbled and boiled and Gramp tried some of the rest of the stuff in the pot, but too much boiling had kind of boiled everything out of it, so we drank more milk, getting really hungry.

When it was fully dark and big fat stars sugared the sky, Gramp said softly, "Let this be a lesson to you, Stevie. That bird spent so much time being in love it hardened his fibers toward the better things in life."

Mamma was really angry now. "I wish I were dead."

"Sari, you show me a man who boasts of being a great lover and I'll show you a clown who's no real gourmet. He spends too much time in bed instead of at the table and——"

"Little pitchers," said Mamma, her code word for me, meaning, I used to think, that it embarrassed her to hear how much I knew about life.

Gramp kicked over the pot and put out the fire. Mamma in her best cutting voice said, "You being such a gourmet, Gramp, I suppose this means all those talks of your lady friends aren't true?"

Mamma could be very cruel when she was unhappy—cold, hungry, and really tired. Gramp said politely, "Oh, go to bed."

That hungry night on a lonely Virginia road was rather a bad time for us. We almost turned back, but Mamma was game at dawn and happy at noon, when we got to Richmond and stayed at the Orwells'.

The Orwells were old friends of Gramp's. Old man Orwell, now "passed over" as Mrs. Orwell said, had built railroads with Gramp. Young Mr. Orwell lived, Gramp said, "in endowed idleness." Lunch was very good at their place. The usual fried ham and sweet potatoes and good apple pie and an okra soup. Gramp said something about "the South showing no imagination in its cooking, the same old ham and . . ." at which point he said *"Ouch!"* because Mamma on her second cut of pie had kicked him under the table. She was very happy with the same old Southern cooking.

The Orwells invited us to a big party at the Confederate Hall that evening, the shrine where the battle flags and paintings of the great generals of the Lost Cause were hung. Gramp said they "lived high for losers" and he for one didn't mind going to see the foe in all its glory. Mrs. Orwell, whose grandfather, a Yankee, had made a fortune carpetbagging and stealing cotton to ship to Europe, said Gramp must be joking. Gramp said he knew the South had been brave in the war, he meant no offense to his noble foes. It was just "a lot of people who hadn't fought or lost anything were getting a lot of fun out of it."

Mamma finished her coffee, yawned, smiled, and said she was going to take a hot bath. Mrs. Orwell said Mamma was very brave to travel so much and Mamma said her great-great-grandmother had helped settle Kentucky with Daniel Boone and Mrs. Boone didn't like it at all. Gramp looked at her, knowing Mamma had made that up, but Mamma just stuck out an inch of pink tongue at him. Gramp sighed and offered his cigar case around. Mamma was going to be trouble before the trip was over. She was not forgetting that tough lover boy of a rooster in the pot. Mamma never was the forgiving kind anyway. She used to say, "I'm too darn human, all of me, to be kind to people who hurt me."

The hall was a blaze of special lights and a lot of the best people (and some of the oldest too) were there. Mr. Orwell introduced Gramp as "a member of the well-known Longstreet family of New Orleans." Gramp wanted to protest he was a Yankee Longstreet, but Mamma gave him *that* look and he just snorted. "Damn hillbilly relatives, that's all they are."

A reporter came over and said to Gramp, "The inner shrine has paintings of Lee and all his staff. Genuine oil paintings."

Gramp said, "Standard Oil paintings. I've seen them."

The reporter said, "All but of General James Longstreet. He's hung in the hall."

Gramp snorted, "What! Damn it, my father and his father were cousins!"

Mamma said, "Now, Gramp, that's *their* problem."

The reporter said, "You see, the general took a job with the Union forces after the War between the States. He became a postmaster in the U.S. Post Office."

"An outrage," said Gramp, "hanging any Longstreet in the

hall. Who is the hanging committee here? A good name for
them, by the way."

The reporter, smelling a story, took Gramp around to meet
some very fine-looking people. After a while someone got up and
made a long-winded speech. Gramp wanted to talk too and
started up from his chair, but Mamma gave him the elbow,
politely but hard—while listening.

It was a bad evening for the old man, and when we got back
to the Orwells', I went up to his room to tuck him in, and he was
lying there looking at the ceiling, very old, tired, and sad. I
noticed how the skin hung loose on his jowls.

"There is fame for you, Stevie, hung in the hall with the old
overshoes and the topcoats. And why? Because he had to earn a
dollar and went to work for it. 'Old Pete' Longstreet, we used
to call him, biggest beard you ever saw and a pretty fair general, and this is his reward. It makes you think, Stevie. I'm
certainly glad I was never anything higher than a major."

"It worries you, Gramp?"

"It certainly does."

"Why?" I asked.

But by that time he was snoring slightly and I let him sleep
and went to my own room. There was an item in the paper the
next day. "The Martin Orwells were entertaining Major S. H.
Longstreet and his daughter-in-law and her son. The Major has
an interesting business history. . . ."

Mamma managed to hide it from Gramp, and after a breakfast of bacon, steaks, pickles, fried eggs, and real coffee, we all
started off again—heading west now, hunting the big rivers.
Mamma drove part of the way and the stray dogs seemed to
know it; they were careful to step aside quickly when they came
out to bite our tires.

Around noon we stopped for lunch at a battered old white
house and had a lunch that started off badly when the large,
limping colored man said, "Today is our chicken day—the
specials of the house, yes sur, chicken."

"*No*, thank you," said Mamma.

"Fried, stuffed with rice, sliced in wine sauce, chicken potpie with spices and candied crab apple, chicken patties, and——"

Gramp said grimly, "The lady said *no*. Goddamn all chickens!"

"The prime delight of our menu, yes sur, chicken à la king with tender baby peas——"

Gramp rose and said, *"No chicken!"*

We had fried catfish that tasted of river mud and boat oil.

KENTUCKY STILL LIFE

*The great pleasure of owning a
dog is that you may make a fool
of yourself . . . and he will make
a fool of himself too.*
—SAMUEL BUTLER
(From Gramp's notebooks)

DOG DAYS AND
KENTUCKY NIGHTS

THAT YEAR WAS A YEAR OF SUN AND DUST. MAMMA'S
spine was a little unstrung from riding in the back, and Gramp
almost lost half his mustache trying to crank life into the car
on a back road; his mustache was caught in the crank. Gramp
shot out a full series of purple curses, danced, and held his face.
Mamma stuffed her fingers in my ears. After that, we were all
hungry, tired, and dusty.

Mamma said, "We should stop for the night."

"Not till we get to Ohio. No decent food till we hit the river."

"My spine aches."

"Only a few miles more."

We got real lost just before dark, and Gramp got out under an apple tree and looked around him. "Well, you'd think the natives would put up signs for strangers."

"Can't they read themselves?" I asked.

Gramp looked at me and motioned me into the car, and we went on and came to an old white bridge and crossed. It was warm and dusty in the hot night on the other side. Gramp put his cap on and said, "It's certainly cooler in Ohio."

Mamma, who was getting that hard look around her little mouth, said, "It must be even cooler in Hades."

Gramp winked at me as if to say "women!" and drove on. The road got worse, and the moon failed us, and far off a dog howled at something until someone kicked him. We could hear the kick, and then the talky dog stopped his monologue.

It was pretty bad in those days—the bad roads, the bad maps, the worse food, the far places, but the worst was the nighttime far from a town. It's an America that is gone now and I don't have too much nostalgia for it; only people who grew up in big cities and never saw the rural old days could collect wagon wheels and cobblers' benches and say, "*Those were the days.*"

After a while, of course, the car ran out of gas and water, and one tire ran out of air. We stood on foot, Mamma gathering her clothes around her, and Gramp, his last match gone, chewed into the neck of a cold cigar.

Far ahead a light gleamed and we started toward it over a field laid out in young peach trees. We came to a barbed-wire fence and went through it. I lost the seat of my pants. Then we waded across a shallow creek, Gramp carrying Mamma and I carrying Gramp's gold watch—for some reason I now forget.

We were on a wide, wild-grown lawn, and beyond was a huge house, looking bone-white in the night. A pack of hound dogs ran toward us, scenting meat, I suppose, and Gramp swung his cane, shouting at the top of his lungs.

"Get back, you hounds of hell, get back! Hello there . . . damn it . . . hello!"

Mamma, who was very brave when her young were in danger, had placed me behind her and was whacking hound dogs over the head with a small shoe she had removed, hopping gracefully on the other foot.

Some big doors were flung open in the white house and a voice said, "What yo' doin' out there?"

"Call off your dogs!" Gramp shouted, banging his cane down on a liver-colored hound's head.

"Git off, Nero, git off, Rufus, git off, Nellie, Cleo! Damn it, Pompey!" We saw a tall, thin man with a gun under his arm drop-kick one of the dogs at least ten feet. The rest got back and sat down with their tongues out, waiting. Mamma had fainted and the tall man picked her up, gun and all, and carried her toward the house.

"Really sorry," the man said to Gramp, "but this isn't the kind of road many people use these days."

"What road?" asked Gramp.

Inside the house the tall man set Mamma down on a sofa and rubbed her hand. He was a handsome young man, and there were more dogs in the house, watching us with big dark eyes. Mamma opened her eyes and saw the dogs and said, "Oh, I wasn't dreaming. Dogs!"

"Gaylord is the name," said the young man. "This is Gaylord House."

"I get the connection," said Gramp, growling. "We're lost, and it's no way to treat strangers."

"I agree," said the young man. "Will yo' join me at dinner?"

"Yes, damn it," said Gramp. "We forgive you the dogs. How about you, Sari?"

Mamma sat up and smiled. "I am hungry. Stevie, comb the hair out of your face."

The dining room was huge, the service fine, and the food—after all these years, I still remember it. I can't tell you who was President then or who won the World Series or the name of the famous murderer of that year, but I remember that meal.

Gramp's journal of our trip says the main course was

tournedos of beef, an old family way of cooking it, the young man told us. His name was Dennis.

Mamma and I were very hungry and Gramp was always a good man with a plate of food. Dennis smiled at us.

"I'm sorry about the dogs but we raise them, yo' know. The Gaylord is a famous breed. Has been for hundreds of years in this state."

Gramp nodded. "The Ohio Gaylord, a fine hound," he said, kicking at a dog under his feet. "I know it well."

Dennis said, "Ohio? This is Kentucky, suh." I noticed a Southern tone suddenly in his voice and I looked up at the dueling pistols nailed to the wall.

"Kentucky?" said Gramp. "Damn, I was drifting south more than I thought. Must get that steering wheel fixed."

Mamma looked at Gramp as if she hadn't come with him and went on eating. When it came time to serve coffee, a tall, very pretty girl came in (with two dogs, naturally), and she was wearing jodhpurs, those imported Indian riding pants. It was the first time I had ever seen any, and I found them amazing.

"My sister Dora," said Dennis, making the introductions. "She's been at a dog show. How did we do?"

"Lost," said Dora, throwing her dog whip into the corner. "They're importing their own judges, Dennis. We haven't a chance any more."

Dennis nodded. "It's hard to find honest men among dogs."

Gramp agreed. "Show me a man who loves a dog too much and I'll show you a person who lacks respect for the human race. Present company, of course, left out."

"I'm hungry," said Dora.

I don't remember much more that night. I slept in a big bed all alone, and I heard the dogs in the hall all night sporting a mouse hunt. In the morning we sent out for help to get our car in order, but something had snapped someplace and it would be some days before the local wagon smith could fix it. The Gaylords invited us to stay on and we did. They were fine people. Much too proud a sister and brother to marry with the decaying stock around them, they raised hounds, kept up the big white family house, and expected to be the last of their line. It was all rather run-down and a little foolish, but to a kid raised on mid-Victorian novels it seemed very romantic and exciting; some would call the Gaylords snobs, Dennis a secret drinker, and Dora frigid. But we saw the Gaylords as wonderful people upholding the family motto, *Disce pati*, "Learn to Endure."

It was a side of American life that, as I was coming out of boyhood, the big Hoover depression of '29 destroyed; it was wiped out by bank foreclosures and public sales. But in the early decades of this century when I was a boy we knew many of these old decaying families, living in deep poverty, given to numbing vices, mild sadisms, comic degeneracies. Often they were just plain fools, holding on to valuable furniture, sweeping their own paneled halls, not paying their servants, but surviving. Old houses full of knobs, termites under your feet already gnawing the old walnut, cracked window glass purple with sun, roofs leaking on handmade exotic wallpaper, and the big copper pots full of only boiled potatoes with soggy green salt to pour over them. Lean men and women smelling of unwashed clothes, often a family idiot wandering around, the gardens run to brown weeds, cancerous roses and chipped statues stained with pubic moss, stable and coach houses, old carriages smelling of long dead horses, rotting saddles, straw dust, and decaying brick walls.

They were sad places, but they gave me as a child a feel of history and the passing of generations. And a kind of pride in family, no matter how foolish or how snobbish it appeared.

Gramp had known many of these people in their glory, in their high tide. I don't think he noticed the patched pants of London tailoring, the first editions put under the cheap table leg, the smell of rotting apples in closed-off rooms, the yellow pallor on faces full of misery, disease, and madness, or uncared-for fingernails on hands that did no work; nor was he repulsed by the reeking breath of neglected bodies.

Gramp could talk to them of faded battles, glorious fools dead a long time ago, or the record time of horses in a race run fifty years before.

Most of these undesired, unpossessed, passed when the banks took over the places, and the people in them killed themselves with clumsy methods, or died off like unwatered ferns, sitting in small parks eating something oily out of a paper bag.

Next day Gramp was smoking his morning cigar when Dennis came out.

"Yo' know the points of a good dog, don't yo', Captain Longstreet?"

Gramp, who had not been expected to be hailed by a military title (even if he had spoken of his war efforts at dinner), nodded. "But certainly. They all have four legs, a tail more or less, and enough ears to hear with."

Dennis said, "Frankly, we're short of judges. And I'm on the committee, and I haven't been able to find a really good judge. Would yo', sir, like to judge in the hound class this afternoon at the club?"

"You flatter me," said Gramp, looking at his cigar as if it were a prize dog. "I know a good dog, but not a dog's good parts according to the texts."

Dennis rubbed a hound's ears. "Yo' yourself saw the points of these dogs. Yo' remarked at breakfast that you'd never seen such hounds."

Gramp had said "hounds of hell," but Dennis hadn't heard it all. Gramp was a sport. He threw up his hand and nodded. "I'll judge. You can say I will judge and judge. . . ."

They shook hands and went inside to try some prime bourbon and branch water. By the time lunch came around they were fairly glowing, and Gramp was explaining the kind of dogs Caesar had in Gaul and the breeding of lap dogs in London according to the shape of their noses.

Mamma and Dora went upstairs after lunch to wave each other's hair, and Gramp and Dennis and I went to the front lawn to pick up the winning team of three hounds Dennis was entering in the show. Dudley, Tez, and Mac were their names, I remember, and they looked just like any other set of three hounds. But Gramp and Dennis were very much pleased with them. I think anything would have pleased them. The bourbon had mellowed them neatly. We put Dudley and Mac in the back of a blue Jordan roadster with me and Tez in the front between Gramp and Dennis. Mamma and Dora would follow later in another car.

We drove off in a clash of gears, the blue Jordan being a very fine car. For the young folk I might explain the Jordan was a real fancy car of the period. This one had a low-slung blue body, red wire wheels, and on the hood Dennis had welded, in silver, a running hound with flapping ears. The horn had been tuned to sound like a braying dog in sight of prey, and the dusty roads saw us pass in gray clouds of glory. Tez in the front seat sat on her round little bottom and howled politely, and Mac and Dudley in the back seat licked my face from time to time and flogged me with their tails.

It was a very nice trip, the car rolling along and the dogs yipping. The towns we passed got out of our way, and it was no time at all before we were at the club.

It had once been a fox-hunting club, but someone had quoted Oscar Wilde about fox hunting being "the unspeakable in full pursuit of the uneatable," and anyway the few remaining foxes got too wise for the dogs. So, Dennis told us, it became a dog and horse club. All the members raised dogs or horses, "or knew people who did."

Gramp was taken over to a lot of fine gentlemen who shook his hand and pinned a blue ribbon on him almost as large as the ribbons they awarded the dogs. He wasn't a winner, however, I saw—just a "Judge," as the ribbon read.

Gramp and Dennis left me in charge of the dogs, who got on my lap, and I sat holding them while they went inside. They were big dogs, and I only had room for one at a time, so the cutest one, Tez, won, and she kissed me on the nose, but I was too shy to kiss her back. I just wished I had her in the city and could walk her in the flower gardens. Mamma and Dora got to the show at last and they took the hounds and entered them in their groups. At least Mamma, who disliked all animal life except raccoon coats from Harvard, went along.

It was a gay time, and they served a few things to charm all dog lovers. A big table had been set up on the front lawn of the club, and while it was just then against the law to drink certain forms of stuff men swallow, they did have a nice odor of bourbon and rye whisky all over the place.

Gramp and Dennis did their duty here, and then Gramp went off with some red-faced characters with notebooks to judge some dogs. All the dogs and all the people loved each other, and when they saw anyone they knew they either barked or said, "Hi, Roger," "Good doggie, Eddie," or "Down, Mike." Gramp was in great form; at least he was doing a fine job of acting as if he knew dog life and its fine points. A large hound was standing in a dazed way in the sun, and Gramp went up to him and grabbed his tail and some skin under his neck and pulled; then he felt along the chest lines. Then he got down for an eye-level view (the eye level of a worm) and scouted the hound dog's angle shots. Then he rolled over almost like a garage mechanic rolling under an ailing car and studied the dog.

Everyone seemed very much impressed. "There never was any judging like *this* before!" The dog seemed bored, then he looked at Gramp as if he were wondering if Gramp were another dog. Gramp got that look and I think for a moment felt a little foolish because he got up, dusted his knees, and said, *"This* is a dog."

People clapped their hands and some of the other judges came over and talked with Gramp and they agreed on something—that it *was* a dog. Mamma and Dora lowered their eyes when two Gaylord dogs got ribbons, but the Best of Show, and the Best in Class went to a big red dog with red eyes and a sensual leer.

On the way home Gramp said, "They outvoted me, Dennis.

But your dogs should have won first. Frankly, the other judges were carpetbaggers, not real judges of dog flesh."

Dennis agreed but said a gentleman didn't care so much about winning; it was the breeding that mattered. Back at the house Dora said "like hell it was"—which wasn't how ladies talked at all, according to Mamma—but even Mamma said, "Damn it, you should have done better, Gramp." Which shows how dog love creeps into people.

We left right after dinner, of which I can't remember a thing any more. I guess the day had worn me down to a mental nub.

We promised to come back real soon, but of course we never did go back. That's the sad part about traveling. You become fast friends so quickly and then it's all over. Dora kissed Mamma and kissed me, and Gramp handed out a cigar and shook hands with Dennis, who looked very handsome in white, his nose just a little red.

Our car was fixed and we piled in and drove off. Mamma held a ham, the bottles of gift bourbon were at her feet, and Dudley and Mac, the good hound dogs, sat in the road as we pulled away. Tez was in heat and had been locked up.

"Sorry I couldn't win first for them," said Gramp.

"It was only dogs," said Mamma, reverting to type.

"The best dogs in Kentucky," I said.

"Don't be too sure, Stevie," said Mamma. "It might be Ohio after all."

Gramp scowled. "I suppose I'll never hear the end of how I mistook Kentucky for Ohio."

"No," said Mamma cheerfully.

That night we had a dreadful meal in a crossroads hotel; the next day we skipped breakfast and lunch, trying to reach a place where the food was fit for human stomachs. But it was two weeks before we really found anything worth eating. Places like the Gaylords' were rare, even if Gramp did have a Dan'l Boone skill in finding good living on the American highways. Food is still dreadful on our roadways, but in 1919 it was even worse. So you can understand why we remember with pleasure, and in great detail, when we had a fine meal.

Things got real bad in the food line, but I knew it was lowest at Cairo on the Ohio River, when we caught Mamma taking a slug of Gaylord bourbon.

"I'm sorry," said Mamma, wiping her mouth with dainty care and corking the bottle. "I could eat Tez on toast I'm so hungry."

I enjoyed the landscape, the wood-smoke-scented air, not being aware I was seeing a world that was soon going to be mistaking speed for progress. The roads were poor, but there was no great auto traffic. Trucks were still of normal size and the farmer usually drove a horse-drawn buggy, gig, buckboard, or work wagon. Garages, if they existed, were mostly old stables, and service and gasoline were cheaply held.

A country town would appear up a dusty road, the elms old and frayed by summer heat; there were still not many billboards, and those that existed advertised products now no longer around. Each town had a water tower, or pumped direct from the river.

The people were more ingrown, looked healthy, but often bored, and the American cowboy of legend, while already on the movie scene, was yet to become the great guitar-playing folk hero.

The hotels gave little service, the beds were wide, soft, and very old, the lobby smelled of tobacco juice, Sen-Sen, and the desk clerks' hair oil. You were let alone, you were neglected, and personal-carried ivory or gold toothpicks finished every meal. It was a world that had its faults, but they seemed errors, not big problems.

Even as a boy I saw that these people did not conform; they were not regimented, not yet set in one dictated national mold, not gripped by a whipped-up fear. The village freethinker sat back on his chair in the public square and quoted Bob Ingersoll and Voltaire to me, the camp-meeting folk got jerked to Jesus and rolled in the straw pen in ecstasy as they came to God. The town crank worked on his perpetual-motion machine, and unpopular causes were permitted to air their views. The

Booster, the Wowser, and the Ex-War-Buddy had already organized, but the people who made their own hard cider, preached Henry George, and voted in town meetings would spit in your eye if you tried to bend their viewpoint to conform with their neighbors'. As a child I remember the newspapers, when every village editor kept a pistol in his roll-top desk and angry citizens still horsewhipped a reporter who wrote a story that shouldn't have appeared in print.

As we rolled through wine-warm, summery towns and listened and watched, and ate the local dishes, Gramp said he was aware that the political parties would do away with the mugwumps, the local problems, the root-hog-and-holler stump speakers, and the native suspicion of big-city lawyers. A man's lungs were a political candidate's main asset in the country we passed through, and his campaign funds were never secret. The party machines let local politics alone. It was disordered, gay, not too dishonest, and native as the arrowheads in the ground and the people whose grandfathers walked from St. Joe to Wagon Wheel County. Gramp was aware of it: this wonderful nonconforming, this lack of fears and bugaboos; he told us, "I have always hated the people who say it was better in the good old days, but Stevie, someday all this will be the good old days, and don't let anyone tell you maybe it wasn't better."

Mamma said, "Don't fill the boy's mind with your ward heelers' ideas, Gramp. You once bought an election."

"Sure. Out in Butte, Montana, when they wanted to elect me judge. I bought enough votes to keep from getting elected. Damn it, Sari, drive more careful!"

Mamma said, "I saw that rut. I *like* ruts."

It began to rain that night. We came to a wide, dirty river in flood. We bogged down in mud. The river rose all around us. A wind came and the white caps danced. The river made clipped, monosyllabic sounds. Suddenly, a last blowsy wafer of sun glanced madly about and went down; wind whirled, the whole river shouted in pelting hail. We sat, blind in a white vestibule.

"Scared?" asked Mamma.

"Not with you here."

Gramp said, "I don't like it."

Sleet or hail beat us and tore at our clothing. An island swam toward us, rammed the low shore, and overhead the cotton-woods and river trees howled as the wind menaced their roots and made a polished expanse of baldness where there had once been grass. I shivered and stared.

We lay under the soggy car top, which was covered with mud. Water ran and mud followed. The whole world seemed in a rage, and never was there such wind. We sat in mud; timber whirled and pranced around us. Naked trees submitted to assault. Logs hit us and I looked out for a moment on a preview of the Day of Judgment. Trees flew and birds lay on the ground. There was no sky, no land, but a lead torrent (like a dulled Venetian mirror at home, I decided) that moved in many directions and, when the hail stopped, the waters came down in fuller force. The water still rose around us.

Mamma said, "We've got to save the boy."

Gramp said, "We'll sit it out. A fool could die out there."

Night came. We sat and waited. Dawn came, a feeble mist against a sky that still poured water. We sat and shivered.

Noon passed and we chewed raw bacon strips and muddy fistfuls of dirty potato chips. Then the fury fell away, the thunder stopped behind the clouds. A draining of water rushed by us. We stirred and looked at the river and the gullies cut fresh in the land. Trees, houses, shivering hens passed on driftwood. The far shores came and went as mist parted and closed. A great sow, "impervious to decency and sanity," Gramp said, with chattering teeth, drifted ashore, half-buried in mud. She grunted and sneezed water out of her lungs and began to give birth to a huge litter of naked little pigs. Mamma began to shiver.

A whole barn came ashore and stood tall and wonderful and near us. Then something happened; the river touched some main beam, some secret cross truss, and the barn melted away with devilish witchcraft into a sudden collapsing pile of old lumber. Gramp shouted, and I cheered.

A dog climbed a floating tree and howled madly through his mud-piled fur and passed, snarling with a wet bark. Fences passed and hayricks. Mamma sneezed.

Gramp said, "It will be safe soon to hunt up a fire."

A privy passed like a vaudeville joke, its three wooden eyes open and staring at a sky turning to brass. We sat drying our faces, our feet ankle-deep in muck. The only dry spot I had was the roof of my mouth.

Gramp doused wet wood with gasoline. We cooked beans lukewarm and shoved them into our mouths while our teeth chattered rather than chewed. We slept locked together, trying to get a little warmth into our bodies. It was no use. We ran races in the mud. We sweated through exercises. The chill never left us. Debauched by effort, cross-eyed with fatigue, the cold dawn found us numb but healthy. Mamma was wonderful in drying our clothes out in sections. We were dry (and hungry). Gramp dried the car motor, spark plugs, and wires, and she started at last.

Three miles we fought the road, then swung over the remains of a horrible, chewed-up riverbank. It was twenty minutes before we could get on real high ground through the glue of mire and river silt and decay. A shack, a monstrous unreality, lay on its side while three half-grown, dirty-faced boys wrestled with it. They gave up the job, and the house fell back in the mud. Dead cows lay about, already bloating. A tall, thin man, watching covertly his mashed world, sat barefooted in the mud. Near him, on a crate, a lean woman, nude to the hips, her long breasts falling limply from her, nursed a rash-covered baby against her ribs, and she made some attempt to sing the fretted child to sleep. Our feet made sucking sounds in the muck.

The man looked up and we saw his red-rimmed eyes, his slack mouth, the white streaks in his wet hair, and that obstinacy of farmers in his taut features.

"Come from the river?" he asked.

"Yes," said Gramp.

"High, ain't she?"

"Yes," said Mamma. "Any hotel still open around here?"

"Down the road a mile."

"Wash you out?" asked Gramp.

"Everything. Ain't a chicken left. Most all the hay gone. 'Hoppers got the corn and everything else last week. Now the house ain't worth a fruit box."

"Too bad. . . ."

"I'm finished. Let the bank take it. I been working for them long enough."

His wife stared, and the infant made puppy sounds. She pulled him off with a sucking sound and sat there with him in her lap, staring. I didn't feel shy or flushed. Disaster had numbed such nonsense.

The three boys sniffled in the mud and rubbed wet silt in their eyes. A dog ate something behind a haying machine, and a wet pig rusticated among broken fruit trees.

The baby began to howl.

The man took chewing tobacco and filled his shaking mouth. He chewed and looked at Gramp emptying our dirty sack full of canned food onto a plank. The boys gathered fence rails and a broken door and poured more gasoline on it and soon a fire burned between cement blocks that had once been a water tank. We all ate, gulping food, stuffing our mouths, looking at one another and chewing. We swallowed and ate on, making intimate tones among ourselves to show we were human.

Mamma sat with the baby on her knees, a punched milk can in her hand, and was dribbling its contents into the infant's pimple-encircled mouth. A pink hue crept into its flesh.

The boys swallowed and stared and swallowed.

The man rubbed his cheeks and put aside the tin can from which he had been sipping black, sugarless coffee. He looked at the mud-churned wilderness.

"Well, let 'em take it. Let 'em get another fool to break his back here on fried mush and greens. I'm going to town. Get me a job in some industry. To hell with razorback hogs and scissor-hocked horses."

The woman wept, "Oh, Ned, the town. . . ."

He glared at her. "Funny, funny, ain't it, mister?"

"I don't know," Gramp said.

I looked up into the sun breaking past clouds. I blinked in the fresh glare.

We went on by a soiled river cleaning itself by rubbing off debris against the backs of islands. The very air was full of decay and the smell of corn plants crushed into the mud. More bloated cows lay about. The next hotel was washed out too. We camped and Gramp alone went on to see what he could buy. He brought back little. We ate stale bread and roasted green corn.

"Why didn't you tell me what I looked like?" Mamma asked, looking into a small mirror.

"You look fine," I said.

"A fine monster. I'm a buffalo."

"Good strong hair," I said.

"Don't you have to shave, Gramp?" Mamma asked.

"I'm stopping at the next town and getting a shave."

The next town, called Penny Crossing, had wisely built a hotel on the ridge of the hill, above the river. We were happy to get there, plastered with mud, dog-tired, and reeking of river muck. The car had courageously come through. We had been stuck in ditches, ruts, bogs, but with the aid of old barn timber and brush, Gramp's skill had kept us rolling.

In the hotel dozens of flood victims were stranded, lamenting and eating, weeping and shouting. Gramp managed to get us the billiard room, and the use of a bathroom with plenty of hot water. Then he took over the bridal suite, and here we relaxed, ate, and Mamma wrote letters home about the great flood. It is from these letters that certain details of our flood experience are taken.

We slept the whole next day, while our clothes were washed and dried, and Gramp, freshly barbered and excited, ran around getting news of roads and bridges ahead of us, while the local garage washed out our car, stripped mud from it, and took apart the engine and somehow got it together again. It ran better than ever. For years I thought this flood was bigger than the famous Deluge, but checking back in old newspapers I find only a few lines: *Flash Flood Hits River Farms.*

When the car was ready, Gramp put the question we had all been expecting. "Well, Sari, do we go on?"

Mamma folded her arms and made a humming sound of disdain. "Hmm, I can just see the family nodding and saying, 'We told you the g.d. fools would come back without finishing the trip.'"

"So?" said Gramp, inspecting a soggy cigar.

"Sail on," said Mamma, quoting part of a poem she had been teaching me.

Our problem in traveling was not where to find shelter, but how to avoid visiting all the people we had letters of introduction to, all the relations scattered like buckshot over the land, all the people Gramp had done business with in a long life. And the girls Mamma had been to school with, who had married and gone West, the strangers Gramp had entertained in New York and who now waited all over the country to grab us and show us how much they had to eat and what passed for fun in their neck of the woods.

Also, Gramp and Mamma were people who could make friends with a man-eating shark if they were in the mood for it. In ten minutes a total stranger was telling them the story of his life and inviting them to move in with him. It was a gift they both had, and I saw it often at work on the trip. The people we couldn't shake were the relations. Mamma's kin in St. Louie, an aunt in Oklahoma, a school chum who married a horse-breeder in California; all these knew we were on the road, and they were waiting. And Gramp had business connections—the men who ran copper mines in Butte, old soldiers who had fought in wars with him, old railroad men who had laid right of ways in blizzards from his plans and had taken high iron over the Rockies on his graded track. We could have passed a life-time visiting on the trip, and I sometimes felt both Gramp and Mamma would have liked that.

AUNT GIGI OF ST. LOUIS

ST. LOUIE FAMILY

MAMMA HAD CLOSE RELATIVES IN ST. LOUIE; FAMILY rumor was that they had moved there with the invention of beer. This was not true. The Fosters were brewers of beer and bottlers of beer, and looked as if they drank a lot of it, but even I didn't think they invented it. Their motto was: *Wer a gelt hat, kann a Bier kaufin; wer keins hat, kann a Wasser saufen* (roughly: The fellow with money can buy beer; without it, he can guzzle water).

Gramp drove us into St. Louis on a windy day, and even after all these years I still remember how Gramp usually entered a town, muffled in his great driving coat, smoking a flaming torch of a cigar, going as fast as the car could go, and looking over the town the way the Goths must have looked over the Sabine women near Rome in the early days of recorded history.

The Fosters, Mamma's relatives, were not Sabines; they were highly respectable, very well off, and a little too sure they were the salt of the earth, the beer of the Middle West, and the fruit of the finest family tree. There were several sets of them, but the main root, the big oaks, lived in a large red brick house that looked like a Rhine castle, with white marble steps and bay windows "as wide and protruding," Gramp said, "as the stomachs of the family."

We drove up to the castle and a large Swede housemaid let us in, and Gigi Foster came to greet Mamma and kiss her. She was Mamma's aunt; Mamma's mother's sister, I got to understand after a while. Aunt Gigi could sing opera in three languages, was the first woman (respectable, that is) to carry a cigarette case, and she looked down upon the beer-makers of Milwaukee as Johnny-come-latelys to the malt and hops trade.

She kissed Mamma. "Sari! It's good to see you. And *this* is Stephen?"

"Stevie," said Gramp. "Let's not get fancy. You look fine, Gigi; been living high off the keg?"

Aunt Gigi ignored that part of Gramp's introduction, and we all shook hands and Gigi phoned Uncle Peter, who was at the brew house, that they had company. Mamma was shown to her room, and she cried a little because she was staying on here while I went on in our car with Gramp to what we hoped would be California.

I was hungry, and the dinner gong was being struck below someplace in the red brick castle among the suits of armor, giant beer steins, and Rhine river art.

Uncle Peter was a little round man with waxed mustache and looked like a minor British general of some African war. He could strut sitting down and had a sporting eye.

"Sari," he said, kissing Mamma and gathering her in close,

"that's a nice big boy you have there. He going into real estate like his father?"

Gramp swallowed a small cut glass of kümmel and shook his head. "No. Hell, that's worse than being a great fiddle player. Stevie will be either an international bum or a professional baseball player."

Aunt Gigi said, "We don't use the word Hell here, or words *like* it."

Uncle Peter tried to look prim and failed and put his arm around Mamma.

Gramp said, low-voiced, as we marched into the dining room, "*How* do they manage to carry on a conversation cutting out the best words?"

Aunt Gigi and Uncle Peter had three sons and three daughters, and they all lived at the castle. There were some sons-in-law, some daughters-in-law, and some very fat yellow grandchildren who looked as if they had been weaned on beer. They were all seated around a long, heavy oak table as big as a skating rink. Three Swede hired girls served this grouping; Aunt Gigi thought butlers sinful. The eating silverware was heavy and had a nude mermaid of solid silver as a handle (but a respectable nude; she was mostly fish scales). The sons and daughters were overfed or perhaps over-beered; they were large and heavy and one could see they had lots of red blood in them. They puffed and panted and took on solid food with serious, silent faces.

With the help of some notes by Gramp, I shall try to give you some idea of the dinner, the average everyday dinner (called supper, of course, *not* dinner) of a Middle West beer baron in the old days, but I don't know if I can remember it all. We all got a dozen raw peppery oysters on the half shell and a special silver merry-go-round contained the sauces, juices, spices, and horse-radish that one bathed the oysters in. Uncle Peter had an extra half dozen and sucked juice from the shells. Then came lob-

ster cocktails in small bowls, and we drank a white Rhine wine.
Next, a huge silver coffin of piping hot turtle soup, very green,
and floating on it were slices of lemon. It tasted of a good
sherry, and the green turtle meat was cubed and just solid
enough to give the full flavor of the turtle. Even the odor was
hunger-filling. The family sweated and ate.

That ended the fish courses, the opening guns of the battle,
while little silver wagons on little silver wheels were placed on
the table by the hired girls. These contained rolls, buns, hot
breads with little seeds imbedded in them, and there were china
dishes of sweet country butter, not the cubed butter of the
modern lean days, but butter from a mold in the shape of a
cabbage rose, good yellow butter that never saw a store. It
came from Uncle Peter's own farm.

Mamma and Gramp were looking at each other, watching the
family teeth at work and listening to the gullets of the beer
family at play among the food. No one talked much except
Uncle Peter, who told us about the girlie shows in town and the
size and color of the show girls. The soup came; it was a rice
soup, the rice wrapped in cabbage leaves, stuffed with beef,
veal, and pork and spices, stewed in the soup, a sort of St. Louie
version of *golombki*. This was followed by guinea hen (which I
called *genuine hen* for years, knowing no better) *en casserole
sauce Albufeira*, served with noodles *polonaise*. Not a son or
son-in-law dropped out. Their breathing grew labored.

It's hardly worth listing the rest of the meal. Apricot sauce
and glacé, a *Le Milliard cherry flam*, and of course coffee in huge
blue cups, a coffee powerful enough to wake the dead. *Mit* thick
country cream. By this time the family was warm and glowing,
breathing hard but game. Gramp looked at me, I looked back
and said I wanted to "unswallow," and Gramp said he would
take me out. Mamma looked at us as if to say why didn't she
think of *that*.

Up in my room Gramp shook his head. "Damn me, where do
they put it all?"

I moaned. "Maybe they have hollow legs, Gramp."

"They're digging their own graves, scooping it out with a roasting pan, pickling it in lager beer."

At which point Uncle Peter came up to us with a balloon of brandy for Gramp, and a lump of sugar in it for me. I began to gag and Gramp rushed me into the bathroom.

We were only staying a few days to get Mamma set with the relatives and then we, Gramp and I, were to go on. It was a good thing too. The family never let up on their eating. At dawn the buffet tables started steaming and boiling, and silver pots of tidbits, tongues, bacons, delicate animal organs, and dissected fish were all ready for breakfast. Everyone took a wagon-wheel-sized plate and moved back and forth from buffet and table between mounds of scrambled eggs, small ham steaks, and always that strong coffee to wash it all down. Lunch was a mere play, hasty attacks on chicken in the pot *Mallorouin*, big pies dripping their heavy berry blood on white plates, whole, angry-eyed fish planked and decorated with aspics and carrot carvings, some jugged eels, a whole flank of bloody roast beef, or a few ribs of lamb were followed by a big cheesecake and little cakes with pink icings.

Uncle Peter used to go to the market himself—and took Gramp and me along—carrying two huge oilcloth shopping bags, down near the river front. There a one-armed ex-soldier who ran a shop where the fish of the gulf were brought in on beds of ice, where the river oyster and clam were damply packed in big barrels, where the local hams and bacons (really wood-smoked by the natives) were to be found, black and sinister, but showing a pale pink meat when cut open.

Old One Flipper Sam, the owner, would fill Uncle Peter's shopping bags very full and then rub the stump of his arm (lost at the first Bull Run) and say, "Got some real French olive oil, some Maine lobsters coming in on ice this afternoon, let you have two dozen squab pigeons, they boil up nice."

Uncle Peter would nod. "Yes, boil up nice *à la crapaudine*, halved, buttered, and grilled. Any Rock Cornish grouse well hung? What about those New Orleans prawns you promised?"

"Boat hit a sand bar down-river. Let you have some smoked cod roe *pâté* and half a crate of Dungenees crabs from the Columbia."

And home we would go, carrying our shopping bags, crab armor clashing and spitting white and blue in the basket I was carrying. Of course, it wasn't all eating. Uncle Peter was a man who also liked the theater.

After dinner he would pat his stomach (as if to say to it, *How good I am to you*) and look at Gramp. "New show in town, suppose we take it in?"

Mamma said, "Fine. I've been home all day helping Gigi unpack the winter silver."

Aunt Gigi shook her head. "Now, Sari, the women here don't go to the kind of shows Peter and his friends go to. Girlie shows, they're called."

"I don't mind," said Mamma brightly. "I'm a girlie."

Aunt Gigi made a small pious circle of her mouth, as if sucking a lemon. "I know, dear, *but* we are a family that doesn't like talk. To the men it doesn't matter. All men are . . ." and she went on telling Mamma what all men *are*. And how they couldn't help it.

Uncle Peter sang: *"Bier her! Bier her! Oder ich fall um. Soll das Bier im Keller liegen—und ich hier die Ohnmacht kriegen?"*

I remember some of the shows Uncle Peter took us to. I guess they felt I was a man. I was twelve, but perhaps we matured early in those days.

The shows' posters all read: "Direct from Broadway with the Original Cast!" But as Uncle Peter said he knew the girls in them, and had known them for years, the boast of the posters didn't ring true. The plots were all about losing somebody's garter and trying to get it back, or about being locked up in a Turkish bath on ladies' night, about two bedrooms with one door, about people who had mixed up their wife with somebody else, about wedding nights, honeymoons that somehow

were always confused in long and short underwear. Very daring,
I suppose, but except for the girls, who had shrill voices and thin
lace nightgowns, and the comic maids in ruffled drawers, and
drinking butlers and jokes about missing love letters, it didn't
make much sense to me.

We used to go backstage and watch the girls make up, and
Uncle Peter would pinch their chins and rumps and invite them
to parties at his beer plant for his "sales conventions." He
usually had one a month, after which Aunt Gigi wouldn't speak
to him for a few days. I wasn't invited to a "sales convention,"
but Gramp was. I remember Mamma wanted to go but was told
respectable women never went to Uncle Peter's sales conventions, and Mamma said, what the h——, living in St. Louie
was like living in a g.d. nunnery. But she didn't say it where
Aunt Gigi could hear it.

I remember Uncle Peter and Gramp coming home late one
night from a sales convention, and something falling down the
stairs. It turned out to be a Greek work of art, pure marble, of a
nude boy pulling a thorn out of his bare foot. The next day
Aunt Gigi and Mamma didn't speak to Uncle Peter or Gramp,
but the men had headaches anyway and didn't eat much dinner, which was a shame as it was as big as ever, featuring, I remember, stuffed turkey roll *poupeton de dindon*, and containing
truffles and sweetbreads. But the men just weren't hungry.

Mamma said, "How about taking a drive along the river
front tonight?"

Aunt Gigi said, "It's a pleasure town, sporting life, not the
place to be seen after dark."

"Let's not sport any pleasure," said Mamma glumly.

I felt sorry for Mamma, to be left here among all these sets of
active teeth eating their way through mountains of food, and
Gramp and I climbing the Rockies and beyond in our Model-T.
But as Mamma said that night, "It's a man's world, Baby
Boy."

I suppose it was. Gramp and Uncle Peter and the sporting set of St. Louie lived a fast, fat life. Perhaps it was really sinful; I hear that vice today has been streamlined and made sanitary. But it had a flair in those days. I remember the red-light district, seeing it only of course at my age from the interior of Uncle Peter's chain-driven Simplex car, and in the daytime. The fancy houses with the white marble steps. And sometimes one of my fat, little boy cousins would point out a fancy dressed lady, all fashionable watered silk, with wonderful titian-red hair piled high over a face colored as an actress in make-up. And he would snicker and say, "That's a real fancy hoor."

"You sure?"

I was delighted with her and would walk around her and inspect her hat and wonderful red mouth, and once one smiled at me and patted my head and said, "Go peddle your papers, honey." I didn't fully know what a *hoor* was then, but if this was sin I felt pretty bad being left out of it. This cousin of mine, Herman by name, was a dirty little toad, with vile habits and a wet fat mouth; he saw something to leer at every place, and he whispered more misinformation into my ear than college professors ever did. Herman grew up to be a congressman and a meat-packer.

St. Louie was wide open; as usual the city government was selling protection and mulching the citizens on street repairs, and everyone seemed to enjoy the graft. At night Gramp said it was a fine frontier town and safe; I think he was only taken for three hundred dollars at faro, but he did make a killing at draw poker, cleaning out two tomato-packers and a river boat owner of all their loose change. His other adventures I didn't know about; and Aunt Gigi, you couldn't trust her as to details. Shining your shoes with a bath towel was a sin to her, or asking why God, if he loved people, made snakes, toothaches, and the pimples on Herman's face.

Uncle Peter was to me then, I suppose, a worthless but happy human being. He did no harm to anyone, and a lot of poor pretty girls ate well and got a few bits of clothes, and used to kiss his balding head and leave marks on it for Aunt Gigi to discover. Uncle Peter was a kind of bundle of joy of life who liked best the laughter, the food and drink of this world. I don't suppose he ever read a book or seriously took any interest in anything but beer-selling, charity fund drives, support of the Republican party cash box, and the young female in all its forms. He carried a pocketful of half dollars and had his route of misfits and bums who got a coin every time he passed them. He hung Aunt Gigi with diamonds until, as Gramp said, "She's so loaded now, the only thing he can do is drill her nose and hang some diamonds there."

Uncle Peter's beer was a good beer, heavy, dark and light in the proper seasons, and he sold it by the barrel; and kids rushed the family tin growler for a quart of it for a dime, and got a free pretzel for their troubles.

Uncle Peter hated bottled beer and refused to make it, and when bottles, a year or so later, came to cheapen beer and make it taste unlike the real barrel beer, he sold out to a big beer combine and slowly and skillfully ate his way to the grave. He and the family kept on eating, rolling to the health spas and baths of Europe, turning up in California or New Orleans, eating, drinking, laughing, giving to their charities, educating young women for careers in opera, founding a hospital here or there, and at last when the inner plumbing had had enough, and Uncle Peter was dead, everybody said he had never done an unkind thing to anyone in his life. Several ladies showed up with children they said Uncle Peter had replenished the earth with, but his will took care of that. He had inserted a clause giving any such proven claims a thousand dollars.

As Mamma explained it to me back in St. Louie, "Baby Boy, it's a man's world, so you just be good and blow your nose often and don't let Gramp punish his *liver* (code words meaning don't let him drink too much) and write me every day."

I said, "Of course, Mamma," and I kissed her because I loved her very much, and because I would miss her when we left her in St. Louie.

Uncle Peter wanted to give us a big send-off, roast half a deer, plank a river fish on an oak door, or something like that, but Gramp begged off, rubbing his gall-bladder region.

"You see, Pete, we're not used to eating so much."

"It's nothing, old boy. Wish I had some marinated bear steak for you."

"Never mind; too old to digest bear."

Aunt Gigi said to Gramp, "Tell Peter we have a bear ham left in the springhouse on the farm." Aunt Gigi wasn't speaking to Uncle Peter. It seems he had given one of the girls in a show a pair of garters with small diamonds on them spelling out "Foster's Fine Rhine Beer and Lager," and the girl showed them every night on the stage on a pair of well-filled black silk stockings. Uncle Peter called it *advertising*, but Aunt Gigi called it—— But let's skip that; maybe she didn't mean it.

"Tell Gigi," Uncle Peter said, "we ate that bear ham last Thanksgiving." When they weren't speaking, they spoke across each other.

"Hmmm," said Aunt Gigi. "I'm sure I never ate a drop or shred of it, but I'm sure the girls at the St. Louie Fun House of All Nations did."

Uncle Peter threw up his hands as if to say what's the use. He did leave two bottles of Hennessy cognac in the car for Gramp. "Medicine," he said. "Take it for colds, chills, and damp. Never fails."

Gramp agreed; said he preferred it to doctors. Mamma kissed us both, and we said we hoped she would have a good time. We had to go downtown to get some spark plugs and then to the express office to pick up a new tire being shipped out to us. And then off to California, with some Hennessy on our knee.

We were missing a big dinner and were happy about it. Uncle Peter said: "Minced lobster tails, baked ham *Jambon en croute*, Caucasian *shashlik*, and *pompano sauté meunière*."

As we drove downtown to get our spark plugs, Gramp said, "I kind of feel bad leaving Sari in that nest of heavy feeders."

"They're her relatives."

"That's no excuse."

"Was the sales convention fun, Gramp?"

Gramp looked at me and then looked away and played with the steering wheel (missing a trolley car by a thin hair). "The older you grow, Stevie, the quicker you'll learn it's all a dream, a bubble, and a snare. Don't be romantic about women, Stevie, like your Uncle Peter, and don't be a cynic like your grandfather. The romantics find them unfaithful, and the cynics see their shabby little souls that would sell a man out for a place to park their tiny feet."

"How shall I treat women, Gramp?" I asked. I wanted to know because one never knew what the future held for one.

"Treat 'em often," Gramp said, laughing. "That's the best advice I can give you, and avoid meeting any like your Aunt Gigi. Avoid at all times women who write or play music, who are sad and a little mad in the head, those that say they adore you, and then tell you how much they *give* and somehow never remember how much they *take*. But hell, boy, you've still a year or two before you're ready to tell something on long legs she's the greatest thing since Helen of Troy winked at an apple. I've got a headache."

Looking back, I guess Gramp and my Uncle Peter led a hard life that didn't always end neatly and romantically. I don't know if Gramp's advice ever really helped me. I feel I've made all his mistakes on my own.

We did pick up the spark plugs and then crossed town to the express office to pick up our tire. And there in the express office, next to a crate of live ducks, stood Mamma, her packed bags at her feet!

"What the——," said Gramp. "Damn me, Sari, they throw you out?"

"I ran away," said Mamma, kissing me on top of the head. "I couldn't take it any more." .

"What will they think?"

"I don't care. I'm coming along with you two. Move over."

Gramp grinned and lit the first cigar of the day. "Well, Sari, I can't say I blame you. I like fat women, but not as fat as you would have gotten there in a few weeks."

"Besides," said Mamma, "Aunt Gigi didn't believe in doing anything but retaining her social position."

"She's got a big one, too," said Gramp, winking, "a beaut."

"Uncle Peter helped me get away. He understands."

We got the tire and strapped it on and started west and kept going. Mamma was very happy and didn't say how much the car shook and how bad the gasoline smelled.

That night Mamma showed us Uncle Peter's last-minute parting gift to her, a pair of frilly garters with small diamonds, set with the letters "Foster's Fine Rhine Beer and Lager."

MY COUSIN SANDORA

7

*Nor fame I slight, nor for her
  favors call
She comes unlooked for, if she
  comes at all. . . .*
— ALEXANDER POPE
(From Gramp's notebooks)

ROUGHING IT
WITH GRAMP

THE NATIVE DOCTOR WAS NOT OFTEN THE SPECIALIST, and when Gramp took a cold we stopped at a small-town doctor's office, walked up one flight, and the bearded, pipe-smoking doc swabbed Gramp's throat, washed his nose in warm salt water, wrote out a fat-free diet, examined his chipped elbow, and strapped up a knee Gramp had twisted putting on a tire; cost: two dollars. A year or two later when almost all doctors were specialists, Gramp would storm out of their offices in a rage, and I myself once heard him tell a hundred-thousand-dollar-a-year quack: "Goddamn it, how do you know what's the matter with my nose? You looked in my right nostril, and everybody knows you are only a specialist in left nostrils!"

I grew lean on the trip, and tanned, and wondered when I would begin to shave. I was taking a good healthy interest in girls, and Mamma hoped I wouldn't inherit the talents of Gramp or Uncle Peter. This led to a talk between Mamma and Gramp as to whose relatives were worse, each claiming that their side of the family was the limit in meanness, depravity, and bad taste. As they really admired their families—even when bored with them—it must have been a futile kind of contest.

Gramp used to say he'd done everything in life twice, but even he wasn't a *cordon bleu*. He didn't come right out and say it, but if you cornered him and asked, he'd have to admit it. Mamma's Aunt Gussie was a *cordon bleu*, and that hurt Gramp. He didn't like Aunt Gussie, and to have her throw her art *l'épluchement d'une anguille* (how to undress an eel) was too much.

"Listen to me," Gramp would shout. "To eat and eat well is enough; to go into the gruesome details of gullet-plucking and liver-tickling is too much!"

Aunt Gussie would nod. "The ultimate in *haute cuisine* is something only a true Frenchman knows."

"Great jumping Balzac!" Gramp would scream. "Get the woman out of here before I stew her in beef broth and cold cream! Don't say *cordon bleu* in my house. It's a filthy word from now on!"

"Easy, Gramp," Mamma would say. "Aunt Gussie was never more than a *demi-pensionnaire* at the school."

"Demi-*what* did you say?" But Aunt Gussie knew he was going to be vulgar and left the room. The family was much given to shouting and pointing fingers at each other.

My Aunt Gussie was a very young girl around 1900, with lots of money because her husband had died rich. She dressed the way they did in the road show of *The Merry Widow* and went to

Paris to see "Art and Life," as she put it. But when she found out the money left to her was in trust and all she got was, as she said, "money to ride the horsecars," she enrolled in the famous cooking school, the Cordon Bleu, in Paris. She felt that if things got real bad, she could always open a railroad diner in Montez, Oklahoma, where her late husband had done well in oil. The idea of good French cooking in a dog wagon in Montez, Oklahoma, never seemed to baffle Aunt Gussie. She said she learned how to make twenty sauces, how to cut a chicken seventeen ways, and she had the amazing power to make a potato look like something else. She did create a dandy omelet; I do remember that.

Gramp's language about Aunt Gussie was amazing, and I learned some of it proudly. Gramp and Mamma, on our prolonged auto trip, had the idea that if Gramp ran his swear words together I wouldn't understand them and couldn't repeat them.

I said, "Where does the damnoldbag live out here?"

"Baby Boy!" said Mamma in panic. "*Where* did you learn such words?"

"_____ _____ __ _____," I said. (I was saving the real good ones for the last.) "I got ears."

"And your grammar!" Mamma said and began to weep. "The child is being ruined! And it's all your fault, Gramp. Oh, why, why did I come and bring that innocent little mind along?"

Gramp stopped the car, looked at his glowing cigar end and said softly, a defeated man who knew it, "Which way is Montez, Oklahoma? We'll go see our *dear* Aunt Gussie."

Mamma wiped her small, pearl-like tears away, sniffed air into her uptilted perfect nose, and purred, "You're not a bad man, Gramp, just careless. Go back a few miles and turn left."

"Thank you, Sari," said Gramp calmly, and we turned for Montez. Gramp knew all about women, and the thing he knew best was to give in when beaten. He hated tears, and he knew Mamma knew it. She was a pretty bright character herself, and she never pushed her gains too far. She acted now as if going to

Montez were Gramp's idea and she was only going along for the view—which was mostly oil wells.

Montez was something you had to see to believe. It was one main street with another one crossing it, some cement-block stores with very high false fronts, a lot of Stone Age cars, some drunk or sleeping Indians sitting at the curbs, lots of hay and feed, and oil-drilling tools, some trees that had died a long time ago—and, of course, Aunt Gussie.

She lived in a big brown frame house on the outskirts of town, a house out of the General Grant period, all gingerbread trimmings, three stories high, low in the porches, narrow in the hips, but with a good slate roof. There was water from deep wells, and Aunt Gussie raised cattle and had done very well for herself. Her second husband had also died. ("She never had any luck with the higher emotions," Gramp said.)

We drove up past a spotted hound dog nursing ten pups, and a brood of Chinese ducks testing a drinking pool of iron, called a stock tank in Montez. Aunt Gussie was seated on the steps of the porch smoking a corn husk cigarette, wearing levis (long before the fashionable fad for blue-jean pants), a man's shirt, and the remains of a weather-torn Stetson resting flat on her head. She didn't look at all like a fancy character from Paris.

"Waaahoo!" she said as she saw us. "Visitors!" She came over to the car, but she didn't say, "Howdy partner," or "Put it thar, strangers." She just kissed Mamma, Gramp, and myself very wetly and said, "It's good to see you all. It's been a long time."

Which shows you how movies let a guy down. She didn't even wear a Colt on her hip or spit chewing tobacco. I had to settle for hand-rolled corn husk cigarettes. (No nice woman smoked in public, and the ads never suggested a lady would ever put tobacco to her lips.)

"It's a nice place, Montez," said Mamma after we got out of the car and up onto the porch. "Such a dry, sunny town. Dusty too."

Aunt Gussie used some of Gramp's run-together words. "If it weren't that beef took a flop after the war (World War I), I'd be out of here as fast as a sparrow could flick its tail. Paris, that's a grand place, isn't it, Gramp?"

"It's a place," said Gramp, not wanting to get committed on anything with Aunt Gussie.

"The food," said Mamma. "The French—they know *how* to eat."

"So do I," I said. "We just visited Uncle Peter."

"That glutton. Come in," said Aunt Gussie, "and I'll rustle you up some grub." (That wasn't such bad-sounding western-style talk, I figured.)

Inside, the house was cool and neat. On the walls were Aunt Gussie's two pink Matisse nudes on sofas, and her real good Picassos, purchased years before anybody in this country thought they could paint better than "an idiot chile."

"Lot of meat on those sofas," Gramp said, looking at the paintings, but he never really got past Degas and the yellow-green of Lautrec's night scenes.

It would have been a nice lunch, only Aunt Gussie said, "You all coming out here reminds me I'm a *cordon bleu.*"

"Why should it?" said Gramp.

A little girl came in just then, carrying a big pencil and looking at us. Aunt Gussie patted her on the head. "This is my daughter Sandora. The late Mr. Hervath Andrassy was a Hungarian."

We lowered our eyelids for a moment in memory of Aunt Gussie's late husband. Sandora stuck out her tongue at me and ran her pencil over it. I noticed it left a purple line on it, and I hoped she would die.

"Shake hands with Cousin Sandora," Mamma said. Mamma was like an Englishman in the jungle dressing for dinner; you had to make the proper social sounds and gestures with her around. I shook hands, and Sandora tried to throw me with an Indian handlock. I was very polite and only kicked her in the shins.

I must say lunch was a real delight. First a huge tongue came in, smoking on a board. Aunt Gussie "grew" her own tongues, she told us. She had some cattle crossed with buffalo, and their tongues, hung and smoked, were the best—her private stock.

"Good," agreed Gramp, wiping his mouth and reaching for the local wine that Aunt Gussie made from native grapes. Gramp and Mamma and myself were very happy to tuck in and eat. Crossing America in 1919 was unkind to a stomach. If I write here of the food we often found, don't think we ate well on the trip. I don't record all the hand-hammered sandwiches, the rubbery fried chicken of the deadly South, the iron rolls, the rusty hamburgers, the tired and limping greens, the river-bog soups, the rancid pork sides, the hot dogs stuffed with decaying mystery, the cabbage steamed to death, the plaster-of-Paris pies, the sand-tasting cakes, the mud doughnuts, the battery acid coffee, the sick blue milk, the eggs that were pure little-chick murder, and the scrambled, fried, and omeletted horrors, fried in rancid bacon fat—all the things that crossing America brought to our stomachs.

We spent several weeks at Aunt Gussie's ranch. Mamma needed some rest, and Gramp had a touch of gout, the first big touch on the trip.

At first it had seemed to me arid land, wet by the few streams that had run on a while and then been smothered in the dry earth; desert held the range. But Aunt Gussie had the bigger streams diverted to the fields and deep wells dug and the retaining dams put up to hold back the spring rain, if any, and so spread its wet throughout the year. Where the sand flea and the cactus had fought stony seasons for a hard brittle existence, timothy, red clover, lespedeza, redtop, and even, in some fortunate spots, Kentucky blue grass sprouted and went to seed and sent down deep roots. Water meant everything, Aunt Gussie told me.

The range had been cattle and sheep country, such sheep and

cattle as no more are seen in the land, wild savage animals, lean, hardy, fighting the wolves and the mountain puma and even wintering on the snow pockets high up when they had to.

Aunt Gussie had pure-stock heavy Shropshire, and Rambouillet sheep grazed at ease with the Merino ewes. I chased with Sandora the wild chappell hen and the hill quail who often joined the gray and white Toulouse geese and the white Peking and Muscovy ducks at breakfast. But the wild ones were beaten, Gramp said, and knew it and kept to their bramble thickets and lost some fear of man and his dogs and his shooting irons now that he no longer hunted the brush life for food.

But there was one animal, Aunt Gussie said, that was never tamed by the range—old Geronimo. He was a huge longhorn steer with a horn spread of five feet or more. His old red hide was worn smooth in spots, his bloodshot eyes no longer saw as well as they once had; but he lived on in the top grazing patch near the foothills, a lonely, nasty old bachelor. Only Pelon, the ranch foreman, could go near him and only Pelon could pull on the stumps left of his ears. Cattle rustlers had changed his ear brand so often that he had almost no ears. His lean flanks, hairy and unkempt, had a dozen brands and half a dozen attempts at brand changes burned into his leathery hide. No one knew how old the steer was. "*Santissima Maria*, the old *mamarrocho* could be any age!" Pelon told Sandora and myself.

"How old is he?" I asked.

"Some say thirty, some say forty, and the Mexican cow hands they think nothing of saying he is the Devil and a hundred and fifty years old."

He was the last of the longhorn steers and he knew it. No one breeds longhorns any more. The bright young college boys wrote books saying too much prime beef was wasted on two long useless horns, now that all the wolves were dead. Gentle Jersey, Guernsey cattle were best now on Aunt Gussie's ranch, and red Hereford bulls. All the rest of Geronimo's tribe were as dead as the buffalo.

Geronimo didn't care what they said about him. He knew he was history, like the covered wagon tracks you could still see on the upper range where no rain ever fell. Pelon told me a wagon party had come that way through Barebone Pass, three hundred covered Congress wagons with a thousand oxen, and all had been caught in the snows, and most had died and eaten each other in the icy hunger, and in the spring only four wagons had come through onto the range. That was the kind of stuff Geronimo stood for, I felt. Sometimes I found a slivered bit of old wagon wood or an arrowhead that had hunted white blood; but mostly history was gone from the range, I decided in the callow wisdom of youth.

The old steer was stiff in his joints and he ate when he felt like it, and the horseflies and ticks did not bother his iron pelt. People came to see him and to say those were the days, and remember how Billy the Kid shot Sheriff Jim Brady, and what fun posses used to be. The old steer would rattle his frayed horns at Gramp's cigar smoke and act hard and chew his cud like tobacco and snort as if saying he was still a hell of a galoot. But nobody really thought old Geronimo was tough any more. Not even me.

When the grazing horses came back from their trip to the hills and danced in the feed lot glossy with health, something snapped in the old steer's mind and he went slightly mad. He never liked the smell of horses and he found a weak fence post and he crashed through it one warm afternoon and tossed a stable dog onto the grape arbor with one twist of his great horns, and then he walked through the garden patch stealing green corn and pushing down the cultivated colored flowers that were alien to him. When he was on the highway he stopped a small flivver head on, and the alarm went out. By that time he had crushed the fenders and punched a horn through the windshield. Geronimo went limping down the road followed by the screams of a rancher's wife jammed inside a mashed flivver. They caught him after he gored a gasoline pump at Moxie's roadside Bar-B-Q and after two kids tried to rope him with department store *riatas*. It took Pelon with a two-ton truck and pitchforks to bring the old warrior home in glory, while he chewed prize carrots stolen from a roadside stand. They mended the fence, and Gramp and Aunt Gussie talked proudly of the old devil's break as if it were the last Indian uprising. In a way, it was.

I enjoyed the ranch, but not Sandora. The night old Geronimo came back I dreamed she was on him and trying to ride me down. The next morning Sandora took me out to see the horses and tried to get me in the right position to get my brains kicked out. She was a real delightful child. I played Indians and tied her to the stake in the barnyard. Is it my fault she fell into the manure pit? After all these years I still can't answer that one.

After lunch Sandora and I played "Hanging in a Mining Camp." I had her two feet off the ground before she screamed. She showed me where the hay was stored, and I almost fell down into the teeth of the hayrack. The score stood pretty much even at five o'clock. At that hour we went to see the new well they were digging, and my shirttail got "caught" in the steam pump, but they stopped it in time. Ten minutes later Sandora was swimming for her life in the sump hole. The deadly wars of children are never fully written about. Sandora had the real Hungarian touch—she did it all with a charming smile. She suggested playing Mummy and Dada, but I remained passionate but shy.

I think everything would have been fine if Aunt Gussie had not tried to kind of rub Gramp's nose in it. We were sitting after dinner one night some weeks later, relaxing and digesting the meal, when Aunt Gussie said, "And to think I owe it all to being a *cordon bleu*."

Gramp did not react. He closed his eyes and put on his rigid smile, and Mamma got ready to kick him in the leg if he opened his mouth.

Aunt Gussie said, "There I was, a green young widow, alone in Paris and tired of the art galleries, but that ugly little building was there on the dirty street with the magic words, reading— What did it say?"

"Do not flush while train is in station," Gramp said.

"No. Cordon Bleu," Aunt Gussie went on, as if she hadn't heard Gramp, and Mamma put an elbow into Gramp's ribs, a hint not to get vulgar.

I think that really tore it. Gramp had been willing to forgive and eat, but Aunt Gussie never could let it lay. "There are of course gourmets, people who know good food; but *only* a *cordon bleu* is the true expert. The rest——" We heard the wind in the cottonwood trees, the horses at the drinking tank, a duck talking love, the late birds under the roof. "The rest," said Aunt Gussie, "they are, how shall I say it? *They* are amat-ooours."

"——— – ——— —," said Gramp, forgetting to run his words together. "I think I need some sleep if we're to pull out early tomorrow."

There were fond good-bys in the morning, Mamma and Aunt Gussie weeping, and Sandora and myself kissing good-by—she got a good grip on my ear with her teeth, but I blacked her eye by butting her cheek with the top of my head.

After that we waved, the car started, and we went off down the dusty road, Gramp feeling real good and smiling. Mamma couldn't figure it out until Gramp said, "We've added something new to our art gallery."

Our art gallery was our windshield. In the habit of those days, we pasted onto it hotel labels, slogans, witty sayings, and trademarks. Stickers reading, "Hi, Chickens, Here Comes the Inspector," "Hotel Tjaden, Running City Water in Season," "Real Steak Dinners—All You Can Eat, Thirty Cents," "Drink Enduro, Be a Man Again."

And there in one corner it was—a card reading, "Cordon Bleu Diploma de Cuisine Bourgeoise, Gertrude Camille Shribheimer."

Mamma screamed, and Gramp smiled grimly. "It was her

scalp or mine, Sari. Never show a Hungarian, even by marriage, any mercy. In the next war I have a plan to get Hungary out of the conflict; drop second acts over Budapest." Gramp could get a little fanciful over Hungarians.

Mamma said, "You're a cruel old man."

"That I am. Stevie, get me a fresh cigar."

"Drive with care," said Mamma.

The car ran along the country roads across the brown and dusty land. It was a much better car in many ways than those we had a few years later. It was simpler; it had no battery, no complicated wiring system, no automatic window-lifters or seat-movers to get out of order. We sat over the gas tank and measured it from time to time with a wooden ruler to see if we needed gas. It was not streamlined to uncomfortable sitting space, and it was high enough to keep its crankcase from being broken by ruts, ditches, or low road crossings. It needed no brake fluids, special gasolines, greases, or doctored motor oils. A healthy man could lift it up by a corner for repairs. The fenders needed no expensive repairing, the body no specialist's body work. A jack could still fit under the car, and no chrome wheel shields, fancy locks, or a collection of many unneeded dashboard dials existed. In clumsy hands, with nonmechanical minds, it ran well. Its illnesses were few, and the average citizen could attend to them with dime-store parts. If the radiator leaked, one dropped in a raw egg; the hot water soon sealed all leaks with hard-boiled egg. If the spark plugs didn't fire too well after cleaning or after damp weather, Gramp filed down the points a bit in the boxlike sparking system. If a hill was too steep to climb, we turned the car around and went up it rear-end first. It could crawl over rough ground. It could run for hours on a few gallons of cheap gasoline. It had handy running boards for standing on and attaching things to; it was high enough above the road so we could really see the landscape; and it bounced enough to give us the impression that we were really traveling outdoors, not in an air chamber underground.

And the other cars we met were each its own kind of steel insect; you could tell a Franklin, a Paige, a Packard, a Maxwell, a Buick, a Dodge, or an Essex by its shape and special hood; soon every car tried to look so much like every other car that the fun had gone out of car designing; fashionably streamlined for the speed of outer space rockets, longer, with more waste space, and impractical for good vision, real comfort, and any traveling away from the super highways. When I was a boy, sixteen hundred different kinds of cars were being made. Even in 1919 several hundred different auto companies made cars. "The Golden Age of the American motorcar already belongs with the good five-cent cigar and Buffalo Bill," Gramp said.

We stopped for gas in a town called Stallion Crossing, and the garage hand tried to sell Gramp an early cigar lighter to attach to the car. As we had no battery, he failed in the sale, and Gramp said, "Damn it, man, the day I can't lift my hand to rub a kitchen match on the seat of my pants to light my stogie, I'll go back to being fed with a baby spoon and taking my drinking mixtures out of an infant's oatmeal mug!"

Mamma was also feeling better, I think, because we had driven out of range of her last relatives this side of California and because she was beginning to enjoy roughing it with Gramp. By later standards of travel we crawled, but we did see all the country, and we were none of us in any hurry to get into the middle of the twentieth century. The years seemed much longer then, and no cigars have smelled as evil as those big, black, tobacco trout-shaped ones Gramp set fire to while the landscape flew past us at a good forty miles an hour on a fair stretch of road.

The land held me. It was my first long American trip. I had not been aware how large the earth really was. Trees looked lonely here. They seemed cut from black tin and pasted against a yellow earth and a brass sky. They looked misplaced even twenty miles away, and below them far away, too, farm buildings stood, waiting for us to rush by. Everything was seen a long time before you were on it, and it fell back fast once you were past it.

And when the storms came, Gramp said, they brought no rain—nothing but the wind tearing up dust around the roots; and they veiled the roads, the trees, and sometimes put blood on the sun, so that you moved like a frightened demon in some nasty, just-finished suburb of Hell. (Gramp could paint a vivid picture.)

And then I felt it too as the wind fell, the dust caked on my sweat, I spit dry cotton, wiped my face, and the wheat stirred past the roadway—so much wheat, so much grain, I wondered who could eat all this bread and why the people looked so poor.

Flat, healthy land, full of wheat, and nothing much more to hold a man here, just a living on this flatness. Even a child could see it.

"The people are good people," Gramp said. "They are the folk who did not get to California, who didn't make it in forty-nine, didn't dare cross the snows into Oregon; or they are the backwash that did not find gold or homesteads over the mountain passes. They turned back, Stevie, found the sod, and cut it and stacked it into a house. They worked hard, breaking more sod, exposing the grass roots, and cutting the black furrows and planting wheat."

They left the naked skin of earth pulled back so that the flesh was taken away by the wind, and the dust that was never to stop came later, in a few years, to make all this a dust bowl. I was impressed by nature.

I LEARNED TO RIDE

8

*I think it was Jekyll who used
to say that the further West he
went, the more convinced he felt
that the wise men came from
the East. . . .*

—SYDNEY SMITH
(From Gramp's notebooks)

ROLLING WEST

WHEN WE HIT THE FOOTHILLS OF THE ROCKIES, GRAMP
ran the car into a tree and broke a front wheel, and we all put
up at Running Horse Ranch till a new wheel could come from
Denver over the mountains. Sheep were in the hills and the
ranch yard was full of young animal life. Gramp polished a
borrowed shotgun and spoke of game to shoot. Mamma, bored,
put up a hammock on a cool, wide porch and read *Free Air* by
Sinclair Lewis.

Summer was really here. The only creatures who did not
mind the changes of season among the sweet fern and Lechea
by the springs were the things built like shaggy nuts—the gilas,

the horned toads, the darting, flame-colored lizards—all of whom, I saw as I explored, had heavy lids over reptile-slanted eyes and slits for nostrils and were colored to fade into the sun-painted landscape. There were snakes, too, and these the cow-pokes on the range killed among the harebells and laurels; and sometimes after a cold night they would find a cold rock, and turning it over, a reeling, rolling knot of snakes would come into view—all coiled together against the chill of the night. I held my nose, for there was a pungent, evil odor like rotting toadstools and bellwort blossoms about these snake nests.

I learned to ride, to saddle up, to rig a horse. In the open near a rotting log there was often a rattlesnake sunning, and the horse would lean away from it. I would whip the horse past the rattler and ride on. I was dimly aware of the family back East in Gramp's house, but I didn't think too much about them.

Behind the wool storage shack the goats were no longer bothering about their black and white kids, and the last colt had been born, and only Gramp went to hunt for jack rabbits in the tall dry grass. The lizards were free to come and go and blink what Gramp called their prehistoric eyes.

In the hills the sheep had been collected, the lambs tagged and gelded and their tails docked and touched with tar, and the heavy coats of wool were matted now with dried brush. Soon they would come down to the streams to be washed and dried and sheared by the Mexican shearers, who could, they told me, denude a sheep in three minutes while they held it between the toes of their *alpargatas*.

Life on the place excited me. The tick baths of vile-tasting creosote and soda and mixtures of darkness stood ready, and I helped push the calves in and they dipped down and for a moment the dip was a mad whirl of calf legs and frightened head. Then the calf walked up the ramp and into clean earth and air and stood there shaking off the strong odor that would not leave.

Even the chickens were dusted, and our last job was to catch the dogs and give them their full share of worm medication. The smart dogs howled and took it, and the dull dogs protested and took it, and only Badimann, the dachshund, held off and ran and hid for a day before we cornered him and forced him to swallow.

Badimann, bought from a passing horse dealer, was Gramp's gift to the ranch. But no one, except possibly his mother, ever really liked him. He was a Waldman *Hund*, a low-breed, low-slung dog the color of stale mustard. He was as tall as a beer stein, he had warped rubber legs, and his head was the head of a fish—some mad breed of mackerel, Gramp suspected—not that of a dog. "He has the weight and shape of a limp valise lost in storage and unclaimed."

He had leering black-framed lips and broken yellow teeth and, like some lecturers Gramp took us to, he could sneer and leer and smile at the same time. Badimann was not a pretty thing, nor did he have a pretty mind. And yet, somehow, I heard, he always had an owner who felt that while he wasn't much to look at, he came of good stock and could have won blue ribbons with a little proper whipping and training.

His mother, his papers said, was the Baroness Elsa von Kimmulorn, and he was related, I believe, to the Duchess of Kent on her father's side, which must have been a remarkable side from all accounts the papers gave us. The Baroness (who had, I hope, the Hapsburg lip) went to a rose farm one warm summer, and there met something secretly during the dull social season and that became Badimann's father. So her last owner swore to Gramp. But you will find no record of this in the blue books, the Waldman *Hund* books, or the listing of the kennel clubs.

Badimann remained a long, low hoodlum who lurked behind garbage cans leering at the white exposed legs of women passing by on their way to the swimming. He had a monstrous ingratitude and the eye of a cynical duke in the Von Stroheim movies Gramp and I enjoyed.

They never housebroke Badimann. They just beat him from time to time with anything they had handy and could lift off the floor. He not only would not learn, you could not teach him. He took a voluptuous joy in laceration, in finding out that it was more fun to do it the other way around. I still bear his scars.

He bit the R.F.D. mailman and lost a tooth, or part of it, from a kick. It showed broken and yellow when he leered. He had attacked his first and last tomcat, and his nose went sniffing through life with a limp from then on. It gave him, Gramp decided, "a certain indelicacy of gesture when he sniffed."

He would come home from some mad night in the open, scratch on the ranch door, and walk into the house yawning. No one dared pet him, for he could slash a wrist like an Italian bravo in the salad days of the Medici. He never liked to bathe (and smelled like spoiled Edam cheese); but often he was attacked with burlap bags by Gramp and a hired hand, trussed up and thrown into a cellar tub full of Lysol, tar soap, sheep-dip, and mange cure. It used to be my pleasure to hold him under in this mixture with a broom handle until death by drowning was near. Then I would let him up and he would sputter, curse, and howl with rage. After stewing in the brew for several minutes, he was allowed to jump out and the hose was turned on him, after which he would run out into the corral and find some decaying rat's nest, some rabbit guts to roll in until he was again immensely untidy, and welcome back the flies that followed him like pilot fish follow a shark.

After he had bitten several people, slashed at them without warning, he was sent into exile to a sheep ranch and there he murdered a few hens and settled down to some vile sort of friendship with a broken-tailed Airedale. They used to run wild during the nights, gathering a canine mob of riffraff of the surrounding ranches. One night, I heard, the Airedale and Badimann came to bites over a white poodle with cropped tail and shaved thighs that a local editor thought of as one of his family. The Airedale, a big bully called Reynolds, made old lace out of Badimann's right ear.

That's how time passed for us at the place.

The replacement wheel for the car came and was put in place and Mamma finished the novel and we got ready to move on west. I made one real friend, a horned toad. All my best friends were animals that year.

He was a small one that looked like a walking oyster and lived in the garden among the fronded poppy pods, and everyone used to stop and pick him up and play with him. He was called The Clinker and looked happy—that is, if a horny stone toad face could show signs of happiness. Since even Mamma loved The Clinker, Badimann used to protest, and one day he found the toad plopping his cold way, like a handful of cinders mixed with mud across the patio, and Badimann tormented The Clinker, but I saved him. General Lee, the Chinese ranch cook, whipped Badimann with the potato masher and Badimann bit General Lee in the leg and ran away. He knew biting was punished by an oiled leather strap. When we left, I turned Clinker free.

Rolling on, we beat it still farther west in our Model-T flivver, running out of cold cream, good cigars, and the soap of polite society. Mamma didn't like the roads along the Arkansas River as we dug into Colorado and headed for Pueblo and Pikes Peak. Gramp didn't like what they sold for gasoline in those days, and I was car-sick a great deal of the time but managed to get better for mealtimes. The pickings were slim: miners' flapjacks, white beans and salt pork, yeast-pot camp bread, and stuff they said was deer, calf, and chicken. Gramp said, "More like grandmother panther and petrified vulture."

The morning we hit Colorado Springs we were a sad lot. The hotel was rather grand, but its food was no better than anyplace in the West, which means it ran from poor to fair. Our beds were large and made of brass, and the clerk said Lillian Russell had

once stayed in my bed. Gramp said that was one way to stay
warm, and shouted that the prices were staggering. A first-class
room at three dollars a night impressed Gramp as flaying alive.
Not that he wasn't a spender. As Mamma said, "He's the best
little spender in the world; he spent my dowry and all the
daughters-in-law's incomes"—which was unfair but true.
Gramp was always swinging railroad stock deals, and sometimes he swung too hard and struck out.

In the morning we had flapjacks and good coffee (they once
knew how to flap a jack in the West), and when we went out to
the hotel yard, no Model-T! Emma, our brass-bound car darling, was missing.

A blacksmith was shoeing a gray mare in the yard, and
Gramp went up to him and said, "Where have they moved my
car?"

The mare and the blacksmith looked at Gramp, but only the
blacksmith spoke. He spit out some of his eating tobacco and
said, "Don't know, don't care."

"Damn it, man, that's an almost-new car."

"Now, horses can find their way back home. Cars got no
horse sense."

"Neither have you."

The blacksmith lifted a horseshoe, red hot from the fire, and
looked at Gramp. Gramp was an old man then, but he was still
six feet three and built, as he proudly said, "like a brick privy."
They glared at each other, and Gramp left to find the police.

The police turned out to be one large man weighing three
hundred pounds and carrying a silver badge labeled "Chief."
There was no police force. They figured size counted, not
number. Chief Ball, as I remember his name, looked over
Gramp and Mamma and liked what he saw—in Mamma, anyway. Chief Ball was one of the handsomest men I had ever seen,
not fat, just big, with a face "brown and beautiful," to quote
Mamma, "with big, icy blue eyes." His mustache was a little
long, but they wore them that way in those parts.

"Oh, dear," said Mamma, playing little girl, "where can our little ole car be?"

She flapped her eyelids a few times, and Gramp looked at me and I at him. It kind of made us sick to see how Chief Ball fell for it; but anything to get our car back.

"Ma'am," said the Chief, "rest easy. We'll get them car rustlers."

"Stranded!" said Mamma, fanning herself with a limp hand.

"Shucks, Ma'am, I've been stranded before; it isn't so bad. When Teddy Roosevelt and I were out hunting elk, we got snowed in for two weeks."

"Dear Teddy," said Mamma. "I used to sit on his lap—when I was a little girl, of course."

Chief Ball almost got down on his knees. "You *know* Teddy!"

Mamma nodded, and they went off arm in arm to look for our car. Gramp lit a fragment of his last good cigar. "She never could resist a handsome face. And there's a lot of it here, twice-life-sized. Come on, let's find lunch someplace."

We found a place called The Hunt Club, a big log cabin filled with land examiners, railroad chiefs, timber crooks, ridge strippers, all of whom had made their pile, or claimed they had.

Gramp mumbled a few words about investigating the ground for some railroad he was thinking of promoting; which was true, only the railroad was in Louisiana, and that's another story.

A large thin man with a gold tooth where it would show the best, introduced Gramp to the boys. "Great to have the General with us," he said. "Call me Chet, but *never* call me late for dinner!"

This killed them, and they laughed it up, showing they hadn't followed vaudeville jokes much. We sat down, and a lot of large colored men in white came rushing in with trays loaded with food. It was mining-camp bunkhouse food, but made for men who had made their pile in the West and were staying there to dig their graves with their forks. "A nice way to die," Gramp said later.

Chet relaxed after the meal and opened his vest to give his

stomach breathing room. "General," he said to Gramp, "this is real fancy camp truck, but wait until we get into the hills and get us a bear. Bear ham is something!"

"I know. I ate it once in the Black Hills," Gramp said.

"Why don't you and half-pint here come along? It's going to be a jim-dandy hunt. No womenfolk and a carload of prime ninety-proof Kentucky mouthwash."

"You're a kind man, Chet."

"You're a real man, General."

"You're white, high, and handsome."

"You're mountain lion and river horse, and I like you."

"You're heap big chief in my book, Chet, and game."

"Put her there!"

"It's a pleasure!"

The two strong men shook hands and refilled their glasses. They couldn't have been closer friends even if they were lovers. It was a delightful afternoon. We got back to the hotel at dusk, Gramp singing "Campfires on the Potomac" and "Don't Cheer, Boys, the Poor Devil Is Dying."

Mamma was dressing to go out, in her best net dress and the little golden shoes. I said, "Have they found the car yet?"

"Oh, the car," said Mamma, putting on perfume behind her ears.

"*What* car!" asked Gramp, sitting down, laughing.

"I'm going out with Chiefy," Mamma said. "Dinner at the Four Aces Club."

"Good girl," said Gramp. "Keep him looking."

"You think the car is at the Four Aces?" I asked.

"He's a fine man," said Mamma, wetting her eyebrows. "What a war record! He was up San Juan Hill two feet in front of Teddy himself. Cuba must have been dreadful."

"With Teddy grabbing the headlines, the rest suffered," said Gramp. "Stevie and I are going hunting in the morning."

"That's nice," said Mamma, putting on her pearls. "Don't let him eat anything to spoil his stomach."

"He'll eat anything that can't eat him."

I could see I was the only adult in the group. Gramp was feeling, as he put it, "no pain," and Mamma was admiring handsome manhood. I got Gramp to bed, then took out my sketchbook and waited up for Mamma. I must have fallen asleep painting a picture of Chief Ball being tortured to death by Indians (in three colors) because I came awake to find Mamma kissing me and her eyes shining as they always did when she was having fun and enjoying life. "Wake up, Baby Boy, Mamma is home."

"Have fun, Mamma?" I said, kissing her.

"Oh, loads of it. Real French champagne. They work hard at fun here. *Aucun chemin de fleurs ne conduit à la glorie!*"

When Mamma tries on her bargain-rate high-school French, it's time to worry. "Maybe I better not go hunting."

Mamma had me unbutton her gown and shook her head. "Chiefy is taking me to see Pikes Peak tomorrow. *A tout prix.*"

At such times one either sent for Papa or stopped worrying. I decided to stop worrying. Mamma was in love with Papa, but Papa had to work hard in the office for Gramp, and he liked to smoke his pipe in the garden when he came home and read the sports pages of the papers. Gramp and Mamma and I hated all sports that were played with bat, football, or golf stick. I figured Papa would have no need to become alarmed, because Mamma hadn't put on her black velvet dress and worn the red feather in her hair. Gramp called it her "painting-the-town-red dress."

Mamma was still sleeping the next morning when we left for the hunting field. Chet picked us up. He was driving a four-horse carryall and greeted Gramp with a crack of the long whip.

"You're a great man, General."

"You're the top of the tree yourself, Chet."

"A man's man and two-fisted drinker, that's you."

"Aces and a full hand and a grip like an eagle, that's you."

"You're a forest fire, not a man; a northwester, not just a citizen!"

"Chet, you're tall timber and a heart as big as Grand Canyon
—and a thirst to fit!"

Grown men can often be pretty sickening.

There were about ten hunters, and all had taken something in
a glass against the morning cold. There were almost as many
colored servants, plus a whole iron camp stove and a carload of
food and bottled moisture to wet throats.

It was a delightful trip into the big timber. I sat by Chet, the
driver, with Gramp swinging the whip. The horses flew, the
timber grew rougher, and the high clear air was good to inhale
and good to shout into. It was the spring of my life. I was very
young, and Gramp was very old but still springy in the joints,
and it was such a day and such a time on earth that is always
rare.

At two in the afternoon we were mounted on pack horses and
still going up. There we made camp, the servants built fires, and
we sat up late eating. The men passed the cheer, and someone
fired a double-barreled shotgun through a new tent. A hunter
fell into an icy cold brook.

There were many versions of the Great Hunt in the family
history, so I might as well tell the truth about it. At dawn two
of the hunters were nursing a cold—nursing it tenderly on Kentucky dew. At noon one of the hunters was lightly shot in the
rump by another hunter. In the afternoon someone shot a
skunk, and the skunk hit back before he died. We had to move
camp in a hurry. The dogs scented a bear at three, and we all
went running along a trail, me carrying a .22 rifle, a Savage that
you couldn't dent a tin can with.

The dogs kept getting ahead and running through streams.
Gramp and Chet and I were second; the dogs were always first
in this race. The bear roared a few times, sounding like no bear
I ever saw. We cornered it in a clearing, but it had cleverly
dressed itself up as a brown and white cow. "Very clever of that
bear," Gramp said later. In some versions Gramp killed the

cow, but this is not true. It's not true either, as Aunt Gussie said, that they cut the tail off.the cow and wore it into camp as an Indian scalp.

At dusk the result of the day's hunt was cooked up—mighty small showings: rabbits, two woodchucks, some real fine rainbow trout the servants had caught, and the rest of the meal came out of the supplies. The hunters came down to civilization the next day, everyone a little tired and with a bad taste in his mouth. "Too much protection against the cold," Gramp said. Everyone was very happy, and Gramp and Chet hugged in the hotel lobby, shouting very loud, each thinking the other was deaf from all the shouting they had done.

"Old horse, you're a real Injun, a regular hair-lifter!"

"General, you're big powwow and son of the thundercloud yourself."

"Wahoo! Oh, big smoke signal."

"Yahooo! Voice of thunder, breaker of lightning!"

"Wahooo!"

"Yahooo!"

Stories that they were both drunk are not true. They had brought nothing back to get that way. It was just fine animal spirits and new friendship.

"Tomorrow," said Chet, "we go after mountain lion. See you in the morning."

"Mountain lions are fun," said Gramp. "We keep them as mouse hunters where I come from. . . . Tomorrow."

Gramp went up to get some sleep. Mamma was out riding with Chiefy, and I went up to our room and found the black velvet dress laid out—and the red feathers. There was no sign of our car, and Gramp was signing a lot of checks. There I was, twelve years old, trying to hold a dynasty together, and rather sleepy myself.

Left to myself the next few days, I wandered around the hotel, watched the bellboys shoot dice, and spent a lot of time in the bar, which was full of badly stuffed deer heads, drinking cherry lemonade and listening to the men talk and brag. And there in the bar one day I met adventure, got a taste of the West's real past, smelled the dust and gun smoke of a just-gone era. Like the Ancient Mariner, he was old and held you with his eyes.

He sat in a well-worn oak chair by the bar and looked at everyone, and his deep blue eyes shone out in the very tanned face. I watched him a long time from behind my glass of lemonade and stale copy of *Colliers*. I knew he had seen Indian smoke signals and ridden hard on sweating pintos. The stiff right hand, rigid now in some disease of age, had once, I was sure, pulled a Colt .45 from shiny leather blacked with campfire grease; he had killed men.

I started my first novel. I wrote it in pencil in the back of one of Gramp's journals. I still remember the opening line. "Burrrr! The shattering clatter of heavy gunplay broke the brittle silence of the desert night." The rest of it (I never got past chapter three) is not so clear. The old man in the bar was my hero.

One day I spoke to him. The old man with the foul-odored cheap cigar wanted a drink. His eyes, his hands, his shaking chops, the very twist of his old body said he was dying for a snort. I moved a little way up the bar, pulled over the bottle, and looked at the barkeep and nodded yes. He slid a glass across the bar, and I said to the old man, "Have one on my grandfather."

"Mighty white of you, boy," he said briskly and businesslike, tilted the bottle, poured out four fingers, and swallowed it with a jerk of his Adam's apple. I nodded again and he refilled and swallowed and then wiped his mouth and sighed, and we just stood, looking at the bar mirror, feeling the way male animals always do with a few slugs in their bellies and their feet on the brass rail and the malt man-smell and man-talk going on all around you—a sort of passive annihilation of the outer world. I took a deep suck of my lemonade.

There was a movie poster pasted on the bar mirror advertising a Hollywood angel's face as "Billy the Kid." The old man stirred against me and said with solemnity, "I was with Sheriff Jim Brady when the Kid got his'n. And I guess I know what I'm yammerin' about when I say the Kid never looked like that girl."

"That's a very popular actor," I said.

"Hain't Billy the Kid. I knew Billy—better than I know this here bartender. Hello, Bart. Yessir, knew him like he was my own brother, and he warn't no doll-faced actor in fancy pants."

"Have another drink on my grandfather."

"Don't mind if I do. Don't mind if I do, at all. The Kid's real name was William Bonney—but on account of his maw marrying someone else you see it written sometimes—William H. Antrim. Never did know what the 'H' stood for. Funny thing about the Kid. He ain't no more a real corral roughhouser and whangdoodler or Western man than William S. Hart is. The Kid was born in New York City sometime before the Civil War. My pap fought in that one. Was one of Hooker's Texans. The Kid, he was a killer early. I hear tell he knifed a blacksmith at Silver City when he was only twelve. Of course the Kid was always tough for his age. Used to hang out in saloons and beat cowhands out of drinks and cash with cards. He didn't play good—just steady. He never was no hero, either. No matter what them pictures say."

"You see the picture?" I asked. I had seen it four times.

"I see all them Western pictures and laugh like hell at all them mistakes they make—them mistakes would pucker a rattler. When Billy was sixteen he had killed twelve men, to hear *him* tell it. Murdered three Indians, too—for their furs. They proved *that* one on him. Of course, Indians was fair game in them days, like college boys—you couldn't honestly notch them on your guns.

"I first met Billy in 1878—yep, 1878. Sometimes I say 1879, boy, but I mean 1878—confuse it with my weddin' date. It was in Lincoln. Billy was under six feet, thin, but full of muscle. Hands and feet like a girl—you wouldn't believe how dainty they was. Brown hair and his front teeth they stuck out a little like a rabbit—but not as much. How the gals loved him! Everyone in town just goo-goo-eyed him to death and he never, nohow, could keep away from any kinda skirt. Women was not so plentiful in them days. I seen men, well you're too young— But Billy, he never had no trouble. Billy was a kinda dude, but nobody ever said nothing about his duds. He changed cow brands a bit for a livin' and rustled a few heads of cattle, but he wasn't really thought mean or dishonest. Just a young boy full of life. He was eighteen—yep, just about that. He was a great shot. I seen him toss a can in the air and fill it full of twelve shots— one right after another—and keep that can in the air high, twenty, thirty feet—until both guns was empty. I used to be a heller in them days myself. Billy and I sort of went around after gals together. Wimmin drove us crazy—that wouldn't interest you. But when Billy was a killer with the law on him, I was settled down and piping in water and growin' a family.

"Wasn't Billy's fault, much. He got mean and trigger-itchy. He was headstrong, and he was working then for a rich Englishman named Tunstall. Tunstall and the Murphy Company was fighting it out for the best cattle land. Them two masterminds fought it out. Only they used mugs like the Kid to do their fightin'. The Murphy mob got Tunstall in 1878—just chopped him down real fast. Never had time to take his boots off an' die proper. Hell was loose after that. There was two hundred killers on each side, pourin' lead at anything that passed.

"I was with Sheriff Jim Brady when he went to see the Kid about something, and the Kid shot him right in front of my own eyes. Of course, Brady was said to be a Murphy man—but maybe he was only hearin' of this thing called law and order, and tryin' to sell the Kid some. Well, they almost got the Kid when they shot down Tunstall's partner, McSween. Set fire to his house, and the Kid left last, killing a man as he got out of that burning house. The Kid was plenty mean—just no Nice Nellie hero—remember that.

"Well, the President—man named Ruth Ford Hayes—ever heard of him? Me neither, much—he called in the Army and they had a general amnesty, and the Kid promised to stop shootin' up people, but he had a lot of hard friends and they liked easy livin' and they began to really hist a lot of cattle, and they killed a lot of folk that said that ain't no way to live. Hard fellas hate to hear that."

I said, "Didn't they catch the Kid and sentence him to hang?"

"That they did. Sheriff Pat Garrett captured the Kid, and they tried him proper and legal, Bible and all, and said he hadda swing. The Kid says nothin' much—just asks his jailer to sit down for a game of monte. Then he grabs the jailer's pistol, kills him with his own shells, and is out and off before that dead jailer could figure out his card hand.

"They had a big posse out for the Kid. Posses *was* fun. He was out two and a half months. Then one night Pat corners him in a house and went in after him into a pitch-black room. Some say he just called the Kid, and, when the Kid walked out, he let him have it. Some say he went in there, shot it out. Anyway, the Kid was as dead as a stepped-on horntoad. He was about twenty-three, but mean as a rattler and never gave nobody no chance."

"Was the Kid really left-handed?" I asked.

The old man helped himself to more whisky and made a systematic hunt for a thought. "Well, he was as right-handed as I am. Some of them old pictures was taken the wrong way first in them days—mirrorlike. That's what started it."

"The Kid have a favorite girl?" I asked casually.

"Well, the Kid was a ladies' man. But he liked José Sedillos' daughter. I forget her name. A smart, dark little trick. But the Kid, he never went to no church and he had a hard reputation, you might say, and the family never let it come to a weddin'— but the Kid wasn't the marryin' kind, anyway."

"Have another on my grandfather."

"No. Thank you, kindly. I never go over my quota, boy."

The old man went out, his high-heeled boots wagging wildly, and the bartender looked at the bottle and frowned.

"Goddamn old mooch. He'd die of thirst if it wasn't for Billy the Kid. He tells that story about three times a week."

"Who is he?"

"His father used to be a big muckamuck cattleman. Owned a thousand acres outside town. But the gang wars and his fight with the Murphy Dolan gangs clean busted him. Raises eggs and friers. Only friend the Kid ever had."

"Charge those drinks to Gramp," I said.

I went back to my room and I wrote out most of what the old man had told me, as well as I could. It was my first sustained writing, and I got most of the spelling right. The facts seemed to check with the little I later read on Billy the Kid, but I've never done any real research on the subject. I meant to ask the old man the next time I saw him how many men he himself had killed, but he didn't come back the rest of the time we were at the hotel.

COOKIE, THE COWHAND COOK

9

History is little more than the register of the crimes, follies and misfortunes of mankind. . . .
—EDWARD GIBBON
(From Gramp's notebooks)

LAND OF THE SAINTS

NOT LONG AFTER, THEY FOUND OUR STOLEN CAR IN Denver. An Indian half-breed had taken it, and we got it back, battered but not in bad shape. Mamma was by now bored by Chiefy, and Gramp was what he called "sugaring-off elbow-bending." So it seemed only fair to go see Salt Lake City. We started for it in our car. Mamma was sleepy and Gramp was grumpy; his big toes ached. I was the only one who enjoyed himself, and Gramp growled and said, "What makes you so bright-eyed and bush-tailed?" I said nothing, and I guess I didn't know it then, but having nothing on your mind isn't a bad state of affairs.

The roads were a mockery of the word *road*. The weather consisted of rain, but the car and its motor kept us floating, never let us down after Gramp had two bearded blacksmiths at the railroad yards hammer out a big hook which they bolted to the front end. After that if we sank into a mudhole, a rope tied to the hook and hitched to any two passing horses started us on our way again.

We wanted to cross the desert country before the full black of summer was upon us. Mamma was wondering if there were such a place as California.

"I don't see how the covered wagons made it," Mamma said, as we changed a tire on a mountain road.

"They ate well," said Gramp. "They ate one another."

Mamma knew Gramp was just trying to get a rise out of her, so she said, "It was better food than you get nowadays on the road."

"Are people good to eat?" I asked.

"Some," said Gramp. "Imagine Lillian Russell in a roasting pan. Meat's meat."

"Gramp!" said Mamma in her low, icy voice.

Gramp kicked the tire in place and said, "Of course *I'm* not much, just bones and old scar tissue, but, now you, Sari, or even Stevie here with an apple in his mouth . . ."

Mamma said, "Gramp, I'm putting you in Coventry."

"Now, Sari," said Gramp, knowing he had gone too far. "I was just teaching Stevie history, about the Donner party that got snowed in and lived off one another, and you, Stevie, you know . . ."

But I shook my head and pointed to my sealed lips. When Mamma put anyone into Coventry that meant no one talked to him until Mamma, like a Pope in skirts, withdrew the interdict.

Gramp had been in Coventry twice on the trip, and he didn't like it. He liked to talk and be talked to. He lit a cigar, sighed, and pointed to the car. We got in and drove on in silence.

Mamma hummed a little tune, I made faces at my reflection in the windshield, and the car ran on over bad roads, past sod huts and ranch fences, ran on, making the only real sounds after Mamma had stopped humming the tune.

It was past noon, and I was hot, tired, and thirsty. I pointed to my mouth and swallowed. Mamma tapped Gramp's shoulder, pointed to her small mouth, and then drank an imaginary glass of water and swallowed in a ladylike fashion.

Gramp held one hand to his ear and said, "Eh? Speak louder."

Mamma cut something with a phantom knife and put it on a fork that wasn't there and swallowed again. It made my mouth water.

Gramp said, "Can't hear a word you're saying. Speak up, Sari!"

Mamma folded her arms, scowled, and said to me. "If some people had any sense they'd know we're hungry."

Gramp said to his steering wheel, "If some stomachs could talk, they'd talk to an old man who never meant anyone any harm. But, of course, snobs and stylish people from New Brunswick, New Jersey, they're too good to talk to the likes of me. I'm just old American stock, fought in the Civil War, raised up a family of sons, and now in my declining years I'm shoved aside, and who the hell cares!"

The last four words were shouted across the plains and frightened two steers who were rubbing themselves against a fence post.

"You win," said Mamma. "You're such a ham, Gramp. I bet you'll be bringing up a few tears next."

Gramp grinned. "Hell and high water, Sari, a man doesn't like to think he isn't fit to talk to!"

Mamma crossed her arms. "I withdraw Coventry."

"Can I talk, Mamma?" I asked.

"Yes, dear."

"Gramp, we dropped our spare tire about a mile back."

"Why didn't you yell out!"

"Coventry, you know."

"I'll break your damn little——"

"Gramp," said Mamma in her Coventry voice.

Gramp finished, "—little piggy bank and buy you some real cowboy boots."

Gramp turned the car around, and we went back and found the tire. Near it we saw a chuck wagon drawn up and some men outside it who didn't look at all like cowboys but more like hobos sitting around, smoking hand-rolled cigarettes while a cook filled tin coffee cups.

"How far to Salt Lake City?" asked Mamma.

"Oh," said a long cowboy (who looked the way Gary Cooper was going to look in a few years), "just about a hundred miles, more or less."

"Anyplace to eat around here?" Mamma tried out her Lord-I'm-just-a-poor-little-woman-alone-in-the-world smile. "It's been a long time since we've had solid food."

"Best place is right here. Come on over." And the cowboy held the strands of barbed wire apart for Mamma to crawl through. "And bring your friends. Plenty for all."

We followed him around to a small fire and met the cow hands (they're not called cowboys, but hands, I found out), and Stretch, as they called the tall one, yelled out, "Hey, Cookie, we got company."

Cookie was a wide, fat, dipped-in-some-soot-and-oil mixture, part Mexican and part mustache. He came over, a flour sack tied around his middle, and said, "Sure, plenty in the chuck wagon for all."

"Don't bother on account of us," said Mamma, sitting down on the saddle Stretch had put down for her.

"No bother, is it, Cookie?"

"No siree," said Cookie.

"Punching cows?" asked Mamma.

"Steers, ma'am. No cows around here."

"Herding steers?" asked Mamma.

"No, ma'am, we're—— Well, we're gathering in the calves, and . . ."

He went on to talk of the process of overtaking a lot of new-born male calves. I guess you could call it "making steers." Mamma nodded and listened, and then Stretch blushed under his tan and said weakly, "Anyhow, that's what we're doin'."

Cookie came over with some frying pans and tin trays and set down his camp cooking before us. Cow hands eat well on the range—or did—or else we were lucky in finding a good outfit.

"I'm sorry," said Stretch. "We haven't butchered a steer, or we could have Cookie give us a mess of steaks."

"This will do fine," said Gramp, as his tin cup was refilled with cow-hand coffee, which experts claim is the best coffee in the world. "Cookie should get a medal."

Stretch picked up a sliver of fire from the ground and set his cigarette glowing. "He'll get a swift kick in the slats if he's got no real grub left for you."

"I got, I got!" screamed Cookie. "I got enough left. You fellas got no sense humor. All the time, lady, they want to kick poor Cookie in the—the ribs. What for fun is that?"

Stretch winked at Mamma. "Keeps him spry and busy."

We ate with cow hands a lot after that, every chance we got on the road, and some of them ate well and some badly. If they had a Mexican or colored cook, they ate well. But no damn-yankee could cook well for cow hands, and a cow hand would leave an outfit and drift around until he found the kind of grub he liked. Cookie was one of the best, even if he did live in terror of the hands who promised him all sorts of fearful adventures if the standard of the food fell away.

We thanked Cookie and Stretch, Gramp handed out his few remaining cigars, and we left the cow camp and headed toward Salt Lake City. We smelled the lake a long way off, then saw the great temple against the hot blue sky, and soon we were in the streets of Salt Lake City. Gramp made no jokes about Brigham Young and his twenty-four wives and six hundred children, except to say that a good wife is like an elephant, "very interesting to look at, but who wants to own one?"

"Gramp," said Mamma in that *cold* voice.

And Gramp replied, "I must buy some new cigars."

"After we settle at the hotel."

We found a very good hotel, with the biggest moose in the world (his head anyway) hanging over a big fireplace in the lobby, his big glass eyes looking down sadly at us as we registered, Gramp writing ur names with a big pen in a fancy hand.

We had huge rooms with high ceilings, and everything smelled of American history. The hot water dripped but would not flow. Gramp and I changed, and Mamma said she would rest her spine on a good bed and forget the bad roads.

We went to buy some cigars, and Gramp found Salt Lake City didn't have any places that sold cigars: "Sorry, but the war, you know—didn't import many." Which shows you how old *that* excuse is, World War I, in 1919, being in the just-gone past.

"Hell and tiddlywinks," said Gramp, "the things they blame on wars. I bet Ajax went to the wars of Troy because he dropped in to buy a few stogies and they told him, 'Sorry, just out, this war business over a woman, you know.' Helen didn't launch a thousand ships, Stevie, but she most likely took a hundred good cigar brands off the market."

The clerk took the gold toothpick from under his mustache and said, "Try that little shop next to the hotel. The elders of the church buy their smokes there. He may have some old stuff in stock."

"Thanks."

It was a dusty little shop, but it smelled neatly of Turkish blends and polished pipes. A little old man with a bright blue eye shook his head when Gramp asked for his favorite brand of cigars.

"The war?" Gramp asked.

"The war. And what I have, I have to keep for the elders of the church. That was a beautiful woman you had with you."

"Oh, Sari," said Gramp.

The little old man leaned over. "Sneaking in an extra wife?"

Gramp looked at the ceiling. "That isn't done any more, you know—at least publicly."

I started to say something, but Gramp gripped my arm and I think he trembled, the tobacco habit had him in such a grip. If there were any way of getting cigars, Gramp was going to get them.

The little old man winked. "A mighty beautiful and comely offering to the codes of the early saints, I must say. Getting married at once? Well, I don't blame you. Other wives getting older, and not so much chance any more of defying the gentiles and their mealymouthed habit of one wife at a time."

"It is to be quite an event," said Gramp, "and I did want to pass out some good cigars. As you say, the custom of many fruitful unions is frowned upon; the good work of Smith and Young is going fast. Just two dozen cigars to pass out would have done it—the important elders, you know."

The little man nodded and climbed up over his shelves like a chimp and brought down a cedarwood box. "Two dozen Belindas, prime Havana leaf."

We went out, glowing, the box under Gramp's arm and a fresh cigar in the corner of his mouth. Gramp looked at me and winked. "It's a man's world, Stevie. Mum's the word. As a famous man once said, 'A woman is only a woman, but——' "

"A good cigar," I finished, "is a smoke."

It was a mistake for Gramp to warn me. I figured out that was what happened—that and three servings of ice cream. For when Mamma heard me muttering in my bed, she came to test my head for fever and to tuck me in, and she found me talking in my sleep about cigars and maidens.

We knew something was wrong the next morning at breakfast. We knew it was real wrong when we took off for the mountain passes. A few miles past the stinking lake Mamma said, "Coventry for the next three days, Gramp."

Gramp, a good cigar in his mouth, asked, "But why?"

"Stevie talked in his sleep last night. So I'm your new young wife? And all your others are worn out."

Gramp looked at me with distaste. "It wasn't that bad at all. He built it up in his dirty little mind."

Mamma put her arms around me. "Now, Baby Boy, you just show Mamma all the jack rabbits."

"You like jack rabbits, Mamma?"

"A jack rabbit is only a jack rabbit, but a good cigar is a smoke," she said.

Gramp inhaled his cigar carefully, flicked the ash off, and said, "Please don't talk to me. I've just put *you* and Stevie into Coventry. Why didn't I ever think of that before?"

Mamma looked at me, and I looked at Mamma, and I showed her the first jack rabbit, but she didn't seem interested. . . .

THE OLD IRISH REBEL

The seat of the soul is the
pylorus. . . .
—ORTUS MEDICINAE
(From Gramp's notebooks)

I MEET THE DARK STRANGER

TO CHILDREN DEATH IS A WIND IN A FAR-OFF COUNTRY. It comes only to other and older people and has the color of a myth that will never become real for them. Gramp used to quote a poem in his cups, about the black camel kneeling at the gate waiting to carry him away in the dark night. But he was not much given to talking of death unless it was in juicy quotations. This was the summer I almost drowned; for the first time death was real to me. I don't know how the knowledge comes to other children, and how they take it, but I was suddenly aware of earthly decay and rapid aging, and of the terror and weight of time passing. I knew suddenly time doesn't really pass; we do.

Our car had been going through rough mountain country, and one day we put in at a camp on a great blue saucer of a lake.

I had been swimming for several years, in my own odd over-hand way. That morning I got up early and listened to the clatter of birds, the lisp of wind in the pitchpole pine trees, the *clap-clap* of water against the bottom of the moored boats. Someplace someone clanged iron on iron. I smelled wood smoke and crushed sere grass and the wet stone paths. I got up. Both Mamma and Gramp still slept. I went down to the lake, mother-naked and carrying a towel. Reflected in the water was the de-parting pattern of the last evening star, and the sun was al-ready coming up like a shout. A loon flew low, skimming across the water, a perch leaped from the mirror surface of the lake and turned jeweled and limber, one tiny animated lump of fish muscle, and fell back with a plop to splash a hole in the lake.

I stood, my naked toes in the damp lake shore, and the water was cool. I walked in quickly, a good ache, like shock, all over me.

The scent of pine and wood smoke and bursts of early morn-ing sun seemed part of me. Life suddenly had a meaning, which I could almost understand. I swam out to the diving raft and felt superficially satisfied. Again and again I dived off, knifing the cool waters, arms, legs cutting through the heavy water that was the early blue lake world. I rested as the sun rose higher. Then, rubbing my chilled body, I watched myself in the mirror surface. I suddenly began to shout. It just seemed to fit the mood of the day.

I dived in again and began to swim for the distant dimness of the far shore, still half obliterated in mist. I had never at-tempted to swim that far before. It was over two miles. With regular motions I began to glide through the water, arms com-ing up, legs kicking, the hug of the chill water on my body. My breathing faltered and I swallowed a huge mouthful of cold lake. I gagged, sank, struggled; seven times (not three) I sank, then began to tread water. It took me a long time to recover. Torso heaved, legs knotted with pain, and no facile imagination sent any visions of past moments to plague me. I just felt: Mamma and Gramp will think me a goddamn fool.

Why had I leaped in this lake? Why had I decided to swim across? I sank and rose and held my breath. The dim, far shore seemed no nearer. Again I began—this time slowly—to reach for it with moving arms and legs. For some time I swam. Then, numb, uncaring, automatically I relaxed my grip on any body control and stayed just awash in the bottle-green waters. My forward movements were slower than the lake drift. The far shore was no closer. But why, I decided, did I owe earthly allegiance to it?

I felt very good, very still, as if in a great sleep. Nothing mattered—nothing mattered but the lake drift and the water and my moist body floating so still, the lap of little waves as I turned in loggy circles on my back and tried to float. The lake entered my mouth, bubbled in my nose, and I felt the cold frog-tasting lake bottom come up toward me. . . . I drifted, was submerging like a ballet dancer in slow motion . . . so good . . . so calm. . . .

Then the clangor and walloping clatter of the first morning breakfast bell sounded from the camp. It came in ripple after ripple of bronze-colored sound. It bruised my ears, stirred protest within me. I halted my sinking, drove the water into white foam about me, and came smashing through the thin skin of the lake to glare wetly about me in the hot dawn sun, frightened, angry, and very tired. Throwing back wet hair, I blew water from nose and mouth; alert, afraid, enraged at this trick my nerves had played on me, I began to swim in swift panic for the camp. Fears communicated themselves to me. I swam harder.

I was busy making heavy gestures, hand over hand, toward the shore. Over the waters the campers, Mamma and Gramp, were moving toward breakfast. I could see them. The lake front was empty of all human aid. I was very tired, very afraid now, wanting to live. All that mattered was that shore. Ineffectual, inarticulate, I floundered on. I never thought of calling out for help.

A great cramp pulled my legs under, my cold stomach heaved and knotted, and the arms seemed torn from my shoulders.

How much better it would have been out there in the lake middle to sink unfighting—not this dreadful terror. Too late I wanted to shout, but couldn't. How Gramp would rage at my damn-fool stunt; even in death I feared his mocking swearing. But there wasn't much strength left in me.

Turning on my side, I gave up and landed in six inches of water on the shelving sand bar that led up to the lake shore. I lay a long time, my body flushed pink as if on fire in the bright sun.

When I heard the people coming down to bathe, I went off wrapped in my towel up a cool, lonely woodland trail.

In a small clearing, I lay down, hearing the laughter of people coming from the lake cabins.

Later, Gramp asked me where I had been; I had no name for it.

Gramp wanted to get in a side trip to Butte, Montana, to see about the copper mine he had an interest in.

As we left one of the dreadful eating places and drove out of town, Mamma fanned herself and said, "What's so wonderful about the West?"

Gramp chewed on a last inch of cigar. "When you say that, gal—smile!"

"Let me know when you're witty," Mamma, dusty, hot, tired, and itchy, said, "and I'll laugh."

Gramp knew mutiny when he saw it. "Man alive, Sari, I don't want trouble with you. I'm a sick old man."

"What hurts, Gramp?" I asked. "Your head?"

Mamma said, "Now, Stevie, you know Gramp hasn't any *gout* medicine."

"Just that little bottle labeled Hair Oil," I started to say.

Gramp gave me the look the eleven other disciples used to throw at Judas. "Sharper than a serpent's tooth is an ungrateful whelp."

"Hair oil?" asked Mamma. "Really, Gramp, you'll be drinking out of the nose of the teakettle next."

"Just a little bourbon I keep for when the gout is bad."

Mamma looked out at the heavy hot day, the tumbleweed, the grim, hard black hills, and sighed. "Not *again*, Gramp."

Gramp nodded and saw he had Mamma on the defensive. Gramp's gout was his only illness. He was tall as a house, strong as a mule, mostly as healthy as a redwood tree. But when his big toes began to send off sparks and an attack of gout was coming up, the family went away on visits, and those who had to stay wondered why they never built a storm cellar. Gramp's gout, Mamma said, made the battle of Verdun look like a tea party.

"Which toe?" I asked.

"Both, damn it," Gramp said. "I got up this morning and somebody was boiling lead inside them. Oh, I can hardly stand it. These shoes are killing my poor toes—the big ones, that is."

"Drive barefooted," Mamma said, "like the Indians do."

"Thank you, Sari," said Gramp, pleased she had forgotten the hair oil bottle. "Now if we can only find the Rockies."

"We passed them days ago," I said.

"Not only a stool pigeon," Gramp said, in a stage whisper, "but *also* a sense of direction." Aloud he said, "I meant the rocks near Tahoe."

I saw I wasn't doing so well with Gramp this morning, so I decided to have an earache. In those days, just a big lout growing up, whenever I got into trouble, I would have an earache, and Mamma would comfort me and protect me from the world. When I stopped having earaches for real and just said I had them, I could feel guilt and sin spread all over me. And I would wonder if God was watching me that morning, or if He'd gone fishing. In time I learned that saying you had an earache when you didn't have one wasn't lying—it was diplomacy. And many of my friends who were good at it are now in the State Department. Some of us who mostly told the truth became novelists.

"Ears!" said Gramp. "Kids shouldn't have ears! They should

have their ears cut off at birth and sewed on when they vote for the first time!"

I moaned. I could do it pretty well then, and Mamma took me in her arms. "Gramp," she said in the voice of a lady lion defending the den of her young, "save your wit for saloons; and you'd better stop before you hit that cow in the road."

Gramp pulled on the brakes, and there, facing us, was a skinny steer taking up all the road there was. I drooled, made a beeping sound, and we saw its dirty hide full of ticks.

"It's a steer, Sari, *not* a cow," Gramp said, and shouted, "Shoo! Yale, ten, Harvard, aught! Three cheers for the United States Steel Company and Teddy Roosevelt! Damn you, get off the blasted road! *Git!*"

But the steer didn't move. Gramp got out of the car and took his shotgun along to scare the animal, but the steer just looked at Gramp as he took aim.

Mamma, suddenly amused, said, "It's killers like you, Gramp, that give the West a bad name."

"I'm only scaring it. I wouldn't harm a hair on its shaggy hide. Get along, little doggie! Newport, Palm Beach, Alexander's Ragtime Band! Get going!"

At which point the steer made a grave and fatal mistake. It stepped on Gramp's sore big toe. Gramp rose two feet into the air, screaming like a ghost in Dracula's castle. He spun around, cursed so hard Mamma covered my ears, and then, weeping pain and rage, Gramp murdered the steer in cold blood (even if he did claim later, when taking on bourbon, that it had pulled a knife on him). The steer fell like a bad man shot by the town sheriff at high noon. Gramp, weeping and sputtering like a whale, staggered to the running board and sat down, nursing a large shoe.

"I've been had!" he shouted. "Oh, my aching toe!"

He pulled off his shoe and sock, and there was the most swollen and hottest-looking toe I'd ever seen. Gramp, as he once said, "always had gout in spades."

"I'm dying, Sari, dying here in this vent-hole of Hell!"

"Don't get melodramatic, Gramp. You've had gout before. Rich living and poor habits."

"Who says they're poor?" Gramp gasped, and hunted for the hair oil. Mamma leaned over, took the bottle from him, and spilled it all out in the sand.

"No drinking during an attack, Gramp. Doctor Wilkin said so."

Gramp turned away and hid his head in his arms; he couldn't bear to see whisky poured out on the ground. He was really in agony now. We got him into the back of the car, and Mamma drove while he moaned. She drove right over the now-dead steer, and Gramp lay in the back of the car and made pain-filled sounds. I sang him "Pretty Redwing" to cheer him up, but it didn't work.

Around four o'clock in the afternoon we were someplace near Virginia City, and Gramp was turning blue-red. We saw a big stone ranch house ahead of us, and Mamma decided to go in there for help. Gramp wasn't even cursing any more. That meant he was at a low ebb and would soon be thinking of additions to his will.

Hunting dogs reeling out tongues ran to meet us, and an iron Negro boy with an iron ring in his hand stood on a stone into which was cut the word *Beekman*. A man dressed like a cowboy playing a hobo came out to peer at us in the powerful sunlight.

"Always welcome here. Jake Beekman is the name. How's the old man?"

"Dying," said Gramp. "I want to make a new will."

"Bring the old coot in," said Jake Beekman. "We'll make him comfortable. What you-all need is a snort of brandy."

Gramp moaned an actor's deep moan. Sari shook her head. "*No* drink!"

"Well, maybe a little dinner would do him some good. We

got a pretty good Indian cook that Mamie—that's Mrs. Beekman—has been teaching French-style grub. Too bad she's in Frisco—Mamie likes company."

Poor Gramp. No liquor. And as we sat down at dinner in the main room of the big ranch house, he wasn't even cheerful enough to greet the other guests. There were four of them, cattle buyers, and they were lots of fun. Gramp had a special meal Mamma had ordered for him.

He sighed as he spooned up crackers from his milk. "Two thousand miles of bad food: cast-iron ham, chicken stuffed with gravel, coffee brewed in cesspools, cheese made of stolen church candles, and bread baked of sawdust, and now when they put *real* food in front of me, I'm not permitted to eat it!"

"Gout," said Mamma to Jake Beekman. "City life, Gramp—all that flowering vice. Well, your big toes just about kill you."

"Gout," said Jake Beekman, "that's a habit, I hear, in England. I wish Mamie were here; she'd be pleased to know we have a real high-class case of gout at the ranch. Well, we'll have the cook fix him up some soft food, something he can just gum."

Gramp eyed a platter of smoked pork chops and the Indian help bringing in big platters of *filet mignon*. "I feel a bit better," he said, grabbing a pork chop and spooning some sweetbreads onto his plate. "That toe hasn't ached for ten minutes."

Jake Beekman nodded. "That's the stuff, old sport. Mamie sets a fancy table here, and I can see you ain't et right of late. Getting puny sort of, and puny types don't last."

Gramp wiped a tear from his eye. "Bless you, Jake Beekman, and God keep you." The knife and fork rattled in his hands as he bent over to cut his food. But Mamma swooped down and took it away from him.

"Gramp, that will just about kill you. You can have another bowl of milk and crackers."

Gramp sighed, closed his eyes, folded his arms, and it looked as if he were praying, but he wasn't. He was remembering, as he used to put it, "how to talk to a mule on a wet night in Vir-

ginia during the Civil War. General Grant used to come miles
to hear me do mule-prayer-talk."

They didn't even let Gramp have black coffee.

Jake Beekman had not only made money in cattle, oil, silver,
power lines, railroads, and timber, he had also been active on
the stock market. And his wife Mamie, he said, seemed ready to
spend most of it turning the ranch into a part of Europe. Jake
told us all this after dinner, as he smoked a rich cigar which
Gramp had been forced to refuse. Gramp, cracker dust in his
mustache, went sadly up to bed, so meek and mild I was really
worried over him. Old age, I decided, is not very satisfying.

He was a little more cheerful the next morning as we left,
and we promised to look up Mamie Beekman "in Frisco."
Jake pumped our hands and the other guests told us good-by.
Gramp smiled and said, "I'm feeling much better; a good
night's sleep and no rich food—the simple life. I think we'll visit
my copper mine. The simple life from now on."

"Yes," said Mamma. "All the way to the Coast and back.
No more rich food for you, Gramp."

"How right you are, Sari," said Gramp, a subdued man.
"The virtues of the plain life are best. The great Greeks like
Plato lived on the head of a fish and a fistful of olives. I shall
do the same."

"Where are you going to get fish heads," I asked, "out here?"

"The ravens that fed the saints in the wilderness, the food
that fell from the skies and fed the children of Israel after they
stomped down the Red Sea. . . . It shall be done. Goddamn,
boy, don't make me sorry for myself. Let me show my best
side, my Christ side."

Mamma looked at me and shook her head. When Gramp was
sweet-talking from the Bible, "*that*," she once told Papa, "was
the time to count your fingers and send the weaker members of
the family away for safekeeping."

But Gramp really seemed to accept the simple life. In Virginia City we found a good eating place run by three sisters who

set a good frontier table. But Gramp just smiled and ordered
corn flakes and milk. He shook his head over the white miners'
beans and salt pork, the roast pigeons, and the Mexican *cocido
Madrileno*. He just sneered at the food and told us, "The spirit
in man is more important than filling his inner plumbing with
the singed young of Nature. Bernard Shaw is right. Let us eat
no living thing. Stop bolting your food, Stevie."

This was a new Gramp, and we didn't know what to think. I
later found out that Mamma's letters home admitted she was
puzzled. Mamma was a fancy writer with a Hemingway kind of
offbeat idea of life and its problems, although I don't think
Hemingway ever got as close to life and its problems as Mamma
did in her letters. She faced facts better than he did. Let me
quote her from an old letter home:

"Odd. Gramp is again red of face and heavy of limb, but he's
eating nothing much. He says he is clean and bright as a dime
inside and out."

Again Mamma: "Gramp is living 'close to the skin,' as he
said this morning. I suspect the old rip when he gets full of his
kind of poetry, but he is so easy to live with now that he doesn't
eat much. He doesn't drink, because I smell his breath when I
lean over to kiss him in the morning. I'm worried—it can't last.
He's been such a china-breaking bull for so long that this version of St. Francis mocking desire doesn't seem life-size."

Again Mamma: "The most delightful Chinese eating place in
Barstow on our way to Butte. Cha Shiu Chow Mein, Hang
Yang Tu Soup, Shiu Ap roast duck filled with anise, Min Shi
sauce and cinnamon. Gramp just shook his head and said, 'A
man at peace with his toes can face life without putting fat on
his front porch and pushing out his backside (he used a three-
letter word) with the winter flesh of small, kind animals.' I
don't know if I can take this version of a cigar-smoking Joan of
Arc much longer."

She didn't have to. One night in a hotel in Cody, Wyoming,
Gramp had another gout attack, and Mamma, over his pro-

tests, called in a local doctor. The lean, dirty-fingered doctor pushed Gramp around, looked at his remarkably long tongue, and asked him to expose his stomach.

He looked at Gramp's navel and nodded.

"Cut out your fat feeding, Mr. Longstreet, cut down your alcohol intake, and I'd give up all the rich dressings. Eat only milk and crackers."

Mamma said softly, "You mean he *hasn't* been dieting?"

The doctor looked down at Gramp's big toes, both glowing like the red electric-light bulbs on the merry-go-round at Coney Island. "The toes show he's been stuffing himself. That will be one dollar as my fee; it's a night call and I had to come fifteen miles."

Gramp was trying unsuccessfully to say something fast. Mamma gave the doctor a silver dollar she'd won in Nevada, and after he'd gone she rolled up her sleeves. Gramp looked at her and said, "Now, Sari—"

Mamma paid no attention. "Stevie, get out that big leather bag."

"Now, Sari, a man's bag is his castle."

Mamma opened the bag and out fell a big smoked ham, the cloves still on its sugar-crisped fat; a whole side of corned beef, wrapped in Gramp's best linen motoring coat; a string of pork sausages; some crisply roasted chickens with wings missing; and a whole smoked salmon, very pink and covered with tobacco crumbs.

Mamma kicked small feet at this food dump. "So, food is a dreadful thing? So, filling one's inner plumbing is vulgar and a foul attack on the simple Greeks! You old two-faced German!" Mamma hated Germans all her life, so it was the worst thing she could call a human being. "You rancid old Prussian, trying to make fools of your own blood and kin, tearing your grave open with your own teeth, chewing the turf away from the family burial vault—and drinking, too! You Teutonic sensualist!"

Mamma dug deep in Gramp's bearskin coat and pulled out a

big bottle with Russian letters and red and gold seals on it. "Vodka! The stuff that doesn't smell or have any color. So you've been drinking a lot of this good clean *water*, eh!"

"Sari, darling—"

Mamma threw the bottle out the window (the window wasn't open, but she threw it out anyway). Gramp stood up tall and calm on his aching toes. You had to admit the old man had his moments. "All right, you win. But just remember, young woman, I'm still the head of this family. You can't talk that way to me in front of the young fry. Respect, damn it! Life without respect and dignity isn't worth living!"

"Then admit what a dirty old man you are," Mamma said firmly.

"I am a sinner," said Gramp, dead-pan. "A deep and hard old sinner. My heart is like leather, and my mind is silted over with almost a century of evil. Now, damn it, let's forget this farce. They serve a fine roast beef here, and I'm buying the wine. Maxim's Chambertin, 1902."

Mamma knew when she had rubbed someone's nose in it enough. She said, "I'd like a Montrachet, not too sweet, to cut the travel dust. And don't let me hear from your g.d. big toes again."

Gramp nodded and put on his good high button shoes, and if the shoes hurt, if his big toes screamed, I don't know, because he was a very brave old man, and Mamma was the most beautiful thing in the world. We went down to dinner a respectable and well-fed American family.

Mamma had the last word. She looked over the ornate hotel menu and said to the waiter, "I see you don't have any fish heads or olive pits. Gramp, you may order the dinner."

Gramp tried to make it up to us and was very kind and polite and a little hangdog to Mamma, and Mamma, to show Gramp she didn't hold any grudge, said we would enjoy Butte, Montana, and Gramp's share in the silver and copper mine, which hadn't been paying any dividends for a long time. I still have

the stock, engraved in fancy scrolls and printed on paper as stiff
as a West Point backbone: "The Queen of the West and Great
Plains Mining Company." I doubt that it's worth ten cents a
share today, or even still mining anything. But this mine was
once the family dream boat for years and years. We all expected
to get millions from it. I must admit we enjoyed our great ex-
pectations.

So we drove up to Butte over cow trails, dirt roads, mining
pikes, and there it was, a city high up, full of smoke and tough
men and miners. And waiting for us in the Hotel de Mineral was
fat little Sean (pronounced *Shawn*) O'Kenna, with the Dublin
Abercorn Road accent still in his mouth. Round, bearded,
scarred, and always smiling.

"Hiya, ol' boyo," he greeted Gramp.

We met a lot of relatives: his prospective son-in-law Parnell
Seumas Michael Hayes, and Sean's daughter, the bride-to-be
Katie, "a big, bouncing gal." Of course we had to come to the
wedding tomorrow. Mamma said she would try, Gramp said
yes, and I was excited.

It was no time, Gramp saw, to talk of the mine, or the pros-
pects of silver or copper. Gramp went to the church for the
wedding the next day and Mamma and I were due at the house
of the bride's father for the wedding feast and party.

Mamma gave me her own short version of Irish culture, folk
art, and native habits, and she dressed me in my tight blue suit
with the long black stockings. Outside the house of the wedding
party some dirty-faced kids were singing a ditty:

> *First comes love,*
> *Then comes marriage;*
> *Then comes Katie*
> *With a baby carriage.*

Gramp met us at the curb as we drove up. Smiling and already primed, he helped Mamma out of the car. He kicked aside
two damp-nosed children from underfoot who were yelling
"Swells for the weddin'!" A fiddle sounded, and good laughter,

and a slap. Gramp nodded toward the house and threw his stogie away.

"This is the place. The chalices are being passed around. Hurry or you'll get no roast pork today. Irish and Jewish weddings are the only good ones."

He pressed the bell and a little man with his left arm off at the elbow opened the door and wiped goose fat off his wide mouth with a napkin.

"Ah, you would be Longstreet." The little man held a hand out—the only one he had. "Desmond is my name, and Parnell's uncle I am—and welcome you are. Your wife?" He looked at Mamma.

"Anyone can get a wife—but a good coast-to-coast driver you have to guard and carry with you to the wars."

"Hell's bells," said Desmond to himself, scratching an ear with a pinkie. "This way."

He led us into a crowded parlor. A long planked table took up a wall, and, on it, suckling pigs and cakes and side dishes fought against an array of bottles and two tapped kegs of foaming beer. People ate and swore and sweated.

And there stood Parnell, the bridegroom, in tight black, smiling darkly to himself and eating pressed ham raw with his fingers, and drinking whisky out of a silver cup only slightly tarnished. And there was Katie, sweet and pink, who this half hour had been Mrs. Hayes, and she fed three children long dill pickles with her own white hand.

(I take all these details from a fat letter Mamma wrote about the wedding; it shows her use of dialogue.)

"There is Father Mangin himself, his well-fed, cheerful face freshly shaved and in his hand two cups of red wine—a proper figure of a priest," Gramp said and took me over to him.

"Welcome, sir," the priest said. "Wine to a newly wed couple. You will drink to their health, their faith, and their future family?"

"I will drink, Father," said Gramp, handing one of the cups to Mamma. "To everything, Father Mangin."

There was Parnell at our elbows. "It's nice of you to come, Mr. Longstreet. You, too, ma'am. Have you all enough to eat and drink? Just ask."

"Oh, Parnell," said someone, "what a bridegroom you make! Such a handsome man!" And she pelted tears down onto her handkerchief.

"Now, now," said Desmond, taking her by the arm. "It's a married man he is now. But if it's for gay bachelors you're looking, Desmond is your man. There's more life in me one arm than in them six-limbed Hindu gods."

(Mamma didn't get it *all* down. Desmond was a bit more obscene.)

Katie came over, followed by the brats. Her skin flushed, and her eyes bright, and she very pretty. This was *her* wedding day. Today she had crossed over and could sit with the older women.

"I am so happy."

Gramp took Katie in his arms. "Don't forget the kiss I'm entitled to from the bride." And he kissed her. A hurray went up. Katie flushed. Parnell was red as a banner.

Sean shouted, "Open up the good wine, Matt. It's the owld gentleman drinking. A bit of the chicken breast for the owld dandy and a proper lad he is yet, kissin' the colleens. He's buried six wives, they say, and one was a black nager princess with rings in 'er nose! Fancy that!"

More food, more drink. More people crowded in and introduced themselves. "Pleased to meet you, I am. O'Malley and Keen, and Mitchel and Kelley and Devall and Murphy and Chassdel, and Cohen and Finkel (They live upstairs, it's their silver we're using) and Rosco and O'Neil and Dirks and Tony Pizzelee, a fine wop and a white man (And how do you like his red wine?), and here are the children (Shake hands, you limbs of evil!). It's Mike and Eddie and Nell, and little John and you, Fenia—the back of me hand to you and kape away from that cake or I'll pull yer drawers down and give you one on the bare arse ('Oh, Mother! And me going on twelve') and this is Mary—sure. Parnell's mother, and you must taste her cooking."

Desmond was shouting again. "Dinner! Dinner! Dinner is

served! Take her arm, Parnell. It's no time for blushes. Hello, no—not with yer weddin' bed clean starched upstairs. After you, Mr. Longstreet. My arm, miss. What? *Missus!* And the saints bless me, but young and buxom you look for it. Well, your arm, and let me tell ya about Robert Emmet's insurrection and the part we Desmonds played in it, cutting English ears off for our stews."

I danced in after everyone—intrigued by these amusing savages so full of fun and fight.

Sean was seating everyone. "Katie, Parnell. Here at the head of the table. Bride and groom. What a couple! Six stories the cake—and faith. I'd uf had more to it, but the ceiling stopped me! You here, sir—in case you care to kiss the bride again, you flirt! You here, Father Mangin, get yer Latin ready for the grace and don't ask me now why I don't appear at Mass more often. Children, *please!* (Get the little bastards out of here!)"

The food: plenty and hot and cold and spiced and baked by a girl that "learned it all in Gabhala. In Kingstown, in Dublin, by the South Bull, Parnell's mother learned to cook for the English (May Jaysus strike them all dead). Sorry, Father, what is on the mind is on the tongue with me. Simple oaths, like simple poems, are best."

Sean was beating off children. "You brats in the other room. I'll crack the pate of any child that licks the icing off of that cake. So help me! And wash yer hands or I'll chop them off with the carving knife. And *take* Ellen, Mag. The child has wet her drawers with the excitement. It's t.b., madame. Tiny bladder, ha, ha. And what's so funny, if I may ask? Were ya never a child?" Mamma said she was.

"So sit you down to the wedding feast of the proud Irish folk —and honored again we are—and try this black bottle. Imported, mind you, and not a penny paid in duty. Dew from Limerick, and try this mellow fire from Galway Bay."

Desmond held up his one hand. "A little Latin, Father Mangin. All heads bow. Ah, now, a toast taken standing to the bride and groom—and faith, now is the time to stand, for later who knows who will be left above table? Your glass, sir. Your glass. The proper way to toss it down, I say. I like me a woman who can drink, for, sure then, who can you fight with if the other party is sober? Hot soup! Hot soup."

I was awed, dizzy, dazed by it all. A tall man came to Gramp. "Monegan is my name. And how are you? They're happy, the good folk, but don't take them for comic characters. A proud race and a gay one even when seeing pixies. A vast sense of living, a great courage for trouble.

"Yes, Father, I've introduced myself. Here comes the big pig—and, lord, it's a beauty—and look at the roast goose!"

Sean shouted, "Just pass yer plate and name yer parts and I'll cut as fast as the wind over Bailey's Lighthouse in Dublin Bay. I'll never stand in that breeze again. Yankee, I am now.

"And for you, sir? Would you care for the Pope's nose? Oh, it's yer pardon I'm asking, Father. I didn't see you there. I mean this bit tucked back here that goes over the fence last. The breast. The flank. The pig loins. How can people not eat? More beer, Mag, and see that little George doesn't choke on the bone again, the little angel, and blow his nose. On the sleeve. I declare, I'll sew your hankies on another time. You'd lose yer . . ."

Sean never stopped talking—even at me. "A fine wedding. We have never done a better one. Don't fumble, man. Don't be ashamed of cheerful jigs. Let the bogtrotter give us a tune. A good ringing one. A foot tapper. The one about Tigernan O'Rourke, Prince of Breifne, or King Sigtrygg of Dublin, or Maelmaedoc O'Morgair. *There* was a cattle thief!"

Desmond came running and grinning. "Pull back the rugs and stand the chairs in the hall. There is a wedding dance to be done. And if they don't like it downstairs, let them move. Back, John. Clear the room, Marge. Oh, you've let the child eat too much. Take him out and hold his head over the gutter. And none of yer sass. And get out of the way, you man-mountain, and none of your lip, my good man, or I'll give you one across the ears.

"You're drunk, man, and in no state to dance with a respectable girl. But, then, who's respectable? Wait, the bride and groom the first dance. Play, fiddler, and it's a glass of bitters ye'll earn, or a clout on the sconce. What a couple! Such grace, such charm—and a man to be proud of. And sure now, and what's wrong with Katie? Marrying beneath her. The Hayes are copper-ore cart drivers—nothing more."

Someone objected to the remark. "Sure now, it's a pleasure to take such a gurl to bed. What wrong have I said? It's my mouth and I'll use it as I feel. Them that are afraid to face truths need not listen."

(I must admit Mamma had a wonderful ear for dialogue. Here is some when the fighting started.)

"And is your mother still taking in wash? Go away. And what is a shanty Irishman doing at a white man's dance? You limping hodboy! You gandy dancer!"

"It's your eye I'll close."

"And your fey gut I'll empty!"

"Fight! Fight!"

"The shame of it at a wedding! No respect, these young ones. Wedding or wake and they are up to their American copper camp tricks. It was a nice punch he gave. He should be in the ring. In two years I'd have the boyo a champ. In less."

Sean said to Gramp, "Ah, would you care to join Father Mangin and the gentry in the parlor? Where is me father? You mean the owld rip? Faith, now, and he's dancing with the bride!"

"What are you saying, man?"

"Right in front of your gin-red nose."

I joined the gentry in the parlor. Father Mangin shifted his cigar and leaned back in the rocker.

Desmond waved his empty sleeve. "I don't hold with monks and priests and, to me, Ireland has too many fat ones."

"Don't be bitter, Desmond," said Father Mangin. "You're a lucky man to be alive."

"That's right. Ireland needs the cloth, the Latin text."

"And why?" asked Desmond. "You smashed Wolfe Tone; broke John Mahoney; drove the great Parnell to his grave."

The doors burst open and a herd of cake-and-dirt-smeared brats broke in. "The cake! The wedding cake! They're going to cut it!"

"Well," said Gramp, getting up, "I wouldn't want to miss that. I may even catch the bride's flowers and get married again!"

Father Mangin grinned. "At your age!"

Gramp dug his elbow into the priest's stomach. "He laughs at wounds who's never been to battle."

Mamma shook her head.

Sean was losing his voice as Katie cut the cake. "The big piece for you, Mr. Longstreet. And here, for you, Mother Parnell, and you, Father, and you and you and you—and *you*. Lend me the sword, Katie. Lads, stand back and keep the young nippers from bawling or you'll all feel the flat of the sword on your pants seam.

"Bung the new keg, Martin boy, and you'll find more bottles in the feather bed. And who put this live cigar in the music box? The low Irish are climbing in everywhere! Well, here's to you, Parnell. Here's to you, Katie. Love and happiness and fortune and health and many children and a good home and a sober life. And where in hell did the corkscrew go to? The best wedding this year in Butte, even if the MacMurtrys had a nager band and shamrock-shaped ice cream."

I was ill that night; too much cake. And Gramp was talking with a brogue ("Begorra, 'tis Himself danced he the bride"), until Mamma stopped him. The next day everything looked grim and smoky in Butte. Gramp went out to the mine and took me along, and we went down in iron buckets into a long, deep hole in the ground—steep, steep dripping stone walls, and then heat. Little lamps all around and the smell of mine mules. Men naked to the hips hammering and little railways and little steel-wheeled carts pulled by the mules. That's all I remember.

Then the roaring smelter with big red bricks of what Gramp called prime copper.

Later Gramp had a long talk with Sean, when he fully sobered up. But there was no use in Gramp's trying to get any true understanding of how the mine was doing. Gramp should have sold out his share, but he didn't, and he sent Katie and Parnell an ugly table lamp made of silver sea shells holding up a red silk lampshade with feathers on the top; it was the best Mamma could buy in Butte.

Then we got into our car and started for California, with no more side trips. We were all still pretty tired from the wedding, and Gramp had a little black bottle in his pocket which he took when Mamma wasn't looking. "Gout medicine, Stevie, a gift from Sean, came from Dublin, and it's doing me a world of good. Someday that mine will make millions for you, boy. Millions."

(It didn't.)

ESME, MY FIRST GREAT LOVE

The chicken is the country's, but the city eats it. . . .
—GEORGE HERBERT
(From Gramp's notebooks)

ON THE GOLDEN GATE

WHEN I FIRST SAW CALIFORNIA, I LIKED ITS BLACK backbone of mountains and the burned-out color: gold, umber, and brown where there was little water, and the crisp salad green of the shiny plant life where there was water. We came in over the mountain roads that had felt the weight of the "forty-niners" and went past Placerville. ("It used to be called Hangtown," said Gramp. "But the damn real-estate sharks didn't think that was dainty enough.") We saw the old hanging tree in front of a saloon that was now a speak-easy. We went over rutted trails to Sutter's Mill, where Marshall had started it all by finding specks of yellow metal in the mill run. Gramp took our frying pan and panned out fifty cents' worth of dust, or so he said.

Then we went south to the grape country, where everything

to me looked as it must have looked under the Spanish land grants. (I was reading Prescott's wonderful book *History of the Conquest of Mexico*.) I dreamed of bloody stone gods and dark savage girls. And of men rimmed in iron who cut their way into Mexico City with Spanish blood lust and cruelty, while the monks fried a few heretics and the Aztecs hamstrung the great war horses who screamed and fell like stones rolling.

We stopped to ask the directions to San Francisco of an old man sitting in an adobe hut in the middle of a vineyard. He invited us in. He was a fine old man, and since the car was overheated, we sat and waited for it to cool off. His name was Miguel Jesús Villa, and he grew ten acres of grapes and made his own wine and sold it by the gallon jug or by the swig.

He was the color of terra cotta and as old as his twisted and aged vines. He had a broad face and very black eyes, and he limped like an old goat.

"Welcome," he said from a patio that was deep in morning glories. He got out his best red wine and filled a glass for Gramp and Mamma.

"Your health," Gramp said, as is proper between men of distinction.

"*Ojalá*—God grant it!" said Miguel Jesús Villa and joined us in a glass.

It was good up there in the hill, and the world below was hidden in an outcropping of mountain. We sat and Gramp drank, and some pigs ate *piñon* nuts and someone was cooking *chile con carne* and *enchilada,* and I wanted to sit there a long time looking at the old man. He was fierce and stalwart like a god of Israel in Gramp's Bible.

Miguel looked at us and shook his head. "You people always drinking fast and rushing off. I see many wars in my time. I ride with my nephew, the fool bandit and hero-patriot, Pancho Villa, but I tell you, war's best to get over quick and come back to wine drinking."

"Sure," said Gramp.

"When I first came here, I was very sad. That's bad—always it's all going to end in death," said the old man. "But to *gente de razón*—people with reason—it can be born. When I was young fellow I sin a great deal. Every night a new sin—maybe six, seven sins a night. I sin with married woman, I gamble, I spit on priests, I steal, I live like a pagan, and then one day . . ."

He looked at me. I was very much impressed and very much interested.

"I am declared a heretic by the fat priest of my village. This is long ago, you understand, before we Mexicans have minds of our own, and priests they are very strong in my village. I remember the dreadful form—the banning of heretics—I remember every word the fat priest said. He said it in Latin, then in Spanish. In English it went like this . . ."

(I have just looked it up—and copied out what he quoted—and it still gives me the shivers.)

Wherefore, in the name of God All-Powerful Father, Son and Holy Ghost, of the Blessed Peter, Prince of Apostles, and of all the Saints, in virtue of the power which has been given us of binding and loosing in Heaven and on earth, we deprive Miguel Villa himself and all his accomplices and all his abettors of the Communion of the Body and Blood of Our Lord, we separate him from the society of all Christians, we exclude him from the bosom of our Holy Mother the Church in Heaven and on earth, we declare him excommunicated and anathematized and we judge him condemned to eternal fire with Satan and his angels and all the reprobates, so long as he will not burst the fetters of the demon, do penance and satisfy the Church; we deliver him to Satan to mortify his body, that his soul may be saved on the Day of Judgment. . . . Fiat, fiat, fiat!

"That must have been bad, Miguel," Gramp said, pouring the dregs off the glass into the myrtle bushes.

"It killed me. I was scared. I crawled home. I lay down in bed and died of fear and no one came to me to oil me, to give me the wafer, to say the words of the dead, and like a pig in a bog I died. . . . Only the ranch's foreman said it was fever. But I knew . . . and when I am dead . . . I got up and went to the church and the fat priest said I could be born again if I had twenty gold coins. And I gave him all the gold I had been saving up to get a married woman a ring with a red stone. And he gave me rebirth and holy water and called me Miguel Thomo Jesús Villa. . . . I know some people say he was a false priest hungry for gold and money, and that he was false to his vows. *Mi hijo*, but why should I take a machete to him and cut his fat belly open? No, I gave some *pitahaya* branches to the Altar which burn like candles but smell better, and since that day I have never been without God. And every year at La Laguna de los Flores I give thanks and now I am old man with not much itch left for married woman. I am an American *caballero* with a *rancho de verano* and my good and bad wine for the soldiers who buy it. And I tell you you are right not to be sad for old friends and old girls. They call me *cabrone*—son of a goat. But this I tell you: What you hold, what you pant after, what you see, what you have, *that* is living. That and a short bow to God; that is life. All else is remembering—and remembering is always bitter and sad. More wine?"

"One more glass." The deep alto of blackbirds came from the fig tree in the patio, and I was young and romantic—and so vividly impressed I never forgot any of it. It haunted me, and years later I put the scene into a novel.

The car performed well as we came down the coastal hills and began to smell salt water. Soon we would be in San Francisco, and Mamma looked forward to some small and large luxuries. Gramp explained to her that it was a town based on the best society. "The Barbary Coast whores married the forty-niners and sired the Native Sons. Ask anybody."

Mamma said calmly, "Little pitchers," and blew me a kiss.

I never see San Francisco without getting a bang out of the lofty hills wrapped in mist, the houses clinging to their steep stone sides, the gray-silver skies, the sweep of bay and the hassle of hills on the Golden Gate. It's like no other city I've ever seen, and yet it stands as part of a culture that is the East, and that is also Europe. It's like nothing else in California, certainly not the daffy pace and the nutty fruitcake complexion of Los Angeles, and the lesser breeds in Brentwood, Pasadena, and points south.

I can remember the day we came to the Oakland Ferry station and looked across at the city of San Francisco. It was a few days before Christmas, and we peered across the lead-colored bay at the populated hills, the fog already dancing on the roof tops, and the deep, bitter green of pine trees clinging to one shaggy hill. Over it all sounded the gawk of seagulls busy shoplifting along the waterfront.

"Big bastard," I said, copying Gramp's army talk as a gull flew past.

"Don't point," Gramp said. "Yes, it's a fine place. Let's get on the ferry and get going."

Mamma shivered and wrapped herself in Gramp's bearskin coat. "Hot water is what I need, lots of it, and good soap and crisp clean towels."

"Now, Sari, let's remember we promised to get in touch with Mrs. Jake Beekman, the rancher's wife."

"People," said Mamma as we drove onto the ferry, "get in the way too much when you want to see a country or a city. I just want lots of hot water."

"Don't talk as if this isn't America, Sari. Cheer up."

"How's your gout this morning?" Mamma asked, expressionless.

Gramp snorted, blew wind through his mustache, and looked at Mamma as if trying to see all the secret cunning corners of her female mind. Gramp's gout had been very bad and his big toes were still hurting him. He knew it was his own fault, and he didn't need Mamma to remind him of it. But she did when she wanted to make a point against Gramp.

"My gout, damn it, is fine; it's doing great in every toe I have. It's a family gift, like long noses and gray eyes. Stevie will get it in time, so don't gloat at an old man sinking away."

"You must learn to decline with grandeur," Mamma said, "like a Roman ruin."

"— ——— —," said Gramp, very low.

The ferry was running in a coat of mist, and the harbor horns were making deep sea sounds. Everything was dotted and soaked with spots of water. This is the best climate you will find in San Francisco, when the weather is what the natives call *good*.

Mamma said, "Gramp. Where are we staying?"

"The Palace Hotel. It isn't what it once was, but in its day . . . *Yahooo!* It was mighty fine, the best thing here besides the Barbary Coast."

"Can't we stay in a modern place?" Mamma asked, showing that even in 1919 people threw the word *modern* around like a loose shoe.

Gramp lit a fresh stogie as the ferry clanked into its slip at the foot of Market Street. The gate went up, the horses started to clatter off (in those days the wagon was often the solid muscles in transportation), and Gramp followed, the car growling with power and fury as it saw the heights beyond.

I said, "Think the car will take the hills?"

"We'll find out," said Gramp. And we shot into traffic and took the highest, steepest hill I had ever seen close up. It was just a city street—standing on end—but the car roared and took it as if it were a walk in a country garden. Mamma turned a little green and said, "I feel ill."

Gramp said, "It's the height. Breathe through your nose and watch out for eagles. Up this high they often carry off a full-grown woman."

There weren't any eagles, and while I was happy that Mamma wasn't carried off by one, still it would have been exciting. Of course, any eagle that got Mamma in his claws was in trouble. Mamma wasn't much over five feet, and the most beautiful strawberry blonde in America, but Mamma was a fighter. She had to be, with Gramp running the family and Papa a fashionable failure in the real-estate business.

The Palace Hotel was big, impressive, and old, with solid marble columns and hanging crystal fixtures in the ceiling singing in the breeze. The rooms were big, the beds long, and from the window you could see almost more of San Francisco than you could take in. The room was full of flowers, candy boxes tied in red ribbons, a basket filled with stuffed olives, smoked hams and hors d'oeuvres in glass.

Mamma said, "They've put us in the kitchen!"

Gramp read a card on the baskets. "No, it's from Mamie Beekman. Says, 'Welcome to our City.' "

"And eat hardy," said Mamma, taking the pins out of her riding hat. "She must think we're starving Balts or something."

I clawed up a bunch of hothouse grapes, and Mamma took them away from me. "Baby Boy mustn't fill his stomach before lunch."

Gramp slipped the aged bellboy a dollar and said, "Put this truck in storage and clear the way to the dining room; we're roaring down to lunch."

The bellboy looked at Gramp, then at the dollar, and stood aside and held the door open for us. The headwaiter bowed at us as we came into the dining room. A band was playing lunch music, and a sad little man was sawing schmaltzy Viennese music on a fiddle.

"Mrs. Beekman has asked me to give you *her* table," said the headwaiter.

"Damn white of her," said Gramp, "but we'll use our own."

The headwaiter looked up over his head (where Heaven must have been) and said, "This is the *only* free table. You'll like it."

We sat down, Gramp's big toe hurting, and Mamma said coolly: "May we see the menu?"

The headwaiter motioned to some of his staff. "Mrs. Beekman has ordered lunch for you. She felt that after your trip you would be tired, and the food here is of the best."

Gramp was going to protest, but Mamma, acting very grand, looked at him, and then at the waiter. "We don't *know* any Mrs. Beekman, and if you don't mind, we have minds and will use them. That is, if you have a chef here who can really cook."

The headwaiter tried to swallow his head, failed, bowed, and stood a defeated man. Mamma doesn't ever miss when she brings up the big guns of her scorn. Gramp nodded and sat silent, and Mamma ordered, in a swift firm voice, the way Gramp had taught her.

The headwaiter gazed at Mamma with the look of a sheep dog in love; he was ready to kiss her toes and let her step all over him. I never saw a man so impressed by a woman's ordering a meal. Mamma coolly waved him off, said the napkins were to be replaced and the butter brought back colder. He backed away, a beaten, adoring man, his face beaded with pleasure, and when he spoke to his help one eye rolled in the direction of Mamma. Good servants are all snobs and true anti-revolutionaries, Gramp always said.

Gramp killed his cigar in a silver ash tray and said, "If I were wearing my hat, I'd tip it to you, Sari. Damn it, you have talent. You have the gift. Too bad you're not a man."

"Stevie," said Mamma, "take your elbows off the table; and, Gramp, save the sweet talk. Anyone who mentions Mrs. Beekman gets Coventry."

"A good idea," Gramp said, as the hot shrimp came. We were a talking family, and to be put in Coventry at mealtime, where no one spoke to you, was just too much. We had dessert, and then Gramp and I went for a walk around the city, while Mamma went up to bathe and rest. Being small, she couldn't take on a load of food and carry it around right after a meal. At the hotel entrance the man in the Swiss naval uniform said that Mrs. Beekman's Cadillac was waiting, and I fear Gramp told him what to do with it. (It didn't seem it could be done, and I would have liked to watch when they tried.) Gramp hurried me off to show me the remains of the Barbary Coast.

Of course our luck couldn't hold. We were dressing for dinner when the phone rang and someone said something very fast that we couldn't hear very well. Three minutes later there was a knock at the door. There stood a large, pretty woman, built along the lines of the original Ark, and with her was a very beautiful young girl of fourteen, with an upturned nose and cruel green eyes. The Ark came in fast, talking quickly, and moved among us with skill and speed, kissing, handshaking, and pressing us close to a twice-life-sized bosom heavily scented with chemical violets.

"Ah, the Longstresses at last, at last! Mamie is the name. Mamie Beekman, but you just call me Mamie, and call me often. Jake said you'd be in Frisco, but that husband of mine, try and get him away from the ranch. Well, welcome to the town, boom, boom, and all that muck. Welcome to the only real city in the real West. Don't bother dressing, I'm giving a party on the top of Russian Hill, and this is my daughter, Esme. Esme, kiss the young man, and stop pulling on your dress. General, it's good to see you. Well, let's roll, time's fleeing and the band is playing 'Dixie.' "

After all these years I can still see and hear Mamie Beekman. Things like this you never forget. Voices in other rooms go, once-intimate faces and painful emotions are lost; the real and false things lived out in small rooms under low ceilings fade, but I shall remember Mamie's voice as long as I live. Gramp said she was vaccinated with a gramophone needle.

I expected Mamma to freeze her solid with a few well-picked-over words, but Mamma was a sport and liked fun. Something in the big pressure play being put on by Mamie appealed to Mamma, and Mamma was a fine actress. She could steer a scene any way she felt it. She slapped Mamie across her yielding acres of behind and put on the grin of a horse hand sunfishing a bronc at a big rodeo.

"Sure thing, Mamie," said Mamma in a tone of voice then being used by a young vaudeville actress called Mae West. "You show us all the way."

Gramp nodded. "We'll get the stagecoach through to Russian Hill come Indian raid, flood, and fire. *Or* earthquake."

Esme Beekman said softly, as she looked me over, "They don't admit it was an earthquake, *just* a fire."

"Of course," said Gramp.

"Take the young man's hand, Esme, and let's go."

"Lay off," I said. "Nobody holds my hand."

"You bore me," said Esme, taking my hand. We all went out, got into the big waiting car, and drove up more hills and down the other sides and went past Chinese signboards and places smelling of tired fish and sun-dried ducks, and along white houses with great big fat bay windows. San Francisco is mad about bay windows, and it has the most I have ever seen.

We stopped at last before a marble and gray stone house, and Mamie said, "Stanford White built it for Jake. I wanted Frank Lloyd Wright, but that Jake, he's a man you can't move without using TNT blasting powder."

Esme said to me, "You walk pigeon-toed."

"Your eyes are too close together," I said. (I wasn't Gramp's grandson for nothing.) Esme pinched me, and I got up a good funny face, rolling my eyeballs back till only the whites showed, pushing up my nose with one finger and stretching my mouth with two more. It usually worked with girls. They screamed and ran for cover. But Esme just shrugged and stuck out her tongue. She made horns of her hands and pushed them into her ears and rotated them. Pretty good for a girl, but nothing fancy.

The inside of the house was as gay as the outside, and that was pretty fancy if you knew San Franciscans when it came to spending money for houses, rooms, and walls. A lot of people were in the place, and the first Dixieland *jass* music I had ever heard close up in my life was being played by seven men on a platform. It was pioneer stuff—and early riff: "Camp Meeting Blues," "Livery Stable Stomp," "Maple Leaf Rag," and a lot that is now forgotten or made sweet and cool.

"Let's dig in," said Mamie. "Esme, show the young man where he can wash his hands."·

"You want to wash?" Esme grinned.

Well, by that time I was in love with Esme, and instead of finding the place to wash my hands, I said I had washed, and Esme and I went behind the trees and she showed me how to soul-kiss girls. I had a general idea, but no real practice. I made my first mistake—I liked it. I don't suppose any of us knows how simple it is to start a habit, but right then and there I fell in love with women. I had good advice in my time. I remember Gramp once, when his gout was bad, talking a whole afternoon about love and women. You would think all this from an expert would have saved me from a lot of trouble, turmoil, and lamenting. But it didn't. In the end I remained a foolish romantic, mistaking the illusion for the real, and the unreal fever of a moment for the true facts of life.

"Now," said Esme, "put your arms around me and say you adore me."

"Why?"

"Why, my foot. Don't ask, just do it. Say: I adore you, Esme."

"It sounds pretty silly."

"You can say it in French if you want to."

Well, that seemed fair. And I was rather proud of my small French. So I said it in French; I may not have been an expert lover in my teens, but I could sound as daring as any Frenchman in the business. Mamma found us after the French lesson and said I had to eat something. It was a real spread.

I note this from Mamma's letters and Gramp's journal to show that Americans—some of them anyway—around the start of the century and from then on were eating rather fancy, the specialties of real *haute cuisine*. And that besides killing the buffalo and Sitting Bull, building railroads, and defeating Robert E. Lee, we were also a nation that had among it people who were real diners *par excellence*. Somehow you will not find much of this in our literature, and even the little that seeps into Henry James's books is written of with a note of being ashamed of good living. I have tried to show that the good life existed even among the oil and lumber and mine kings of the just-ended West.

I must have eaten a lot. But I did get some wine spilled on my second-best pants, and by then Mamma was for taking us back to the hotel.

Mamie pinched my cheeks, twisted my arm, and said to me, "So you and Esme are going to get married?"

"So we think," I said. "In about ten years."

"He *is* such a sweet boy," said Mamie.

Mamma said, "The Longstreets all have mean streaks." Mamma didn't seem to like to talk about a future daughter-in-law.

Gramp later, taking off his shoes to rub his toes, said, "I hope he makes all the mistakes I made with women. Looking back, only the mistakes seem to have been fun."

Mamma said, "Foo!"

"HOW YOU GONNA KEEP 'EM DOWN
ON THE FARM?"

*The magic of first love is our ig-
norance that it can ever end.* . . . .
—Disraeli
(From Gramp's notebooks)

LOVE MAKES A
YOUNG HEART JUMP

There is nothing duller, except to the recovered
victim, than a young man in love. Love, Mamma swore, is
wasted on the very young, "for they are too banal and brash to
take it calmly and in leisure, to study its every facet and with
patience enjoy each morsel of it in subtle detail." First love,
I found, is hot and itchy, painfully uncomfortable. One sweats
and with graceless emotions makes a damn fool of oneself. I
suspect I was like all the rest, but I have no memory of anything but the bittersweet agony of the pleasure of suffering.
Love is the willing acceptance of suffering, Gramp said, at least
in its first stages, and Esme certainly kept me at the huddles,
panting and bug-eyed.

Gramp was aware, I think, of my torment, and he took me out car-riding with an ex-mayor of San Francisco: they had once done something cunning together in railroad stocks. The Mayor was large, wide, and given to brooding in his late middle age about the people he had served in politics.

We used to go riding in his big red car and drive along the ridge of the town hills. He would talk to Gramp and me about what was happening to California. Mamma suggested I write down what he said and use it when I went back to school as an essay in my English class. Every afternoon, after the ride, I used to write it down, but I never used it in my English classes, as we had to write on George Eliot and her novels, on Long-fellow's dismal poems, and about the Pilgrims' First Thanks-giving. I'll copy out some of the Mayor's talk, cleaning it up a bit and guessing at some words I got down wrong, or spelled in my first Elizabethan manner.

The Mayor would light his and Gramp's cigars and say, "You take these ranch and city folks; the native here is an indi-vidualist, preyed on by Hearst press and railroad politics, but there is very little hope of changin' him into a thinker. He hasn't time for it, he says. He feels he can work his way out of any trouble, and he loves this place that gives him food; college professors only confuse their dry intuition—and their children don't want much more than a gin joint, a movie, college clothes, and a new flivver now and then. The Californian is a hard man to change. Ah've tried.

"In politics he is an innocent, and any voice with beef and holler in it will impress him if the right keys of Land, Farm, People are pressed from time to time, and he is told of all the opportunities he has to die as rich as Henry Ford, Jesse James, or the oil kings. Part of *that* will come true—the dyin' part.

"You know California politics down here is as Ah always say, somethin' to be enjoyed and seen, a side show like the two-headed boy or the rubber lady.

"Under it all there is a complete, democratic individual who, once he starts to think, will make things hum. Walkin' along the coast roads, seein' the groves and people, feelin' the winds and the scent of forage and orchid crops clingin' to a sunny field, there is a feel of the folk doing things the way they did when Ah was a boy.

"The steers have most of their horns removed and a change has come over them. The fight has been bred out of them, and the old longhorns are as dead as Davy Crockett and Lola Montez. Oil sprouts here, thick as the crimes the oil kings commit to get it. But the towns are still the same—full of the guitar refrains and hard livin'. A hot collection of tin and tar-paper shacks, thousand-dollar carriages sinkin' in mud up to the wheel hubs, and gay ladies and hard, heavy men with pin-feathered faces gettin' as drunk and as loved-up and as loud as they can between bringing in gushers.

"Ah'm happy that the most popular stance in San Francisco is to palaver at a bar with a full glass of bourbon against our livers, even if it's against the law now. . . ."

But all I cared for was Esme Beekman, a girl with something about her that made her different from any other girl I had ever known.

Gramp came into the ornate lobby of the Palace Hotel, his cigar smoke trailing him by half a length, and he sat down at my side near the newsstand and took my arm.

"Damn it, boy, stop acting like a sick cat. The girl isn't worth it."

I said, "Gramp, what's between Esme and me is, well, it's personal."

"Not at your age: twelve!"

"Thirteen," I said with dignity. "I've started a mustache."

Gramp felt my upper lip, looked closely at it, and shook his head with a new respect.

"Welcome to puberty."

"She's wonderful, but I don't understand her."

"You're in for it, boy. The women already have their claws

in your heart and tail feathers, and you're going to suffer like I have all my life. When you read Proust you'll see how right I am. He said, 'Those who have never been in love think that a man of intelligence should be made unhappy only by a woman who is worthy of the agony she causes.' But it isn't like that at all. The more unworthy, the more we like 'em. Stevie, you're too young yet; give it up."

"Gramp, could I have five dollars to take Esme to China-town?"

Gramp sighed and handed me the money. "Not even going to *try* to break the woman habit?"

I said no, and thank you. Mamma came in just then, looking fine in her feathered hat and little colored shoes and trailing several men's admiring glances. I looked very grown-up in my long pants, tie clip, and cuff links.

"I'm hungry," Mamma said. "I've found a fine place, the Blue Court, so buy us a lunch, Gramp."

"Your new-found places serve such bad food, Sari, and such small portions, too," Gramp said.

The Blue Court was a good place near the big pin-point tower of the ferry station where the bay spreads out so you can see Oakland across the water and all that atmosphere of mist that makes the town such a fine place for hues of gray and off-white. The Blue Court (not to be confused with the present Blue Fox in San Francisco) was dim, with good wall panels, proper pictures so dark you could only enjoy the shine, and waiters who didn't mind waiting while Gramp and Mamma looked over the long hand-written menu and asked just how their wine was stored, in casks or bottles? I was above it all; only boors could think of food while I was in love.

Mamma looked up through her glass of red wine and sighed. "It's such a fine town."

"Sari, we have a problem. Stevie is in love with Esme and suffering."

"What did he expect of love?" asked Mamma, who had emotional scar tissue of her own.

I said, "I'd rather not talk about it."

Gramp looked up. "Stiff upper lip, eh, lad?" And to the waiter he said, "A good cigar."

Gramp poured some wine into a glass, two drops, and added water and handed it to me. "A man in love must eat, must drink."

"Thank you, Gramp," I said. "I'd like to leave now and meet Esme."

Mamma shrugged her shoulders. "Don't ride the cable cars, don't talk to strange Chinese, don't eat litchi nuts, and wash your face before you go. Neatness in love impresses us women."

"Oh, Mamma," I said, and kissed her.

"Yes, dear, go meet Esme. And wash."

I said it was all to be done as Mamma wanted, and then I excused myself and went to meet Esme in front of a bronze and bird-dropping-stained statue to some man who did something for (or to) San Francisco. Esme was ten minutes late, and when she came up to me I guess my liver jumped and my lungs flapped like blacksmith bellows, and the whole town danced a little in front of my eyes. Before love I would have gone to bed for a week if I felt like that; but I was learning misery is the sauce of love.

How can I tell you now about Esme? It's over thirty years since that afternoon, and a great many other emotions, ideals, personal events, have packed in like veils between me and that time. She was a woman even at fourteen. She made no sense to me—and she was delightful. She knew her values and held herself, if not above rubies, at least above ice-cream sodas and hand-holding on street corners. She was as wise as Eve full of apple pie, and as evil, I suppose, as Lady Godiva tempting white horses and Peeping Toms. I guess she was really just a bright, budding girl with all her erotic emotions in proper order, and I was just a goof—litmus paper to test her reactions on.

I said, as I handed her a wilted fifty-cent bunch of violets, "Good to see you again, Esme."

"Wipe your chin."

I wiped my chin. "How would you like to see some paintings? Gramp and I found some fine Degas at the museum."

"Look, we're going to hear a real razzmatazz jazz band."

"What's a razzmatazz jazz band?"

She looked at me and probably thought, as you must be thinking now: *Doesn't the fool know about jazz?* I must explain that jazz in 1919 was not only unknown to most Americans; to the few who knew it, it was not respectable and was usually played only in houses with odd upstairs rooms for rent, with contents, for an hour or so.

"Jazz," said Esme, "is the most wonderful music. Can you bunny-hug?"

"I can hug," I said, the willing victim.

"This is a dance, and it's better to jazz. Jazz," she explained to me, "is from New Orleans, but now it's spreading out. There are two kinds."

"You're smart, Esme," I said, taking her arm. "Very smart."

"The darkies play it Creole style and it's barrel house. The white people play it their way and call it Dixieland. But the real Negro stuff is very blue and *jazzy*. That's my own kind of music."

I suppose I made the first mistake of our courtship. I stepped back two paces and asked, "Are *you* colored, Esme? Not that it matters."

Esme just said, "Really, Stephen, you are a fool. Mother and I spend our winters in New Orleans and go to the joints to hear King Oliver play."

"What's a joint?"

"Where they jazz it. Oh, come on, you're very stupid today. Thanks for the violets."

We went down toward the place where the bridge is now built across the Golden Gate, and the little cafés were unpainted. Across one café front was a large sign:

ORIGINAL NEW ORLEANS JASS [not *jazz*] BAND

I looked at Esme as if I were St. Anthony and she were luring me to the devil, or asking me to light her opium pipe. I acted brave and opened the door for her. We went past the palms in brass pots and into a back room. On a platform were four Negroes playing something very exciting. I knew all about ragtime that Mamma played, but this wasn't ragtime. This was a new beat, a new kind of voice in the trumpet and the cornet, and the string bass wasn't being played by a bow; a large fat black man was beating it with his hand. I had no idea you could play a string bass by hand.

The cornet player lowered his horn, the man at the battered upright piano ("You can *never* play real jazz on a concert grand," Esme told me) did something to the beat, and the cornet player sang:

> *My baby is down and out*
> *So I'll get one and go toreckly.*

The waiter was at our elbow, and Esme peeled off her gloves and said, "Two gin rickeys."

The waiter nodded, looked at me, shrugged, and the singer sang:

> *If you like me, honey baby*
> *You've got to leave this town.*
> *She said, Don't you leave me here*
> *But sweet papa, if you must go*
> *Leave a dime for beer.*

Our drinks came, with the bootleg gin, and we drank and Esme smiled. "It's the real biggity-boogity. Don't you like it?"

"It's better without the gin."

"The jazz, *not* the drink."

"Oh, I don't know, Esme. It's loud."

At which point she gave me some hep talk of the period, but I was stoned cold by the gin and no longer remember a word of the jazz slang of 1919. It ended up with my saying that if she liked it, why then I liked it too. I held her hand and touched her knee lightly with my finger tips. (Oh, Helen, three times carried off to Trojan glory, were *your* kneecaps silky?)

"You should have heard Bunk Johnson play it. And there's a young man, Louis Armstrong, down there in Storyville." Esme sighed and sipped.

I looked shocked. "You *haven't* been in Storyville!"

Esme looked at me and finished her drink. "You are such a child, Stephen. A very nice captain of police took Mamma and myself around, and we went to a place where the jazzmen meet and play cutting sessions. Playing together without printed music. They don't read music very well, you know; it's all ear."

"That's the way I play," I said.

"Listen to that beat!"

> *See see rider*
> *See what you done*
> *You made me love you*
> *You made me love you.*

"I love you, Esme," I said, grabbing her knee again.

The waiter was back. "How old are you kids? Boss wants to know."

"Listen," said Esme coolly, "don't try that. You knew Stephen was only a boy when we came in. You could get in trouble if I raised a fuss."

"Finish your drink and get out."

Esme said to me, "Don't you *dare* tip this geek."

> *I thought I heard Buddy Bolden say*
> *Dirty nasty butt, take it easy*
> *And let Mister Bolden play.*

We left the café and went to a public park. Esme said, "You may kiss me."

"Thank you," I said, and I kissed her and held her arm and I could smell the crushed, dying violets. I felt I was ready to die

myself. Everything was so sad and so wonderful and so full of
lights that I knew for danged sure I was in love grown-up style;
nothing else could make me feel so dreadful on top of that gin.

"Mamma is giving a jazz party tonight," Esme said, "and
they'll really let out and play. 'Livery Stable Blues,' 'Dipper-
mouth,' 'Young Woman Blues.' The real thing, not this Tin
Pan Alley stuff."

"You're real smart, Esme. Can I kiss you again?"

"You're cute, Stephen. You *don't* ask for a kiss. You do it."

"Suppose you don't want me to kiss you?"

"Oh, then I just slap your face."

That seemed fair, so I kissed her again, and then I took her
back to her place. I went back to the Palace Hotel feeling there
wasn't any use growing up or going on living; no other afternoon
could ever be as wonderful as that one with Esme Beekman. It
just towered over everything else in life. I could understand the
bliss of youthful suicide.

Mamma had a new gown and had hired a maid from the hotel
to help her into it. I dressed with Gramp—black dancing
pumps, hair oil, a dark suit with short pants and black stockings, and a real hand-tied bow tie that Gramp grunted over.

"You look worn out, Stevie," he said as he tied the tie. "You
are taking this love too hard. Take it from an old horned stag
who knows. There's a lot more, and maybe better, later on."

"I don't want to go on living if Esme doesn't love me."

Gramp nodded, grinned, and pulled the wings of the tie out
and stood back to look at me. "Well, there he stands: the climax
of life, art, and science at thirteen. Stevie, wiser than Don Juan,
Casanova, and Catherine the Great's guardsmen. He has tasted
of love and his head is full of colored steam. Here, blow your
nose."

I blew and asked, "Is that Casper Casanova, our iceman,
you're talking about?"

"No. Now listen, someone once said, 'All living is hunger;
without hunger we perish.' That goes for love, too. Don't eat it

all up at once like the three big bears. It's here to last, and you're just small fry and it's hit you hard, but take it easy. There is a lot around. It's good and it's bad, and you suffer, but I suppose it's like doing without your right eye to miss it."

I said, "I don't think you've ever really been in love, Gramp."

"Oh, hell," said Gramp, just slightly angry. "Get my shoehorn and let me put my unloving feet into these goddamn tight shoes."

There were seven Negro jazz players at the Beekman suite. They used derby hats to mute their horns, and the piano player was smoking a cigar. Mrs. Beekman kissed me, kissed Mamma, and shook Gramp's paw and said, "The real gully-low gutbucket, isn't it?"

"What?" asked Mamma, wondering what primitive rites she had stumbled into.

But Mrs. Beekman just said, "Wait and see; jazz is going to sweep America."

And Gramp said, "Like hell it is!" (Which shows how wrong he could be.)

"Where's Esme?" I asked, as someone sang:

> *Oh I love to hear my baby*
> *Call my name*
> *She can call it so easy*
> *And so doggone plain.*

"Esme," said Mrs. Beekman, "is dressing. A little French gown from Worth's I ordered for her."

"Esme is spoiled," said Mamma. "She's too grown up for her age. She's putting ideas into S-T-E-V-I-E'S head."

Mamma always spelled things out when I was smaller—even later when I was there and already educated enough to understand.

Mrs. Beekman smiled. "A little knowledge can do no harm. Now this dance is called the Grizzle Hug. Listen what they do to the music: how they take a melody and change the form, and the solo horn takes over and the others play around him, free style."

> *If your house catch fire*
> *And dey no water round,*
> *Throw your trunk out the window*
> *And let the shack burn down.*

Just then I saw Esme. She was wearing a blue gown with a blue band around her hair and was carrying a small feather fan. This was nearly 1920, remember, and fashions were odder and, in a way, more amusing.

I went over to her and said, "Gee."

"Gee, what?"

"Gee, you look peachee."

"Ask me for a dance, oaf."

I said, "May I have this dance, Miss Esme Beekman?"

"You may put your arm around me. Lower."

> *I hate to see the evening sun go down*
> *Cause my baby she done left this here town.*

After two dances some local youths with long sideburns took on Esme, and I joined Gramp at the bar and buffet. Gramp let me eat a pear.

"How's your love life?" he asked.

"Fine, thank you," I said, reaching for a napoleon.

"Here comes your little charmer now. I wouldn't trust her not to ruin Bluebeard."

Esme came over and said, "Good evening, General Long-street."

"Flattery will get you nowhere," said Gramp.

Esme and I went out on the balcony. There was the town, and the hills and all the harbor and the fog, and I loved it. Lord, how I loved that town then—and still do.

Esme said, "I've got some money, and I've an idea. Let's go to Europe, just the two of us."

"Sure," I said, a little dazzled. Nothing seemed real any more; I was a victim of destiny.

"Of course we'll get separate staterooms, and you can let your mustache grow and pass as a Princeton man. You're tall for your age."

I tugged at the feeble down on my upper lip. "Sure, but why separate staterooms? We'll get married."

Esme looked at me, and jazz drifted out on the balcony.

> *Now I ain't rough*
> *And I don't fight*
> *But the woman that gets me*
> *Got to treat me right.*

Esme said coldly, "I'm *never* going to marry."

"Why?"

"Look what it's done to my mother, and to *your* mother."

"What?"

"I'm not going to hand my whole life to a man to step on. I thought you loved me, Stephen."

"Sure. I want to marry you."

Esme said, "Boor!" and went inside. I didn't dance with her any more that night. I got back to the hotel, and Gramp came out of the bathroom rubbing his bald head and found me weeping into my pillow. He sat down and patted me on the shoulder. I turned over and said, "Esme has no morals."

"No woman has; they only use morals when they need them to gain their end."

"I'll never love again." (I take no responsibility for my teen-age dialogue.)

"Put it in writing and sign it," said Gramp. "Now get some sleep. Tomorrow is Christmas, and we'll go shopping and I'll buy you a twenty-two hunting rifle. And then next week Sari is giving a New Year's party for just us three. Lots of fun ahead."

I said no thanks; I was finished with life. I lay down and slept

and dreamed I had sent Esme a golden spider with a ruby heart
in its mouth for Christmas. The next day I found a golden
spider in a store (no ruby heart) and I sent it to her. She sent
me a set of early jazz recordings, and I sat weeping (and winding
the early Stone Age victrola) and listening to:

> *It takes a brown-skin woman to satisfy*
> *my mind.*

(Some months ago I was lecturing in the Middle West, and
a very wide fat woman with gray hair, curled and tinted blue,
puffed her way up to me after the talk and held out a ham of an
arm and said in a loud fat voice, "It's certainly good to see you
again, Stephen. Meet my daughter, Mrs. Sperman, and my
two sons, Doug and Jim, and this is my husband. Arthur, this
is Stephen Longstreet; we were childhood sweethearts in
Frisco. My name is Mrs. Arthur McCary Foyle now. Been
married twenty-eight years. It's good to see you again. Not
that I liked your lecture; all that nonsense about modern art.
I say it's all Russian propaganda, all modern art. What I like
is stuff you can see and know, like the *Post* covers. You did grow
that mustache, didn't you? Well, you must come over and have
a drink at our place. . . . Arthur, put away the cigar and find
Stephen's rubbers. We live in Park Heights. Arthur's father
developed it. Good American names, no Catholics or Jews.
Everybody there voted for Ike, but some dirty Red gardeners.
Damn it, Arthur, don't light another cigar. I'm a grandmother,
you know. Three times. I'm going to read all your books. I
want you to autograph them for me, something very personal.
You must speak at our Liberty Belles Club.")

> *Bliss was it in that dawn to be alive,*
> *But to be young was very Heaven.*

GLORY GIRL, EARLY FILM STAR

*The motion picture industry, like
the mule, is an animal that has
neither pride of ancestry nor hope
of posterity. . . .*
—GRAMP, in his notebooks

13

LAND OF
NO SANE RETURN

NEW YEAR'S NIGHT, 1920, WAS SAD AND YET SOMEHOW cozy for us. The Beekmans had gone out of town to be with Mr. Beekman on their ranch. Gramp had champagne sent up to our San Francisco hotel room, Mamma put on her best dress, and we all held up our glasses and clicked them, even me, when the noise in the street grew louder and the fiddle music from the grand ballroom seeped up through the old walls. We felt lonely, on the tail end of a continent, far away from the family, but making a tight unit of a group: just the three of us and the old world spinning into a new decade.

None of us was too impressed by or interested in the miserable history of the year just gone; Gramp had long since discarded more than a morning glance at newspaper headlines. He thought the cheap printing press the worst thing that could happen to a nation. "Cheap printing will raise up millions of morons and lower the level of everything; literature, art, the theater, and good taste will go to hell in a hack, and vulgarity will be king, for it brings in the most money." Mamma felt the world was always making more history than it could consume; and I was a young punk already living in a personal world, a private world of my own whose fringes barely touched reality. The year just gone had seen a great destroying world war not yet forgotten and its victims and heroes already boring us. Women wore tight skirts and could hardly walk. Female underwear was disappearing; people said the skirts were to get shorter and shorter and hit the knees, and stockings were to be rolled; and the flapper was to appear in the art of John Held, Jr. Drinking of alcohol was on its way up and the hip flask was a social must. (Joke in vaudeville: "This stuff right off the boat?" "Yeah, scraped off!") The HC-4 had flown the Atlantic. The Peace Conference in Paris had just finished and a dying American President had come home to have his League of Nations flung in his face like a wet glove. Women were going to get the vote soon, and Mamma said, "This means good, clean government, no lobbies, no national stealing any more, no wars, and the end of crooked political machines." Already men called Harding and Coolidge and Hoover were taking bows, and the stealing of the great national oil reserves and public land and resources was starting. And women were about to vote for the same wrong reason as their husbands. Henry Ford in a libel suit had just called Benedict Arnold a writer and placed the American Revolution in 1812, and was already putting his anti-Semitism into high gear, and "Hate the Jews" was as much his love as Ford cars. Gramp almost wrecked our poor flivver when he read the early Ford lies on the subject.

So we stood there in the birth of 1920, drank our slightly corked champagne, and peered a bit into the outer darkness for things to come. Babe Ruth, a young pitcher, had excited

Gramp and me that season. Jack Dempsey was the new world champ. The High Cost of Living worried housewives. The bands still played "The Long Long Trail," "I'm Always Chasing Rainbows," and a song no one ever forgot, if they heard it, in those days: "Avalon." "Smiles," "Dardanella," "Hindustan" were also popular.

The first mah-jongg sets were already in the shopwindows, and Mamma was reading *The Four Horsemen of the Apocalypse* and *The Magnificent Ambersons*. There was a Big Red Scare, and the cartoonists had a field day drawing bearded bums carrying bombs.

I am trying to catch again the feel of that night the new decade got born because it was to see me grow from a puppy to an adult, and just ahead were my tests in the artistic revolts of Sinclair Lewis, F. Scott Fitzgerald, and Ernest Hemingway, all fine artists, to go up so fast and peter out in their later works —somehow always the fate of the American novelist. I was to find Picasso, and Stravinsky, and James Joyce, and reject Gertrude Stein, Thomas Benton, and Rudy Vallee, and the world of the banal dullness of Herbert Hoover.

Two days after New Year's we were rolling down the dusty coast highway, not yet, and not to be for some time, the perfect ribbon of concrete that follows the California ocean. We were going south toward a place called Los Angeles, a frontier town, booming and busting, tearing its pants as it expanded into the bean fields and orange orchards.

We stopped off at the Bartlett horse ranch. (Mamma had gone to school with Nell Bartlett.) We had decided we would only say hello to the Bartletts, maybe have a meal with them, and move on to Los Angeles. But Lou Bartlett, big and handsome and very sunburned, made us stay over.

"We're running the horses down to the sea tonight," he said.

"Why do that?" asked Gramp.

"Salt water good for their hoofs. Hardens them."

"How are horses selling?" asked Mamma of Nell Bartlett,

who was a big silent girl, the kind they grow so tall in the West.

"Oh, we manage. We almost made money last year."

"Don't brag," said Lou. "Come meet the folk who are riding down to the sea with us tonight."

We met a lot of other patch-pants horse-lovers, all breeding horses and not making money at it, but keeping it up because they loved horses. The women were brown and weathered, but exciting, and were able drinkers. The men were silent mostly, but they too could belt the stuff away. The Bartlett's place was a rambling ranch house of boards, adobe bricks, whatever had been handy; but it had a charm, and it was taken care of. But it needed paint, new fencing, and some terracing. Only the horses got the best of everything—wonderful horses as I still remember them. Mexican horse hands took care of them like children and forgot they hadn't been paid for some months.

We were all to ride, with the horses, down to the sea. Mamma and Gramp rode well, and I had tumbled off and on enough farm horses at Gramp's summer place in Pittsfield to know I could stay on, even if my form was not all that Western riding was supposed to be.

I walked around the ranch, taking it all in, walking tall, for I had borrowed some high-heeled boots and a battered brown Stetson that Mamma had padded with newspapers under the band so it would fit.

The Bartlett ranch was on the rising coastal highlands that stood over the sea, that climbed on up toward the snow-topped mountains behind. It was a good farm for horses, and horses had been bred there for many years.

The Bartletts bred horses for the fun of it and were poor—for they were bad business people, breeding horses the way some people breed puppies or show dogs or raise canaries. They enjoyed having all kinds of people living on the farm or, as they said, ranch. There was a row of ranch guesthouses that were always filled, and a pool. We had the last guesthouse under some flowering mimosa trees, and there was a bank of snap-dragons on the ridge above.

At four o'clock we went out into the long slanting sun of the afternoon. A great many people were sitting around the pool, none of them swimming, and two little Mexicans in white jackets were passing out drinks. A dozen ranchers sat down to dinner.

The horses were making a great clatter. They knew they were going to the sea. Perhaps they remembered last year. Mamma, in a tight riding outfit with a black turtle-neck sweater, her hair caught up in a wide white scarf, stood at the patio door under the roofed arbor that the trumpeter vines grew on and watched the activity of mounting.

The chuck wagon had left right after dinner. The wagon had topped the public road and went along into the gathering dusk above the umbrella pines, its axles still making a small squeak, although they had been well greased. The whole coast seemed to be sleeping.

At midnight, the moonlight furnishing the illumination, the geldings were moved up from their meadow and started off toward the coast. In an hour the mares and colts followed.

"*Buenos días, amigos*," said a little Mexican, and poured a bucket of water over the embers in the patio fireplace. A hissing rose angry and white, and steam puffed up into the night air. A last few coals blinked, but they too died.

Gramp said, "Just hold on tight."

"I'll be all right," I said.

Mamma said, "No bronco-busting stuff."

I promised.

Wood smoke and charred logs filled the air. The stallions were very restless. The stars had multiplied to millions when we all moved toward the corral.

I was riding a russet gelding called Red Mike. He was a comfortable horse, not so young as he had once been and lacking the sense of humor that would have, in any other horse, tried to toss off the man who didn't ride for a living. Mamma was to ride a mean horse called Baby. Gramp—looking heroic—was on a big gray one.

Baby had refused the bridle at first, but once the bit had grated between his huge yellow teeth he accepted the saddle, and when Mamma swung up he pranced a little, churned foam around the mouth steel, and settled into an even rolling.

Lou Bartlett was not as bad a rider as he had claimed. He was on a big paint-colored horse with a hard mouth, and the other guests who were to come with us were all on horses according to their skill. There were stallions called Pat and Mike, led on coiled leads of braided horsehair; a pair of horses that gave the least trouble; a red-brown stud horse called Man of Peace; and a small slim male that had very little Arab blood in him—but it showed. He was called Al Jolson, but his record book listed him as Achmid Jihud.

The night had remained clear, and no mist had come from the sea. We crunched up the private road leading to the main gate. The horses, some of them still shy of the saddle or the lead rope, advanced sideways, their back legs seeming to precede their front ones. Mamma fought Baby to a slow pace.

Once we were on the enormous snake of the public road, the clop-clop of hoofs calmed the horses, and we advanced in a column, Lou leading and the prancing steps of the last paint pony bringing up the rear. Red Mike stayed where he was put, kept up his cow-poke pace, and never seemed to wake up. He walked into every step without a jolt of any kind.

The night-blooming flowers were sweeter than usual, perhaps because there was no mist, and we went down across the range, stopping sometimes to let a long milk truck with its glass-lined tank go bouncing past, the horses rolling their eyes and sharply kicking the roadbed as the snorting engines ground into high. Most of the milk trucks had already rolled away hours before, draining the udders and dairies, moving toward the butter and cheese factories. Lou rode beside Mamma, his horse ignoring Baby's bared teeth.

As the road dipped to the left it grew in pitch, downhill, and the men had trouble with the stallions, who, feeling their great limbs tossed forward by gravity, wanted to break free and run for it wildly.

Gramp grinned. "Like it?"

"Sure," I said.

"Both hands going downhill."

A man would calm the horses with a word or a curse in low Spanish, or would move among them laying on his hands, patting a rump, or pulling an ear. Some tried to bite his fingers, but a slap across red flaring nostrils stopped them, and we went on, until the wide, white coastal highway was below us full of thrumming, thumping sounds.

Even at this hour the trucks were moving up the coast with their cargoes of lemons and oranges, their crates of wine grapes, the casks of olives, and the bales of vegetables, grown in the sloped fields by people "who worshiped on dirty knees the fecundity of the coastal plains," as Gramp put it.

Mamma rode on ahead, Baby seeming to skate onto the road, and Lou waved his arm. We cut across the highway and piled onto a sand road still marked with the scars of the chuck-wagon wheels and the piled leavings and dainty horseshoe tracks of the mares and geldings. I could hear the casual voices of the horse hands unseen ahead in the night.

This had once been a royal highway when Spanish kings ruled here, and men in tin hats a long time ago had ridden dusty war horses. Before that perhaps the savages had toiled up from the sea, bearing shells and the rancid flesh of beached sharks. (I was wallowing in history books and daydreaming of the past.) Few people used the old road. We turned north and rode along this trail, the muffled beat of the stallions' hoofs like drums all out of time, playing music. To the right the great mountain ranges, full of fierce gulches and gaps, were marked in the moonlight. The white houses, the pine shapes, and the limbs of oaks and cork trees stood out.

Lou dropped back to my side. "Can you feel the land and the people in it, as a punch in the nose?"

"I know what you mean," I said, feeling grown-up.

"Look at it." The big man turned in his saddle to look back; feather-duster clumps of pepper trees, the neatly marked scars that were the vineyards, the very heavy black olive trees, and the rows of plum and lime and apple catching a waxy shine on their leaves when the road above us was lit up by the headlights of the grinding trucks. The hum and bark of motors would labor around some point of rock and then a line of freight trucks would elephant past, sometimes to be passed by a late bus, its lights dim, its seats way back, and the tired crumpled shapes of passengers seen through the breath-misted windows. But mostly we just had the mountains on the right and the sea on the left—a purple sea with a thin oyster-white fringe of foam, and the heavy solid rocks where seals, pelicans, and herring gulls sat on their guano mounds and slept restlessly to the beat of surf-driven waves, tangled with pungent seaweed and ocean-bottom wrack.

I think even the horses felt it, this mixture of sea slime, citrus blossoms, night-blooming jasmine, and sea life. We rode for three hours, the land growing a little wilder, the big road above us creeping away to the hills, and the coast lower before us.

Gramp kept riding up to me. "Still with us?"

The few gates we had to open and close behind us became rarer and rarer.

I rode up to Mamma. She was holding Baby still by the pressure of her legs around the big expanding barrel of the black horse, so terrible and beautiful and powerful. She rode well, that careless riding that is expert and yet not fancy, but much better and more skillful than show riding in England or in Boston or New York.

"Like it?" I asked.

"Love it. Where's Gramp?"

"Coming up."

Red Mike shied at a night shape. Baby took a nip out of my horse, and the stallions almost had a stampede. By the time we were back in order, we could see the camp on the meadow above the sea, the shape of tents and the log fire burning by the chuck

wagon; then we came down to within twenty feet of the booming sea and stood over it in the tall grass, the hissing breakers
ten feet below us, more and more pasture always being eaten
away by the slow action of the sea. Gramp helped me dismount.
Lou helped Mamma down, and there was a sort of corral of
wire and poles and brush and timbers. I was very tired and
drank my *café au lait* and rubbed my thighs and fell down on
my blanket; and the last thing I remembered was the swish of
sea sucking softly among the rocks and the whinny of surprise
as the mares scented their menfolk. Then the leg pain and body
stiffness acted like a drug on me, and I slept against the big
shape of Gramp.

The sun hit me between the eyes, and I got up and saw everyone was bathing in the sea. I went down below a point where
I wouldn't need a suit, stripped, leaped into the sea, and floated
way out, turning to look back at the land.

High on a path leading to the pine trees I saw Mamma on
Baby and Gramp on his big gray. They were climbing slowly,
as if in no hurry, taking their time and talking very earnestly
about something. They looked free and happy.

I turned back to the sea and swam around in a great circle,
and when I looked back they had been swallowed up by the
massing of many tall, dark pine trees.

I got out of the water and shivered until I dried, and when I
looked up, they had passed the first belt of pines. I saw the two
horses slowly grazing, but there were no riders with them.
Mamma and Gramp were sitting on a great rock looking out at
the sea below them.

I went to see if I could hunt up some breakfast.

A rough corral had been built for the stallions, and I patted
their shiny flanks as I passed. They were restless; some sort of
grapevine had let them know something exciting was up at this
seaside. Red Mike had tried to kick the dark brown horse
through the fence twice. The stallions were not the friends they
had been. Some latent hate stirred them.

A fire burned between two stones and a coffeepot hissed from its hook over the embers. Eggs and bacon fried. Two horse hands named Dom and Ric sat at the fire, pulled off the coffeepot, and drank boiling cups of it, sugarless and creamless. They played games with cards. I ate and drank with them and listened while they spoke.

Dom rolled himself a homemade cigarette and removed a stick from the fire to light his twist of tobacco. All was suddenly very still from the stallion pasture. The gulls were overhead and the wind from the sea was just cooling enough, not cold. There was still no mist. The great heat of the day was yet to come.

"I'm always restless when I'm moving horses," Ric said, puffing on his tobacco and nodding. "Always something she can happen. In the old days my uncle he blamed a *guanta*, sorcerer."

"Remember when we used to take the herd down to the sea before the war?"

"The owner is a great lover of horses, but no damned good at collecting bills. *Boca cerrada*, closed mouth."

"The stallions were making money in those days."

"I remember a waiting list of real horse-lovers wanting to buy a horse. Now they are all rich, and the poor poorer—it does not matter."

"Those were the days," said Dom, watching the flames catch new wood.

There was a clatter of hoofs in the stallion meadow. Everyone got up to look, but the horses settled down again. Dom and Ric refilled their coffee cups. Ric made himself some cigarettes and handed me one. We smoked (I had been doing it secretly for some time). Dom lay on his back, spurred boots crossed, his hands behind his head, and sang one of those old songs he dug up someplace in Mexico where he had herded bulls.

El diablo te espera, La Floreada!

There seemed to be fifty verses of it and he sang them all, and the sun grew hotter as the last cloud went away. The coffeepot was empty and the last cigarette smoked out. Dom ran out of verses. Mamma and Gramp could no longer be seen from the shore. I stood up and hunted the hills with field glasses. Not even their horses were in sight.

They came back very late, very happy, having been free souls all day. We left two days later, and I dreamed about horses for weeks, always waking up and feeling the horse under me, and Mamma would run in and ask me if I were sick.

One morning we hit a town called Santa Monica and tooled the dusty car inland over the foothills that came down toward the sea.

When we got to Los Angeles, it was not the daffy, exciting, and brainless giant it is today. We had been four days out of San Francisco, traveling muffled to the ears to keep out dust and grinding past burned hillside and very blue sea on roads that cattle and Spanish dons had made badly, and where often the word "gasoline" was unheard-of. But we made it.

We rolled up from the sea onto what is now Sunset Boulevard but was then a goat trail among wild growths, bean fields, and the small huts of Mexican field hands. There were a few ranches, but not very active ones. And what is now Beverly Hills was a series of rising slopes, mostly overgrown with native herb and bush, and here and there someone was thinking of making this a lush heaven on earth by laying out tapelines and putting up signs—but not very actively.

Gramp looked over the landscape and sneezed. "Damn it, God never meant this for human beings! It belongs to Digger Indians, Gila monsters, and rattlesnakes."

Mamma brushed the native soil off her dress and nodded. "They should have left it to the desert cactus and the sand-storm."

Mamma was tired from the long ride, Gramp was out of cigars and whisky, and I was too young to be anything but thrilled by new things, the color of places—sights never seen by an Eastern boy before.

"Hollywood," said Gramp, "should be right ahead."

"I hear it doesn't exist," said Mamma.

"It better," said Gramp. "Glory Girl has been writing me to come on and try out the climate."

"Glory Girl," said Mamma, "is vulgar. That is why she's such a success out here among the jumping snapshots."

We passed billboards advertising Charlie Chaplin in *Shoulder Arms*, Douglas Fairbanks in *Knickerbocker Buckeroo*, Mary Pickford in *Daddy Long Legs* (a dismal bore, again being remade). And such names as Pearl White, D. W. Griffith, Norma Talmadge, and Elsie Ferguson were lettered on small theater fronts. We drove over the county strip toward where the shacks of Hollywood were scribbled in the distance. I must explain that Glory Girl (that wasn't really her name) was one of the great silent movie stars, as well known as Theda Bara and other glamour pusses of the day. She was an old friend (not so old, really) of Gramp's. He had known her when she was a thin little earnest actress on Broadway and (he always admitted it) had helped her up in the world. "Nothing like lobster and a good clear wine to put meat on a beautiful girl."

By 1920, she was a great motion-picture star, had forgotten all about acting, and hung on long legs from airplanes, was dropped from tall buildings, fought sharks and wild bulls, and led (on the screen) the most dangerous life in the world. I used to sit on the edge of my seat eating my fingernails when I saw her films; and when the Chinese or the Spanish heels tortured her, or threw her in front of speeding trains, or from the decks of boats, rage and love and pain would fill me, and her beautiful tormeted image would blur in front of me as I dreamed of saving this shapely white body and fighting off the bad people who hunted her. For me, motion pictures have lost a fine violence and epic purity since Glory Girl stopped appearing on the screens of the world.

So there we were on a hot, dusty day (before the famous smog) looking for Orange Grove Drive. At last we found it and a white Moorish monster of a house, with iron railings and colored awnings and a lawn big enough to launch an elephant race. There was a Japanese butler who led us into cool, perfumed darkness over red tile floors. Suddenly, at the top of a curving staircase (which, I later learned, had been designed by Cecil B. De Mille), appeared Glory Girl. She was dressed in white, with a cocktail shaker in her hand. (Everyone seemed to have a cocktail shaker in his hand in the twenties. I've checked with old friends and they seem to remember it that way, too.)

"Jesus, look at the old bastard. Darling!" she said.

She came down and kissed Gramp on the top of his bald head and was introduced to Mamma and myself. I smelled my hand where it had pressed hers, and it smelled of bootleg gin and orange blossoms and well-bred dogs and linen warmed in the sun.

"Well, you really made it," Glory Girl said, pouring three glasses full as the Jap held them out.

"We did," said Gramp, "but the roads almost beat us."

Glory Girl winked and said, "Hell, we don't like roads—don't want strangers and agents and tax collectors out here."

Mamma said, "You talk like a Native Daughter."

Glory Girl nodded and picked up a fourteen-inch cigarette holder. "I was born in California at the age of twenty-two. Five years ago."

Mamma took that statement with a shrug. Gramp lit her cigarette, swallowed his drink, and coughed and said, "Now that's good gin."

"Just off the boat," said Glory Girl. "Scraped off." And we all laughed at the famous joke of the period.

Mamma said, "I'd like to wash up."

Glory Girl said, "Sure, and we'll have lunch, and then we'll run off my new picture, *The White Slave*."

Mamma said, "That would be fine." After she washed and Gramp and I rubbed ourselves with Colorado River water, we all went out onto the sunny patio where the lunch was spread out on cool, green linen.

Hollywood in 1920 had not yet gone fancy, arty, cultured, and dull. Good taste, real writers, and taxes were missing. It lived a free, wild life of fantastic movies, huge, untaxed salaries, drugs, and casual love, and hadn't even one toe dragging in reality.

But of course I wasn't in touch with reality myself then—so I liked it.

Little Japs served us and kept the plates filled. The water was tossed up in the Spanish fountains, and the sun blinked in the swimming pool. That day all was well with the world. We started with clam broth Santa Monica, a local favorite, a spoonful of whipped cream sailing on the broth. This was followed by a steaming clay dish that two boys had to carry to the table. Glory Girl grinned.

"This is a Mexican version of *cassoulet*. We cook it in a clay in our own back yard for two days."

Gramp closed his eyes and ate—a sign it was very good. He said, as he held up his plate for more, "This was the favorite dish of Rabelais, and who can blame him? 'A dirty mind,' he always said, 'is a continual feast,' but he also knew a lot about eating."

The lunch was almost over, and our eyes were hanging out on stems (after the roadside feedings of the last week, we were hungry for real food) when a short balding little man dressed in a polo-player's outfit came in. I found out later that riding pants were the uniforms of the best people, and that most of them couldn't ride a horse. They just liked tight pants and boots.

Glory Girl kissed the little man and said, "Darling, these are the Longstreets. This is Egon Hutz, my director. If you have a Hungarian for a friend you don't need enemies."

"Your slave," said Egon, nibbling his way up her arm with continental kisses. As I remember, they talked like their film titles in those days. "What's to eat, baby?"

Glory Girl said to a little Jap, "Toka Nobunga, serve Egon anything he wants."

The littlest Jap served, and the director ate, looked at Mamma, rose, and clicked his heels. "Mrs. Longstrassee, you ought to be in pictures."

Gramp smiled. "She is. She used to pose for Charles Dana Gibson before my son married her."

Mamma said, "I don't think motion pictures will last as entertainment."

"Entertainment," said Egon, rolling his eyes at me and swallowing food. "We don't make entertainment; we sell dreams. Rose-colored dreams for people who can't dream their own dreams. Come out tomorrow morning and we'll try to fit you into Glory's new picture, *The Dark Woman*."

Glory said, "That's to follow my new picture, *The White Slave*, which we are going to see now right after the General finishes his brandy."

Gramp nodded, and she kissed the top of his head again and called him "darling." I found out later everybody was called darling out here, but it impressed me then.

The private projection room was dark and cool, and we all sat, Egon holding Mamma's hand and explaining what a great picture it was. I don't honestly remember much about *The White Slave*. I suppose there is a print around someplace that I could see, but that would break the skin of personal dreams, and Glory Girl is dead, and the motion-picture business as dreams go no longer really exists, and even the Hollywood Hungarians like Egon are opening teashops and real-estate offices.

I slept after lunch on a twelve-foot-square bed under mirrors, while Mamma, Gramp, and Egon went around to see the town. It was smaller then, dusty, hotter, and everybody knew everyone's scandals. Tom Mix drove a Dusenberg with a Texas saddle on the hood and a set of a steer's longhorns over his bumper. Doug Fairbanks, the father of the present one, never forgot to smile, and Mack Sennett was inventing with Griffith and Chaplin the only art forms that Hollywood ever had, for which they were later crowded out of the industry.

That evening the family and Glory Girl and Egon went to a dance hall on a pier at the sea, and I sat home and played poker with three little Japs.

Breakfast the next morning on Glory Girl's patio was calm and delightful.

Gramp's gout was not bothering him much (just a little headache), and Mamma had bought a new hat with a long black feather and was wearing her high button shoes, still in fashion in 1920. Egon was going to pick us up in his car and take us to the studio.

The horn blew out front and we all piled into Egon's Franklin. They don't make that car any more, but it was a good one. It was air-cooled and had a front end like a bulldog's jaw. Egon drove it like a race horse. We went out toward what is today Culver City, where Ince and Sennett were active. There was no Metro-Goldwyn-Mayer in those days, and Sam Goldwyn was still named Goldfish.

Egon's company was already standing on a desert set with old palm trees and evil-looking Arabs reading the horse-racing forms. The harem girls were drinking cokes and comparing last night's dates.

As soon as Egon, dressed in shiny black boots and switching himself with a braided riding crop, came in, someone yelled, "Quiet!"

Everyone else yelled, "Quiet," and this went on until someone blew a whistle. A camera was nailed to the ground (cameras didn't move in those days; the actors did), and a dark man dressed as an Arab chief stood scowling while Glory Girl got into an Arab evening gown of silver beads. Egon chewed on his riding crop. Someone covered the sunlight with muslin shades (outdoor shooting was cheap and sure) and two men, one with a fiddle and one with a small piano on wheels, stood around until Egon said, "Mood Music!"

The music started. Egon said, "Action! Camera! Keep it rolling . . . more fiddle there. Reggie, grab her . . . *closer.*

Bat your eyelashes, Glory. That's it . . . closer. Now sigh. No, *sigh*, don't blow out a birthday cake. More fiddle, that's it, now turn, and weep. Damn it, cry! You're kidnaped; you're about to meet a fate worse than death, or something. Now struggle; no, struggle, don't shimmy. Oh hell, cut!"

It was very interesting, and a camel almost bit me. Egon threw away his riding crop and they tried it again, and I stood in front of the cameraman and watched Glory Girl and Reggie engaged for moral combat.

The party that night was a good one, I remember. Mary Pickford came, and Cecil B. De Mille (looking almost as he looked some thirty years later when he hired me to write the dialogue for *The Greatest Show on Earth*—(for a minute, when I faced him, I thought I was back again, a boy at Glory Girl's pool). There was Will Rogers, I remember, and that's all. I no longer remember all the other handsome young men and women tanned by sun and flushed with drink, or the leather jackets and the fine flannels, the famous teeth, the popular hips. I suppose they all had names and were famous then. But I just don't remember them.

We did go to a dinner in some popular male star's house. I think it was John Barrymore's, but I'm not sure. It may have been one of the stars of the period who tried to act like him; but I like to think it was John's house. My total recall is often very good, but when it has holes in it, I give up trying to remember. I think Gramp had cause to remember the Irish cocktails, which he noted were made of Irish whisky (Jameson's), absinthe (no idea whether it was real or just Pernod Veritas), curaçao, and cherry juice.

Ordinary Hollywood food, I remember (with the help of some items from Gramp's notes), was tepid fruit juice with the pits left in, eggs fried in stale bacon fat and brown around the edges, sheet-iron ham, bacon crisp as wood ash, steaks rare but tasteless and tough, salads very good, but often limp as an old school tie. Fake smoked meat, faked charcoal flavors, potato chips flavored with shrimp, pink popcorn dipped in cheese mixes, and fruit soaked in bad·rum and decorated with colored toothpicks with soggy cherries on the ends of them. Cottage cheese was mixed with ground peanuts, whipped cream was made from marshmallows, and the soups all seemed to have been brewed with well water in which mule shoes had been steeping.

We should have stayed longer in Hollywood. But I remember Gramp's saying, "Stevie, we leave at noon today. Your mother has promised to act in a picture."

"Will she flop, Gramp?" I asked.

"No, I have a feeling she will be a famous movie star. And can you think of living with Mamma rich and a success?"

I saw his point. Mamma's charm lay in the fact that she was always yearning for things. Mamma as a success would really have made living with her hard. So we pulled out that noon, all of us waving at Egon and Glory Girl, and Gramp talking fast about Tucson, Arizona, where there was a big oil strike and he held some leases.

"Sari, I need your help and business head. Really."

"Do you like this country?" Mamma asked.

"I do," I said. "California is big."

"I suppose so," said Mamma, "but some of the people——"

"Oh," Gramps said, "there is lots that is fine out here. I can overlook a lot. That coast line turning from green to umber from Oregon to Mexico. A thousand miles of the most damn beautiful coast. The redwood forest, the untouched terrain, and those brooding, empty, man-killing deserts. Those spaces beyond space—eh, Stevie—those dry worlds where no man dares to go in his right mind."

"Go on," said Mamma, closing her eyes. "Don't stop."

"And the Sierra Nevadas, white slopes, pitchpole pines and spruce, and two great cities—San Francisco, sophisticated, cosmopolitan, compact, full of a past, full of a future, full of names and places and hills. Gusty with life, full of a wine of interesting living. To stand on its hills and see the Golden Gate, the prison island, to remember old heroes, lousy forgotten glories—there is *something* about San Francisco that no other city in the world ever had."

"Go on," said Mamma, and took my hand in hers.

Gramp lit a cigar and went on. "At night, driving . . . seeing that fine backbone of mountain walking, with a thousand dining-room lights around the city, seeing the beauty of drives and streets and the houses clinging to cliffs. . . . Oh, hell, you know."

"What else?" I asked.

"What else? Everything—the houses over the Pacific, the people who come at night, miles of them facing the sand and sea. I like the little children, chubby and loud and not too innocent, bathing naked in the salt-spumed breakers."

"A little cold for it," I said, remembering Esme.

"I like the young girls in their bathing suits singing on the sands at Santa Monica, their voices coming up over the rocks, and the heavy pelicans flying high and the girls lifting tanned limbs while they laugh."

"You like a lot after all, Gramp," I said.

"What else?" asked Mamma, half asleep.

"I like the Mexicans, the old drunken wine-muckers smoking *pitillos* and scratching their few acres of hill field and their broods, ass-naked, snapping at flies on the kitchen floor. I like the music of ignorant people trying to understand things and taking no gaff from any *hijo de puta*. I like real black voices and the sound of a plucked banjo. I like fruit pickers lying around a fire and talking about farms that once were theirs and will be again some great day in the morning. Why are you asking me all this, Sari?"

"Keep talking."

"I even like Los Angeles at night—the canyons, Coldwater, Laurel; I like the big parties and the small parties where movie girls stand around with highball glasses in their hands—those beautiful dumb girls who are there only to smile. I like those parties where the producers gather to settle the problems of the world, and they unsettle everything, even their own stomachs. See, I like things."

"Sure you do," said Mamma softly, close to sleep.

"I like that dark girl who played gypsy music and sang Spanish songs and I like her black hair. I like that home high up on the mountain so that when you look down you see the ribbon of streets running for the sea and the cliffs black and hidden from the glare of the street signs."

"You sure like a lot, Gramp," I said.

"I like avocado trees and the wine grapes of the San Joaquin. I like the way the orange trees grow, the golden globes; I like the valleys and the snows and the people on the little ranches watching a vulgar purple sunset. I like the fishing fleets and their catch and the nets torn by sharks. I like the fishermen drinking their wine and eating their fish chopped in oil and telling great lies."

"You can stop talking now, Gramp," I said. "You've put Mamma fast asleep."

THE MEXICAN COUPLE

14.

*Here dead lie we because we did
    not choose
To live and shame the land from
    which we sprung,
Life, to be sure, is nothing much
    to lose;
But young men think it is, and
    we were young.*
    —A. E. HOUSMAN
    (From Gramp's notebooks)

THE TALL HORIZON

AS WE MOVED DEEPER INTO THE SOUTHWEST I KNEW I
would come back to it someday. Grown up, adult, if I could I
would come back and find a place in the sun and settle down;
make of myself whatever a man could within the limits of his
time and of the goodness and the badness stored up in his
genes. I was aware we were hunting something that could not
be found, that Gramp, Mamma, and I were circling like the
great condor we saw one day far up in the limitless sky, heeling
and turning on the air currents, circling, hunting.

In the end I sensed we'd go back home, become part again of what had made us fit, if not neatly, at least with resigned acceptance, into the expected groove. Gramp was very old and he wanted to circle on in whatever time still remained for him. But Mamma was braver and would be ready soon to settle down to what to her must have looked like a dismal trap. Yet she went bravely toward her destiny, protesting a bit, watching the condor in the sky, high, free, and struggling for a living on the arid plains and the burned-out heights.

I too was growing up a bit. I was dipping into Gramp's book bag. I was observing and understanding a little more. Callow as I was to remain for many years, I was already aware, with the poet, of the skull beneath the skin, the brevity of man's endeavor, and the fact that the majority of mankind was weak and foolish, and that I could without much practice become a bigger fool than most.

Gramp always had an idea as to why the covered wagons went West and didn't come back. We were crossing desert country, heading for Arizona, leaving California, and the car was roaring along the sand roads when he said it. Loud. "No wonder they never went East again in them covered wagons. . . ."

"Those covered wagons," said Mamma, "not *them* covered wagons."

"I'm talkin' Western style, gal," Gramp said, biting into the two-inch stub of his last good cigar. "Once they traveled these-here roads, podner, they sure never wanted to try it again goin' that-a-way, that way East again."

Mamma sniffed the dry desert air. "You call that Western talk?"

"Ma'am, we ain't polished out yar in the West, but we plumb are right respectful of men and women. *Ouch!*"

The last was because we had hit a rut in the road. Roads were pretty bad. I sat watching the desert landscape, and Mamma refused to carry on any of Gramp's Western-style talk. She was angry at Gramp because she had wanted to stay in

Hollywood and maybe work in the old silent movies, which weren't old then and weren't silent, as there was always a weeping fiddle and a choked-up piano to carry on with the action.

"This the way to Tucson?" Mamma asked at last.

"It's the only road there is."

Mamma thought a while and asked, "Why don't we go to Texas? I have friends in Dallas."

I said, "I like Texas."

Mamma said, "Don't talk, Baby Boy. The air is too dry to open your mouth. You'll dehydrate."

Gramp tossed away his last cigar butt. "Ever hear what General Sheridan said about Texas, Sari?"

"I'm sure it's vulgar," said Mamma.

"Tell it, Gramp," I said, risking dehydration for a bit of vulgarity.

"Sure it's vulgar."

Mamma didn't answer, so Gramp went on. "Seems the General got angry at Texas people and Texas ways, and he got up on his hind legs and he said, 'If I owned Hell and Texas, I'd rent out Texas and live in Hell.' 'Well,' said a Southern gentleman present, 'I guess the General knows where to find his friends!' Pretty good, eh, Sari?"

Mamma didn't open her pretty lips. Gramp looked from her to the jack rabbits on the road, and then at me. "Coventry?" he asked. I nodded my head, and Gramp frowned. By the rules, if Mamma put him in Coventry, even I couldn't talk to him. It hurt the old man a lot because he liked to talk and I thought he was worth listening to. This time I could see Gramp was really angry. He didn't even protest. He just clammed up his mouth into rigid lines and drove the car, bent over, as if he were a jockey. At last we came to a frontier-looking town called Victorville, and we pulled up by a roadside gas station and eating place.

Gramp looked at Mamma as if he were giving her a last chance to say something. Then he got out of the car and ambled over to the Mexican and his wife who ran the place and asked, "Howdy, podner, anything eatable in these yar parts?"

"My wife, she make a fine *enchilada*, real *orégano* and *culantro* flavor. We also have it the *mole de guajolote*, turkey with pepper sauce. My wife, she fine cook."

"Any desserts?" asked Gramp, peeling his gloves and ignoring Mamma and myself.

"Ah, yes. *Pudín de coco* and *camote y pina*, sweet potato and pineapple, she very fine."

"Good, set one place for me. Any *cerveza* or *vino?*"

"But of course. They are not eating?" He pointed to Mamma and then to me.

Gramp looked at us and borrowed a thin Mexican cigar from the stand owner. "Sad cases, podner, real sad. Deef and dumb. Both of 'em."

"Sacred Virgin," said the Mexican, crossing himself, and his wife touched her holy medals. "Deef *and* dumb?"

"Born that way, most people think. But it's not true. Seems they were once very cruel to an old man. A feeble, dying old man who had made their life soft and easy, who had worked and toiled for them. And then, in his old age, they took his earthly wealth and turned him off, out into the cold world. The next morning they were rigid and when they came out of it, they were as you see 'em—stone deef and no tongue, dumb."

Mamma's face turned red, she choked, recovered, and stared ahead of her. For years the family never got the true story of how Gramp turned Mamma's act of Coventry against her. Even I never knew why she didn't shout at the Mexican and his wife that it was all a lie. But I think Mamma had a code about life, and one of the rules was if you were beaten you took your wounds and didn't whine for mercy. Mamma hated any idea of mercy, for herself or others. So she just sat there, boiling inside.

The Mexican came out with a soiled plate on which were two stale sandwiches, with a paper-thin ham slice and one sad black olive on each. He also brought two paper cups of black coffee and a kind of store-window doughnut broken in half, each on a crumpled piece of paper napkin.

The Mexican gestured to us, trying to make us understand, and he talked very loud, the way people do to deaf people and foreigners.

"The gentleman sent this out as you don't like our style of cooking. It's the only gringo food I have here. *La topa chisera*, it is sad to be like this. Would you like to try *caldo de pollo con aguacate*, chicken soup with rice, *arroz Mexicano?*"

Mamma didn't break the rule of the game. She wolfed the bread and ham and stale doughnut and drank the coffee after giving me my share. I was too cowed to protest. The Second War of Coventry wasn't going to be easy to live through.

The Mexican wept for us. "Try, please, lady, a leetle chicken *tamales*, some *mole de olla*. Or just our eggs with black beans."

It was no use. Gramp came out from his lunch wiping the last sign of *frijoles* from his face and carrying a bottle of wine and a fistful of Mexican stogies.

"Tucson straight ahead?" Gramp asked.

"Yes," said the Mexican, and then looking at us, "But these poor ones turned to stone, should you not raise the top to keep sun from them?"

Gramp started the motor, lit a stogie, and shook his head. "They don't feel a thing, *compañero*, not a thing."

"Fatherblood-of-Christ, it is sad. You are a kind *caballero* to take such care of them."

The rest of the trip into Tucson I'd rather not write about. The food along the American roadside has never been much good, but in those days, in those places, it was worse than ever. I don't know why Mamma didn't defy Gramp and just leave the car and order her own meals—that is, I didn't know until we were near Tucson and I remembered that Mamma had no money of her own. She had bought some hats in California and had run out of cash, and Gramp held our fortune in his money belt hitched right around his well-fed stomach. So we ate what he allowed us: stale bread and leftovers. But Mamma didn't break Coventry. Gramp bought a Stetson and cowboy boots on tall heels, and his talk grew more and more Western, and he ate indoors and he ate the best he could find. He showed no sign of weakening in the war. He told a great many stories about us as we sat in the car. The best one was that Mamma had taken a vow of silence and that she was a saint, a real saint. Mamma disliked all the saints (except a few mad ones), and this didn't help the trip. Gramp really was enjoying the Second War of Coventry.

By the time we got to Tucson the trip was about to break up. I could see that Mamma was going to grab me and her luggage and take a train East and home, as soon as she figured out how to get the railroad fare. Gramp also was set in his whim of iron. And he was going to finish this trip his way, even if he had to go alone through the hardest part of it—which was just ahead. He was no longer a young man, but he was just as stubborn as Mamma. And Mamma was pure stubborn, which meant she didn't let emotions or facts stand in her way. She was stubborn right down to her tiny shoes.

Me? I had learned by this time that in this family when the battle flags went up, one just tried to act like an innocent bystander and kept one eye open for a good getaway.

I knew this wasn't going to be a short war because Gramp left us at the second-best hotel in town and said to the desk clerk, "Is there a good lawyer in town? Pardon me, I know there are no good lawyers, but one who can read and write?"

The clerk thought. "There's old man Rogers. He used to be the lawyer for Billy the Kid."

"He sounds dishonest enough. Ever hear what Abe Lincoln said when he saw a tombstone with the markings on it: 'Here Lies a Good Lawyer and an Honest Man'?"

"Nope, what did Abe say?"

"He said, 'Since when are they burying two men in one grave'!"

The clerk laughed. "That's pretty good."

Gramp nodded and went out. We both knew what the trip to the lawyer meant. Gramp was changing his will again. He had sons and daughters-in-law and grandchildren to fit, and every time life got too complicated, or he lost his temper with one in the family, Gramp changed his will. Mamma had been in and out of Gramp's will more often than a fiddler's elbow. It looked as if this time she were out again. I must say that Mamma never really cared, because she, of the whole family, was smart enough to think that Gramp didn't have anything to leave the family. He had been a very rich man in his prime, but he had lived "high off the hog," as he called it, and there wasn't much left. Mamma proved to be right, and while the last will was a beautiful literary document, about all we got were his bluestone cuff links, and he had long since replaced the stones with glass.

Anyway, Mamma and I scooted right away to the dining room and sat down and said a little prayer and picked up the menus and ordered rich, thick steaks, fried onions, apple pie, two kinds of potatoes, and a beautiful pot of coffee with thick cream.

"Food, it's wonderful," said Mamma.

I nodded and cut into steak and ate. Mamma finished a pint of rich coffee after spooning in three good measures of sugar, and sighed.

"Now, Baby Boy, we've got to think of some way of getting railroad fare home."

"You don't think we'll make up with Gramp?"

Mamma took a personal oath on crossed teaspoons. "Not as long as I live and ten years beyond *that!*"

"He's an old man."

"He's evil, he's vulgar, he's sensual-minded."

"What's *that?*"

Mamma patted my head. "Something I hope you haven't inherited. All the Longstreets as far back as you can throw a vice are sensual-minded. Have you any money, Stevie?"

"A dime from Canada."

"We'll tip the waitress with that *after* we sign the check. Finished?"

"Yes."

"Well, let's go find railroad fare. I'll do anything within reason." Her eyes teared and she held me to her. "My poor baby, I'll do anything, even scrub floors."

Mamma talked of scrubbing floors, but when she really got on her knees, I remember, it was always to show some gentleman what a poor little woman she was, looking up at the great big man. I don't think Mamma ever found out how to scrub a floor. Anyway, we felt better after the food, and we went out into the dreadful sun of Tucson. It hasn't changed much since. It's hot, dry, stark, and everyone is tanned, serious, and making a lot of money (except those who don't care to get rich) in oil, cotton, hay, or minerals.

I don't know how Mamma *cased* Tucson, but about four o'clock she said to me as I sat reading the local paper in the hotel lobby, "We're going to tea. You see that big mountain outside of town, where there used to be a fort? Well, a charming lady lives under that hill and she wants to meet some of the grandchildren of the Lost Cause."

"What cause?"

Mamma slurred her voice a bit. "The Wah between deh States."

I knew enough history to know our branch of the family called it the Civil War and not the War between the States. I looked at Mamma.

"Stop looking at me, Stevie, like your grandfather. I only phoned her and said the word *Longstreet.*"

"In what accent?" I asked.

Mamma said briskly, "Come up and wash your hands, you damn Yankee."

I have never been a fighter. I followed Mamma upstairs, got washed, combed, and brushed. Then Mamma told the hotel clerk we would be at Mrs. Rodney Clark's and would he please get us a taxi.

I didn't know how Mamma would pay the taxi driver, but she only said, "Put it on our hotel bill," and gave the taximan a smile and added, "and figure in a dollar for yourself."

Mrs. Rodney Clark's was a beautiful old place of colored pink clay and red tile roofs and gardens and fountains kept cool by use of lots of water.

Mrs. Clark was young and pretty and raised dogs. She said she was "right glad you all had phoned that you all were visiting us." I remember best her Chinese cook, who served a very fine tea in the shade of a vine-covered patio. Mamma and I were still catching up on our meals. The Chinese cook came out to meet us, smiling, and when Mamma said, "This is really very good," he bowed and hid his arms in his sleeves and said, "I cookee boy on big boat for velly fine people. So happy you likee."

"It was divine," Mamma said, "the best food we've had in a long time."

I saw Mamma had her fingers crossed—and that Mrs. Clark was very earnest in her hunt for our pasts. She said, "I've been here, buried, just buried alive, just planning food and cleaning house, while Fred, that's my husband, worries over his cotton here. But now, Mrs. Longstreet, we'll talk of the past."

I went out into the garden, and a nice-looking kid in blue jeans, with blond hair, was playing with an old spotted hound dog.

He said, "I'm Bud Clark. Hi."

I told him who I was, and I figured out Mrs. Clark was his mother. I was right. "Want to see my twenty-two?" he asked.

I said I did, and we went to some old stables, followed by the old hound dog, Fatso. The kid was a little mad about the old dog, the way kids get when they are nine or ten. He was also crazy about deer hunting, as I found out when he showed me his twenty-two. It was beautiful, with a walnut stock, and we shot at tin cans while the fat old dog hid himself in some hay.

"I'm going deer hunting up on the mountains someday," Bud told me as we polished the gun with an oily rag.

I said, "My grandfather is an old deer hunter, and maybe he'll take us both up if you could borrow a gun for me."

Bud said I could borrow a gun that had belonged to his uncle, who was now dead and had given the dog to Bud when the hound was much younger. I liked Bud; he was one of those simple, earnest children who seem keyed into their life with an ease and an interest that I often wished for. My life was perhaps more interesting than Bud's, but it was certainly more hectic.

We talked about rattraps, taw-eyed marbles, the books of Henty and Ralph Henry Barbour, the kissing habits of small smelly girls, the proper training of dogs, and the collection of beetles, stamps, and Indian-head pennies of very early dates. The more I talked to Bud the better I liked him. I saw us as roommates at Lawrenceville prep school, chums at Yale (with a guy named Stover), drifting down the Amazon on a raft, and saving each other's lives in far places. He even took off his shoes to show me how his little toe grew bent around the toe next to it. A very rare thing; the kid was real lucky. I went indoors to see how Mamma was doing. She was still pitching charm at Mrs. Clark.

I went out into the sun, hoping it would kill me, because I had a feeling Mamma would fail to get the railroad fares. (I still dream at nights sometimes about this time and how brave Mamma was.)

After a while Mamma came out looking very pale, and I wondered if the lunch had disagreed with her. She took my hand, hard. "Stevie, it's a phone call from the hotel. Gramp's been hurt. Bad."

"What happened?"

Mamma bit her lip. "He fell down some stairs going to see the lawyer. Mrs. Clark is sending us back to the hotel in her car."

We found Gramp groaning in bed, a bandage around one eye and a doctor twisting one arm while Gramp howled. Gramp looked up at us and held out a hand.

"I'm dying, Sari. I want to say I'm sorry. Real sorry. Kiss me before I go."

"Gramp! Oh, doctor, how bad is it?"

The doctor stopped pulling. "Well, he's got a nasty knock over one ear. And this arm. And maybe there are some internal injuries. I can't tell yet, and——"

Gramp moaned. "Am I going to die in peace?"

The doctor bandaged the arm tight and said he'd be back, and Gramp sat up in bed and even let Mamma talk him out of a cigar. "It's all my fault, Sari. I went and changed the will and felt so bad about it that I went back to change it again, and I'm not used to wearing cowboy boots, I guess, and I fell head over teakettle. Well, you can't leave me now, Sari. Not until I die. Then you'll have everything, and don't say bad things about me when I'm gone."

Mamma took off her hat. Gramp said, "It's a lucky thing I bought that cowboy hat and cowboy boots. If I hadn't fallen down those stairs we wouldn't be together now."

Mamma patted his hand and I could see she was back on our side in the Civil War.

Gramp was feeling better that evening, and we all went back to Mrs. Clark's for dinner. Gramp met her son, Bud Clark, and his old hound Fatso. Gramp offered to take Bud and myself up to the mountains to hunt deer.

A frightening thing happened on this deer-hunting trip, my first real bout of adult terror, when Bud was lost up there. Gramp and I had left Bud in camp with the pack horses. We hadn't shot any deer and a storm seemed to be coming up in the mountain forest. An angry vein of lightning shot across the mackerel-colored clouds. But it was only heat lightning. It did not rain.

When we got to the camp there was no one there. Gramp was worried. He fried fish cakes and made up some biscuits and got out the last of the canned milk. When everything was brown on the fire, I hammered on a tin pan. I couldn't roust Bud out.

The food was ready, so we ate our share and buried the rest between two plates in the embers and went over to the horse meadow. Bud wasn't there; neither was his horse. His horse was loose somewhere, Gramp decided. I went down past the brook where there were a lot of stone piles left by some ice age or upheaval a long time ago. Bud had wanted to hunt Indian stone axes here. There was no sign of him and I went back to camp a little angry. I would put him in Coventry when he came back.

Gramp said, "I'm worried."

"He'll show up."

His gun wasn't in the tent, and a very valuable mouth organ he took pride in was missing from its ledge where his toothpaste and brush stood. I went out of the tent and called him. Only a foolish worried echo came back to me.

We went part way down the trail. Maybe Bud had gone down to meet us. But when the trail struck a soft spot we looked for his tracks and there were none. No marks of his shoes or the lighter patterns of the dog.

The sun was slanting away into the west when we got back to the camp. The place was empty. No sign of the boy, or Fatso. The tent swayed in a ghastly way in the light cool breeze coming from Lake Loon about twenty miles away.

A lost child is a fearful thing to another child, and I stood by the cold fire and the cold food and shivered. The sun was beginning to dip deep into the blue sky, and I knew Bud was lost, or worse.

I would fool myself for a while and feel that any minute the kid and the fat, foolish dog would break from the shelter of the woods and come romping up to me. Bud was playing a game, he was fooling Gramp, he was punishing us. But no boy appeared. I could not move. I could just wait. And he didn't come. Every leaf that stirred, every wood noise was him . . . and then wasn't. Gramp began to shout, "Bud! Bud! Oh, Fatso! Bud!"

"Bud! Bud!" said the echo.

"Bud! Bud!" A loon mocked us from the ridge, reproducing Gramp's voice.

"Bud! Oh Bud! Fatso!" I called out.

"Let's go hunt him," Gramp said.

The gloom was thick between the trees, below the crags. We could see only the scuffed trail; no marks, no footprints. No one. Nothing came. We took bearing by the big peak, cut into the side trails and tried to make a ten-mile circuit around the camp, calling all the time into a rising opaque mist that was beginning to shroud the mountains.

We tripped over logs. Once I went up to my knees in some rotting pit of forest decay, and shadows multiplied and grew heads. I tore my face on brambles. We got tangled on wild grapevines. I could only tear ahead and call, "Bud!" Gramp followed, also calling.

My heart was bursting. I could no longer calm it, and I rolled over in my tracks and began to sob, the dry sob of a boy who is beaten, winded, and very much out of condition. Gramp calmed me. "I don't want any trouble from you."

The gnats ate from me and a beetle crawled on my torn knee, and slowly, slowly, sanity seeped back into me, my chest stopped pumping, and I could breathe without gulping. We stood up and decided we would complete the circuit around the camp. We went on slowly, panting, but no longer rushed in panic. It was dark when we had made the ten-mile circuit around the camp. Night birds mocked my call in long sustained tones.

"Bud!"

"Booood! Boooodhooooo . . ." the echoes and owls said after me.

Gramp patted my shoulder. "Steady."

My hand was bleeding from a bad fall, and one leg of my pants was ventilated by tears. New faint stars appeared. The mist no longer advanced, but had stopped below me and sat very still, like a quiet night sea.

We got into the tent, gulped water from the tin canteen, lit

the gasoline pressure lamp on its hook, and sat down. There
was no use hunting. We had been lucky to find our own way
back to camp. We didn't know the country too well even in
the daytime, and at night we knew it even less.

Gramp said, "I'll stay here to hunt. You ride down trail to
the rangers' station. Right?" I nodded.

Night insects danced around the light. I stood up and picked
up the lamp and stuffed a section of cold, soggy bread into my
jacket. I had no trouble finding my mare, called Gasbag, who
had broken her halter and was roaming free. She came over to
my light and rubbed against me. I saddled her and, holding the
light ahead of me, started across toward the forester's lookout,
ten miles away. Gramp waved me off.

I rode. There was suddenly a break in the underbrush and
two pairs of eyes stared at me. I yelled out.

"Bud!"

The flashlight in my hand held the eyes, and as we came
nearer I lifted the light. Shiny black noses showed me a doe
and her fawn; they stood there watching me with huge,
frightened eyes. The mare's shoes hit a stony patch and that
broke the spell; the deer bounded crashingly into the underbrush, two white buttons of tails bobbing in the light of the
lamp.

The mare was suddenly frightened; the deer may have done
it. She reared, and I dropped the flashlight, heard it smash,
and as the darkness closed in I grabbed the horse's head and
in rage kicked her sides with my heels. She twisted, tried to
throw me, tried to mash me off against a tree trunk, but I tore
her head around, beat home two more kicks, and got her gal-
loping down trail.

It was dark and we might easily have killed ourselves. Then
as the woods lessened, the moon came out silver and gave
ghastly light and a glimpse of zodiacal constellations, a faintly
remembered schoolroom chart. I pulled the mare's head left
and we went on slower, on the rise, between second-growth
timber and the butt ends of trees long since sawed for lumber.

I could see the lookout, a small pin-point of light. I swayed and almost dropped, but the mare went on slowly and the pin-prick grew. I felt what I was—a scared kid, terrified at the thought of Bud lost someplace up there.

A forest ranger, a young man with a short haircut, much tanned, with eyes deep-set behind a broken nose, called the central office. To me he said, "Take it easy. I've been through these lost-person hunts before. You can't last if you don't calm down. I'll call the neighboring stations and have them phone it out."

I went to the door, pushed it, and opened my shirt collar to let the cold night air blow on me. I stood there a long time, and the ranger finished his calls and came and stood by my side. Neither of us said anything.

I slept that night at the ranger's. The coffeepot was bubbling over the little iron stove when I awoke. Larry, the ranger, was sitting at a table with two highway patrolmen drinking coffee, and the sun was filling the windowpanes. The atmosphere was very male and rough.

I got up and tried to straighten my crumpled clothing.

"Hello, Larry," I said.

"Sleep good?"

"No, but I slept. Anything?"

A road patrolman shook his head. "We have just been up to your camp. Your grandfather is organizing a hunt."

Larry was looking at a red-veined map spread open on his lap. "It's a lot of country. But he's in here somewhere safe, I'm sure. He's a smart kid."

"Yes," I said, "he's a very smart kid."

"And has a smart dog."

"But very old," I said. "How's Gramp?"

The door opened and a ranger came in, beating morning dew off his heavy twill jacket. "It's all set. There will be dogs up this afternoon. Meanwhile, we'll divide the ground and begin beating away from the ridge. Two men with each party."

"I want to go," I said.

Larry got up and buttoned his leather jacket. "You can come with us, kid. We're taking the point that's over the ridge behind your camp."

I swallowed the scalding coffee and stood up. Through the door came the smell of resinous pines. . . .

The land was heavily wooded, the trees tall, and the underbrush matted thick, intergrown; and hundreds of trails and paths led through the mountain slope, ending here and there over cliffs and ridges. Our feet went ringing among the clods and stones.

Years of sheep grazing in the hollows, cattle in the valley, and the passage of hunters, herb collectors, rangers, and campers had created many pockets into which a child could wander and not be found for weeks.

Larry had driven way past our original territory for hunting. "It's simple," Larry said and opened his map. "The kid was after deer on his own. Maybe he hit a buck and started trailing it. Maybe he saw a herd and started after it. He's the kind of kid that doesn't give up. He got deeper and deeper into this wilderness."

A ranger shook his head. "Deer are fools. You can't tell where they go."

"Any salt licks around here?"

"Hm? Well, not salt but some kind of black metal-filled rock that tastes sour. I've seen deer licking on it."

Larry folded the map. "If he was trailing deer maybe they headed for that black rock. Where is it?"

"Pretty near all around the peak—to the left."

The ranger shook his head. "Suppose he gut-wounded a buck?"

"With a twenty-two you can't hurt a deer much. I think he got lost trailing a herd. Shall we start?"

We got to our feet and went on into the dark wood. Every fifty feet we all yelled "Bud!" and stopped and waited for an answer. It didn't come. On the other slope we could hear the barking of the dogs that had been brought up to help the hunt.

At midnight we had to admit it looked bad. Larry sat down on a stump and chewed a twig. "Listen, this kid is no fool. Let's keep thinking the way he would think. He's lost, he's lost all sense of direction in these trees. Even if he knew where camp was, the directions of rises and cliffs would throw him off."

"Ranch boy, isn't he?" asked a ranger.

"That's my sure hope we'll find him. He'll find some stream and follow it. He knows water is worth having, and somewhere he'll hit a hut, a house of some kind built near this water."

"We tried that with the streams around the camp."

"That was too close. What's the nearest water around here?"

Maps were again looked at. "Well, we should be near a creek that drains out near the hollow. They put a lot of concrete retaining walls up along it to keep the floods back from the towns when the snow melts. Makes a lot of big pools behind the walls."

"What's the nearest we are to it?"

"About a mile, at least, from here should wet our feet."

"Shall we try it?"

Larry walked ahead and I followed, and soon we were plunging down a steep slope that grew thicker and more overgrown than any we had met all day. I began to worry over Gramp. He was an old man.

There was a roar ahead, and we found ourselves by the side of a waterfall that was hitting white stones and gleaming in the glow of our light. We followed it with great difficulty for about a mile. It was very hard going. We passed the first of the retaining dams; a huge pool had backed up behind it. We went on, yelling every fifty feet. Our voices were absolutely lost in the swift clatter of the creek. There was no answer except from the stones dancing on the swift stream bottom.

I put down my cupped hands from my lips and turned sadly

to watch the waters rip past. There was a small fire burning on the other bank. I turned to Larry and suddenly back to the fire. I grabbed Larry's arm.

"Hey, look! There! Fire!"

"I just saw it, too."

We waded into the creek and then fell deeper into holes and were wet to the hips. The water was as cold as an axhead in a blizzard. We shivered ashore in some of the most broken-up, rocky land I had ever seen. Our ankles were almost turned over and twisted off under us. We moved quickly toward the fire, which disappeared, then winked on brighter, and we stood suddenly where the rocks fell away in a sheer drop of twenty feet, open on the side facing the creek. There below us slept Bud, huddled by a burning log, and across his chest was the shape of a fat old dog. And facing him was Gramp! Dirty, torn, but grinning. Gramp waved to us.

We almost leaped down the drop, and the child awoke. Tenderly he laid aside the dog and looked at us. He had been weeping, as the streaks on his dirty face showed. But he was not weeping now and his voice was small but full of trust.

Gramp said, "I knew you'd come."

"Sure," I said, sinking to my knees and putting an arm around Gramp. "Sure, sure. How are you, Gramp?"

"I'm all right. But take a look at Fatso. Something happened to him."

I looked. Larry picked up the dog, and with very tender fingers probed the off-white spotted body. The dog did not protest the delicate touch.

"What happened to him, Bud?" I asked.

"We were crossing higher up and Fatso jumped and a branch brushed against him, and he fell down here, and he howled and then stopped. Is he hurt bad?"

Gramp turned to the boy. I set the light down on a stone. "Listen, Bud. He is gone . . . he's dead. You're lucky we found you."

"But he was just licking my face."

"You were asleep when I found you," Gramp said.

"Just *before* I was asleep."

"He's dead now, Bud. He was a very old dog."

"He was a very fine dog."

"A very fine dog," said Larry.

"I couldn't leave him here alone, could I? I had to stay."

Larry got out the small ax in my belt and began to dig in the leaf mold.

"He was too heavy to carry. I had to stay with him."

"Old dogs die, Bud, just like horses, just like people," Gramp said.

Larry had a hole, deep and wide. Gramp helped him lift the old dog's body down into the grave. Bud was eating a chocolate bar I was peeling for him and crying again.

"I can't eat."

"Just one bite, and drink this container of soup. It's nice and hot."

"I can't, Gramp, I'm all lumps in my throat."

"All right, just two big sips, then."

The dog was covered. We placed big stones over the mound and built a platform of rocks around it. Bud, thin, wide-eyed, limp, stood pensively staring down. I don't think death had ever meant anything to him before.

"Ready, Bud?" Gramp asked.

We stood close together.

"In a minute." He took his worn mouth organ from a pocket and tenderly placed it over the grave, its luminous pearliness winking in the light. "The Indians used to leave bows and arrows on their graves, a teacher told me. That's all I have for him."

"Ready?" Gramp asked, looking very tired.

"Yes."

We turned and walked quickly away as Larry poured a hatful of water over the smoldering log. We crossed the stream again, Bud between us. Gramp kept pressing the child's shoulder tenderly, but Bud would not let us carry him. He walked between us holding our arms, and I shivered. We topped a rise and went on slower.

Gramp said, "If I were a praying man, I'd offer up a prayer."

Perhaps it was not as dreadful an event as I have carried it in my memory all these years. I reached a kind of maturity there in the mountains I think, and I may have made too much of it. Kids get lost up there for a few days ever so often, and perhaps my terror has colored the event with my personal reactions.

When we got Bud home everyone treated it all as an adventure. I was a little confused by this reaction, but I may have been too young to notice that it may have been a covering reaction to two nights of terrible waiting.

NEW ORLEANS GIN FIZZ

Life has taught me to think, but thinking has not taught me to live. . . .

—ALEXANDER HERZEN
(From Gramp's Notebook)

ON THE DELTA

I WOULD LIKE TO SAY SOMETHING ABOUT GRAMP, MAMMA, and God. Gramp and Mamma did not worship any of the popular organized godheads, but were closer, as Gramp once said, "to God than most who went through the sterile ritual and the mumbled motions and believed in nothing but the pious show and the social position it gave them." They disliked those who felt they had the only One True Answer and felt so safe in having a stranglehold on God, "as if He were," to quote Gramp, "a classmate from a good school."

Gramp and Mamma—as I remember—had little interest in ordinary reality. And while both were not fools and understood that materialism gave great pleasure and that money bought much, both were also aware of a spiritual mystery which they respected but did not attempt to probe. Gramp's God was like a buoy that marked a magnificent wreck, a buoy that was well aware "that an instinct does not exist unless there is a possibility of its being satisfied." Gramp would have made a great preacher, or a remarkable Pope. Certainly he would have worn the purple better than most; he would have been amused at the French king who changed his religion with the remark: "Paris is certainly worth a Mass."

God, in those days, was too casual a friend, and so both Gramp and Mamma wanted a sterner fellow, a wraith out of the Old Testament who could punish and reward, could bring back the moral thunder of a great code of ethics. If they did not live up to all of it, they knew it was there. They retained the ironic sense of omniscience and a feeling of the boldness of human life under watching eyes. If the world were made by Satan and not by God, Gramp figured, "Satan was after all a fallen angel." Their old-fashioned God made them aware of the sense of doom that overhung all popular success and fame. Gramp was a follower of many schools, as his notebook shows:

Alas, I shall never be a Tolstoyan. In women I love beauty above all things; and in the history of mankind, culture expressed in rugs, carriages with springs, and keenness of wit. Ah! To make haste and become an old man and sit at a big table. . . .

—ANTON CHEKHOV

After our mountain adventures, New Orleans was a good place to visit. We lived very high and saw all the famous things. There seemed no way of getting Gramp out of New Orleans, and when Mamma would try, Gramp would change the words of a popular song of the period, and say, "You can get the boy out of New Orleans, but can you get New Orleans out of the boy?"

He was an old man, aware that his world would not last much longer, and he was in no hurry to leave a place where there was so much fun and bourbon and branch water. He wallowed in chicken rice à la creole at Didee's on Market Street; Solari's on Royal Street made special hotcakes for him; the Patio

Royal mixed a good gin fizz and deviled a crab and baked a chicken liver he couldn't resist. The old man was eating his way swiftly toward what Mamma and I dreaded—an attack of gout. Pompano en papillote with Chablis, crabs boiled in beer, and for dessert eggnog with champagne.

One morning Gramp came in and said to us, "Just had a real New Orleans breakfast."

"What's that?" Mamma asked.

Gramp sighed and sat down. "A bottle of bourbon, a steak, and a dog."

"A dog?" Mamma said.

"Yes," said Gramp. "The dog ate the steak, and my pals and I finished the bottle."

Mamma, who disliked dogs, dog stories, and dog-lovers, sniffed, and Gramp suddenly grew very red in the face and gasped in pain. Mamma said sternly to me, "Stevie, take off his shoes."

Gramp said weakly, "Now, Sari, I can still undress myself."

But I took off his shoes and pulled off his socks. Both Gramp's big toes were glowing red, like a circus light bulb.

Gramp said, "Been walking too much."

Mamma said, "Eating and drinking high off the lobster. That's gout."

"Gout!" said Gramp. "All I need is a basinful of ice water to let the swelling down. Gout!"

"Gout," said Mamma.

Gramp looked at me and I said, "Gout."

Gramp tried to put a cigar in his mouth, but Mamma took it away, smiled, and said, "No fancy food, no whisky, no cigars, no late hours. And as soon as the big toes go down, we're leaving New Orleans."

"I was looking forward to some crayfish court bouillon this afternoon, a bit of chicken *cacciatore*."

"Stop drooling," said Mamma. "You're going to take a nap, and then soak your feet in ice water. And this afternoon we're going to see the sights."

"We'll be the sights," said Gramp, "if you treat us like just tourists."

"New Orleans must have something to see besides menus and waiters."

"How about the jass joints, Gramp?"

But Mamma gave me one of her frozen looks, and I didn't carry my research into early jazz forms any further just then.

In the afternoon we went out in the car. Mamma had a folder and we went to see the open-air markets; Lafitte's Blacksmith Shop, where Mamma bought some candlesticks I still own; and the old U.S. Mint, where we didn't buy anything (the dollar even in 1920 being worth only seventy-four cents, I think). We saw the Church of the Immaculate Conception, where Gramp made a small cynical joke (as you can imagine) and the St. Louis Cemetery, where, as in all burying grounds in New Orleans, the dead are buried on platforms above the ground, for the whole town is below sea level. Gramp said the cemetery had one fault, and Mamma bit and asked, "What is that, Gramp?"

"Not enough doctors and lawyers buried in it."

And so we knew that Gramp had been to a local doctor and been told his gout came from food and drink. We got tired of burying grounds and places where Andrew Jackson had beaten the British, and so Mamma, who was driving, headed for Lake Pontchartrain. It was a fine lake with sailboats on it, and Gramp suddenly came to life and said, "What I need is some catfish fat—that always helps my gout. The fat in the head of a catfish rubbed on an aching toe will cure the gout."

Mamma said, "That's pretty unscientific."

"My toes, Sari, were created before science."

Mamma said, "We'll drive to the market and get a fatheaded catfish."

"No," said Gramp, "Stevie and I will hire a boat and gear and go fishing. You can catch up with your shopping. They make a fine shoe down here."

Mamma was torn between keeping Gramp's gout under control and visions of handmade shoes. She fought the good fight and said, "All right, you can go fishing, but Stevie—you know what he can eat and can't eat. And no drinking at all, just filtered spring water."

I had handled Gramp before during the gout season and I nodded. Gramp smiled and said, "I'll buy lunch."

"And watch *us* eat," said Mamma.

We drove back to Iberville Street in the Quarter, found a real old-fashioned place, and Mamma ordered the lunch. Gramp got cold milk, melba toast, salad with no oil or dressing, and two hard-boiled eggs.

Gramp chewed on his toast and shook his head. "Rome fell, Sari, because its citizens ate it down. Their teeth scooped out its walls. Their overstuffed stomachs dragged the Empire into the dust."

Mamma nodded and said, "I know, Gramp; the head of a fish and two olives made Greece great. Food and fine living doom us to the decline of the West."

"Oswald Spengler," hissed Gramp. "He said it all. 'Feed a culture and starve a civilization.' "

I said, "How do you eat a fish head, Gramp?"

"Sharper than a snake's snout is an ungrateful whelp," said Gramp. He was always full of good juicy quotes when they took his food away and he could only chew on words.

While Mamma went to visit a very pretty friend named Alice, who collected modern art and knew where they made the shoes Mamma wanted to buy, Gramp and I went down to the docks. Some shrimp boats were in, and the ladies of the shrimp town were entertaining the crews. Gramp muttered something about "the fall of Troy" but asked one of the ladies where he could hire a boat and crew for fishing. Agnes, as her name turned out to be, had an uncle who rented out fishing boats, and she took us to him. Her uncle seemed very young to be an uncle, and he kissed Agnes as if they weren't related.

Emile Fouchet Toursel Bornay was the captain's name, and

Agnes had a full name, too—Agnes Ninette Gabrielle de Salignac. I know because they both wrote it down in my autograph album. That is, Emile wrote it down. Agnes could only make a cross; she hadn't been educated—not in writing.

"I want to catch a catfish," said Gramp.

"Foo," said Emile. "I catch you a million."

"One will do, a big one."

"We go down to the delta. I catch plenty cat there. You buy wine for the trip, no?"

"No," I said. "Gramp has *le gout.*"

"*La goutte,*" Emile corrected. "Well, that is too bad, but fun to get. No drinks on this trip, no?"

Gramp coughed. "I hear the native medical brews are very good for fever and pain."

Emile said, "Up the dock, there is a small store. Ask for Big John—the best fever and pain mixture you ever take for *la goutte.*"

We went to the little shop and bought the fever medicine, Big John. It came in pint bottles, and Gramp bought six of them. He read the label and nodded. "This will do for my toes, Stevie. Big John, secret remedy of the natives. Certainly wine and brandy are evil in our society. Pure sassafras root, ginger, boggie juice."

"Could I see the label, Gramp?" I asked.

"Later—we've got to pick up some bait."

Big John was certainly a healthy mixture. Emile and Gramp drank it all afternoon and lost some valuable gear; and Emile fell into a bayou and we had a bad time steering the boat home. But we made it back at nightfall, all of us with our noses peeling from sunburn and Gramp glowing a Chinese red—but feeling fine, "just fine." Emile had a black eye where he had run into the fist of the bait-boat man in some little fight over the charges. But Gramp had a few pounds of catfish fat wrapped up in the New Orleans *Item,* a newspaper. We took a taxi back to the hotel, and the room was full of shoes, new shoes in pairs—but no Mamma.

There was a note on the dresser reading, "I'm at Alice's for dinner."

Gramp said, "Don't want to go out. Any Big John left, Stevie?"

"Just a short three fingers," I said, copying Emile's talk.

Gramp took it and said, "England expects every man to do his duty. Kiss me, Hardy."

I took his shoes off and put him to bed.

We went out on three- and four-day trips into the bayous for catfish fat for Gramp's toes. Mamma led a fancy social life off Jackson Square, where the bronze general sits on a horse.

We got to know the Cajun life very well. We met all of Emile's relatives and friends. The Cajun world was a world within itself and few outsiders ever saw it whole and saw it true. Lived along the bayous, among the oleanders and twisted oaks, "it was a tested way of life," Gramp said, "hard and hard working, but with a charm and a glory all its own." Lived close to the water, close to the crackling sound of the fiddler crab, the spread of the oyster beds, and the brackish waters of the bayous and inlets. I was a happy kid.

It was a tropical world of angel-trumpet trees, banana plants all elephant ears, and often, a stranger transplanted, the swaying palm among the crimson and splashing yellow flowers. Cows moved in the grass near the surf or bayou shores, reflected in the phosphorescent waters. The old houses watched and grew older, their heavy batten windows and the mosquito bars tightly in place, in memory of yellowjack, the shakes and miseries of that fever that had once been here. *"Mon Dieu,"* said Emile, "how the fever hit them in the past!" Like the treasure talk of Lafitte's loot, the whole mad talk of hidden buccaneers' plunder. That and fever were part of the Cajun past.

The Louisiana scene, I decided, was good to watch—gulls
and clumsy, comic pelicans in the sky, and the Cajun fishermen
tossing long nets over the side. And the great day I attended
when they blessed the fishing fleet. "*Deus, qui dividens aquas ab
arid arida. . .* ," I wrote out, the holy Latin blessing of the
shrimp seas. The peasant fishermen knelt while the priest
prayed, just as they had done, Emile explained, in Normandy
and on the Brittany coast long ago. The Archbishop himself
did duty in golden cape and tall miter, outshining the gold
green and lavender of the hyacinth plants. Chanting the Litany
of the Saints, the altar boys from the oyster boats marched in
white and Emile's *Maman* and the family were there moist
with pleasure and even his *Grandmère* was smiling.

. Then came the feasting—shellfish boiled pink as baby bottoms, cooked just right with red and green peppers, salt, pepper,
onion, lemon juice, bay leaf, and clove. (Gramp cheated and
ate.)

The Cajun was half farmer, half seaman, I saw. He liked the
sea life, the sea horses and the flounders and catfish, the bobbing
bubble of the squid, the clattering crab life. Crabs fascinated
me. And I too said, "Damn the porpoise," that enemy of the
shrimping fleets, when he tore the net.

The Cajun shrimp villages still existed on their high stilts
and looked down on the Chinese, Filipinos, Malays, Spaniards,
and Mexicans who also shrimp; but there was plenty for all.
Three quarters of all the shrimp in America comes from Louisiana. "It's a good thing," Emile said, "the female shrimp
drops three million eggs at a time, almost all the time." Shrimp
life, Gramp decided, "was rather monotonous."

The best eating is the crab, the Cajun soft-shell crab caught
in a dozen moments of his life when he drops his skin, molts to
fix himself into a bigger suit of sea armor. Then he is good eating. Hard-shelled, I remember, he is called "green" by Cajuns;
when ready to shed, a "buster"; undressed he is "cracked";
just growing a shell, "paper-thin"; and getting hard and horny,

"clear." One can't be too careful in understanding the soft-shell crab and his rooming problems.

The Cajun, Emile said proudly, hunts the sea as well as the land. "He takes from it the sweet-tasting pompano, redfish, and flat-faced flounder, bluefish and drum, Spanish mackerel, white trout, sheephead, and sea bass. The markets of the nation eat this up and ask for more. And often the great ray fish, the giant manta, appears, the bat of the Gulf, and he weighs any-where from three hundred pounds on up to three tons. What a life, eh, Stevie?"

But the Cajun loves best the land, I decided, the inlets and the flat fields, the long roads through the swamps, the home of M'sieu Muskrat, the animal who helps make an off-season liv-ing for the hungry Cajun and his brood. In corduroy and cap, in heavy high boots, the Cajun goes after the pelt-bearer. And I went along a few times. It's hard, ill-paid work, but a man must feed his family. He digs long canals called trainasses, a shallow ditch in which his pirogue can be poled to the lair of the muskrat feeding on the three-cornered grass that he loves. Hundreds of traps are set out; each hunter is allowed two hundred and fifty traps a day; and when the muskrat is caught and brought home, his skin is dried on metal stretchers. Good weather or bad, the pelt-hunter goes out to trap, his family on their high-stilted camp passing the time by pelt-cleaning and packing, playing cards and making guitar music, and eating *tac tac* (which is only Cajun for popcorn, for all its fancy sound). I wanted to stay here forever.

And they eat gumbo, a pot of which is always bubbling on the stove. Some eat a pungent dish, well seasoned with a heavy gravy made of M'sieu Muskrat himself; but Gramp and I thought of him only as a rat and did not care for the taste. Rattlesnake meat, 'gator tail, as well as a few waterfowl grabbed when the game warden isn't around—they are something else.

The land deep down is also rich in great rock salt deposits, and here, Gramp said, in the solid salt are found prehistoric fragments, the bones of the ground sloth, the mastodon, and the three-toed horse—long gone, "even if there is a local legend that they voted for Andy Jackson when votes were short."

Tabasco peppers were brought in long ago from Mexico and they are part of the flavor of Cajun living, and the condiment canned and bottled is a product to export.

Looking up from the pepper fields, I was attracted to the bird life. The Cajun life always had wings around it, not just the clown pelican, but the roseate spoonbills, the snowy and delicate egrets, a dream walking. I used to see the egret (protected by law and man) walking the country roads. Gramp taught me bird names. Blue-winged teal, geese from Canada's snows, the gray duck and the spoon-billed mallard and scaup. And many found their way into our cooking pot. Meat is meat. The heron winged his way in heavy grace, and all the birds filled Louisiana with song and color.

But the home is the real palace, the castle of the Cajun. He's the master, the father, the husband, the citizen of his small private world. Isolation and concentration make Cajun life rich and warm in its limited wealth, and its strong habits. Some villages smell of fish and oil, some of furs, some of cowsheds and roots of the field. Gramp said one could almost be in Normandy, Picardy, Brittany, or Saint Tonge.

The Cajun system may be patriarchal, but it is mellowed and full of frankness and joys. The Acadian, Gramp said, is no sourpuss, no bluenose, no puritan or repressed wreck to his own emotions. He loves all of *les petis habitants*—as the bayou people call themselves. Not rich, of course: a cow or two, hogs, and chickens. And Emile bragged, "In the old days it was a simple life: hook the breakfast from the front porch, shoot the dinner from the back door, trap the supper in the next field. I not like the change. *Je fais comme mon père.*"

They fight, they dispute, but the priest was usually the

universal arbiter, even if the young fry were turning more toward a modern world.

"So one raises children, tends the land, fishes the sea, and eats well and takes a little drink from time to time," said Emile. "Digest and sleep, they round it all out, and in the end there is the family plot and the family priest and plenty of relatives to weep during the last Mass and the planting in the good ground." The *greniers,* or attics, are filled with old pictures and old letters from generations that have lived and moved on. "One regrets their passing. We Cajuns feel the bitterness of going oneself, but one must not think too much of that or one would not enjoy life here and now."

Gramp could not drink the *café*—the coffee—and Cajuns can drink ten, twenty, thirty cups of it a day. "The doctor say it is bad for the heart, the stomach, but *café* is *café* and good." Perhaps it is good for them. No non-Cajun can care for the native brew, black and strong as tar. "One must become used to it from birth and take it gladly as mother's milk and just as naturally." This I was never able to do. It stains the pot, it bites deep, it comes in two colors—black and white. Black is *real* black, and white is just a term for the weaklings who drink it polluted by milk.

We always went back to our hotel in New Orleans with regret, and England expected every man to do his duty, every night.

One evening Gramp rubbed his toes with catfish fat and we got dressed and went to visit Mamma's friend, Alice. She had a beautiful house, "seventeenth or eighteenth century, before dah Wah," said Gramp. It was on Moss Street, with columned porticoes, embrasured French windows, and in the back, for all who cared to look, what had once been slave quarters. A grove of moss-hung live oaks floated over the house in those days, and flowers were every place. Inside, we met Alice and some of the guests. She had a cubistic Picasso and some of the more modern flat school of Paris paintings. And that in 1920 was really *avant-garde!*

Mamma came over and sniffed at Gramp and asked, "How is your gout?"

"Fat of the catfish drove it off. You don't think I've been drinking!"

Mamma said, "Now watch yourself at dinner. I've had them make you some nice custard and some very dry toast. And only spring water to drink."

Gramp nodded and said in a low voice as Mamma walked away, "I wish I had some Big John. Stevie, why do beautiful women have such mean ways?"

"I don't know, Gramp."

"That's right, always answer right out what you think."

Alice came from an old family, which meant, Gramp supposed, "Newgate criminals, bonded servants, and other riffraff that settled in the South." (I'm quoting Gramp; I don't think he was entirely wrong, but he was settling the South too easy. A lot came for liberty, and to grow tobacco, and to marry Indian princesses who saved their lives. But I have to quote Gramp from time to time to show that if his arteries didn't harden, his prejudices did.)

It was a kind of lazy life in those days, after a romantic World War I. People were coming off the plantations, the old Dixie battle flags were tattered and faded, and they were admitting the rest of the United States back into society.

The dining room was old wallpaper and polished silver and furniture rubbed down like a race horse. Candles burned, on the walls the old family faces behind coats of yellow varnish watched us eat, and the last of the "white-haired old darkies" served us, wearing white gloves that grew green thumbs as they served the pea soup and turtle stew in sherry.

It was a dying culture and Gramp hated it; but I liked it. It had manners, it had taste, and it didn't use life for too much hunger after money and power. Perhaps it was out of date, but

I, as a boy, liked it, and I'm sorry to see it today a cold civilization of big politics, oil wells, meanness, and petty hatreds. The
South was—Gramp said—the closest we ever came to a true
culture in this country—a breed and an interest in things above
the herd animal. Democracy may have been pushed around,
but as one sees the greed of the modern Southern cities, one can
again wish for this nation of planters and riders who added
something lost to us by the invention of mass-production thinking and packaging. "I would gladly trade the telephone and
the airplane for an American Gauguin, or a new sauce," Gramp
once said.

Of course I wasn't thinking that when I was a boy sitting in
that Moss Street house watching the dark butler with the three
chins and voodoo tuft of hair on his lower lip.

Gramp ate his toast, and Mamma beamed at him. Later there
was polite music. Negroes in red coats played French waltzes
as if they had never jammed in the jazz sessions on Bourbon
and Basin streets in red-light Storyville. Nobody blew a slide
of the real stuff or took a riff.

We all slept late the next day. Gramp and I went fishing with
Emile for the last time. It was a sad time for us. Emile kissed
Gramp and hugged me, and the crew nearly wept. Gramp
bought a round of red wine and a few more and I had to make
him swallow four cups of Cajun coffee so Mamma couldn't
smell his breath.

Alice also gave us a farewell party in Jackson Square, and the
Negro jazz men were back but too well mannered and respectable. Jazz was not respectable. (A few years later, when
I was in a New York speak-easy, I heard jazz in the North and
something was already phony about it.) But the red-coated
waltz players at Alice's never let on that they knew the jive.
I danced with Mamma, and Gramp danced with Alice, who was
a fresh-made widow thinking of going to Paris to start a literary
magazine. (She did.) Then Gramp danced with Mamma, and
I danced with Alice. Of course I fell in love with her for an hour.

I was always in love in those days, and I don't think it did me any harm. I almost never told the objects of my passion how I felt about them.

Mamma was very pleased with Gramp when we got back to the hotel, and he showed her how he rubbed his gouty toes with catfish fat, and she showed him all her new shoes.

We left town the next day, heading for Florida, where the papers said a big blow was coming. But Gramp wanted to do some big-game fishing in the Gulf from the west coast of Florida. The old boy had his reasons: "I wouldn't give a dime for the whole east coast of Florida. The sons of the robber barons are dying in Palm Beach, and the sons of the Yahoos from Ohio are breaking Miami up into lots that I wouldn't let a dog live on. I can buy half of that town for peanuts, but I'd rather have the peanuts."

(Which shows how smart Gramp was. The boom in Florida came in about five years and his peanuts would have been worth millions, but then the boom broke so Gramp wasn't out anything, anyway, if you figure it that way.)

The car ran, more or less, and we had the usual number of flat tires. But near the Florida state line, Mamma fanned herself and said, "My, we must have run over a herd of skunk."

Gramp sniffed the air. "*Something* gamy. Stevie, you carrying any white mice this trip?"

"No, Gramp. But I've noticed the flies are following us."

Mamma said, "Something is dead and I'm for burying it."

Gramp stopped the car, we walked around it, and suddenly Mamma shouted, "Oh, my new shoes!" and pulled out a package that dropped out shoes and bits of what I saw was catfish fat.

Gramp said, "Don't drop my game-fish bait! They love that catfish meat!"

Mamma said, "double d-damn!" and began to cry. We dumped all the valuable catfish fat out by the roadside. It was a good thing we found some good shoe shops. It cost Gramp a lot of money, and later we went after deep-sea fish without catfish bait. But even his toes didn't seem to miss it by then.

Mamma suddenly developed a fever. We stopped our journey down the delta, at a bayou village, and put her to bed in a big white old house now turned into a hotel. Its sign read: "For the Gentry, by Day or Week."

The local doctor looked wise and said, "It's the native misery. Yo' should be fine with a week in bed and some beat-up milk punch, with an egg in it. Yo' can't beat a milk punch, maybe a spoon of rum in it too."

Mamma didn't get worse, but the fever hung on, and Gramp decided we'd stay there till Mamma was able to travel again without fever. We worried, but then grew bored, and as they took good care of Mamma, Gramp and I explored the vast life of the delta, the coast, the gulf, the bayous, and the islands. Mamma sat in her wide brass bed in a beautiful bed jacket and read the poems of Lord Byron in a small blue volume that belonged to the people who ran the place. She hated to have us hang around and routed us out early every day.

Gramp and I found the decaying neighborhood plantations, the remains of pillared houses among now-lost bayous, dried up, Gramp said, in time and forgotten in history. We saw weeds and chipped marble pools, sunken paths, and trees dying of neglect.

Gramp hired a boat, and we floated out past the cypresses dying in salt water and past the orange flower and the indigo iris. The shore was thick with growths. We could count water hickory, tupelo, bald cypress, and locust. I still remember all those names. Over everything were ferns and creepers, palmettos and the green gold, the silver white of choking vines. Gramp said it was like Indo-China, where he had once built a railroad.

The greatest trouble to the out-boating was the orchid of the bayou, the water hyacinths, beautiful, thick-growing, and choking up the waterways. I felt I could almost walk on them. They were not native, and one story told me was they came from Japan, escaped from a potted plant that took over the bayous. They made a mat of flower and leaf that hid lakes and streams, and hundreds of unmapped bodies of water were under the bayou orchids.

On shore Gramp had me watch my step. There was the *prairie tremblante*—that jello-like land, a quavery land that, a native told us, "will suck yo' down. Suck down a man or an animal and lick its lips for more." The canny native respected it and walked with care. A stranger is doomed if he walks across it—to me it was like strolling in a bad childhood dream. Floating surface of dead matter, long-gone greens, and a mudlike glue. I sweated at night thinking of it.

But it was fertile, Gramp and I had to admit that. Alligator grass covered it, salt cane, patches of oyster grass, the waving cattails. I did simple water colors of it. A native could read the condition of the bogs by what grew on it. Humus, ooze, and roots made a nightmare world of its own and tormented my dreams for many years.

The bogs went on to the rim of the world. On the Gulf the salt marshes sat, and beyond that, sand ridges with sparse plant life, places called *chenières*, where a stunted oak fought for life and learned to like the salt taste of the tides. Gramp loved it all. After a day of crossing from land to island, from swamp to peaty shore, it was good, Gramp said, "to sit in a cabin kitchen and spoon up *shrimp jambalaya*." And I remember the native rice and pepper, shellfish and tomatoes, and the quick color of scarlet plants under the yard chickens' feet as they pecked at the cadavers of skinned muskrats whose hides, now on stretchers, lined the cabin wall; I drew the Spanish dagger plant proudly erect in the sun.

Gramp taught me about nature. "The peninsulas of earth and man made by the bayous bear a rich, full life, not an easy life, but a life for the hard worker to get it out of the rice field or the Gulf with nets. Look at it all. Oysters and shrimp, fish twisting their jeweled tails in the brown waters and inhaling the minute plant life that feed, in the end, bigger fish, and, at last, us."

"Who eats us?" I once asked.

The old man smiled. "God eats us."

Everything grew rich and strong and there was plenty of it. Spanish moss hung from oaks, tabasco, peppers, diamond-back terrapin; ducks to be taken out of season, soft-shell crabs, and lots of alligators. Gramp knew the history of a favorite alligator from the Bayou Teche.

"One-Eyed Louie—he must be two hundred years old, Stevie —and the great-great-great-grandpappy of all the 'gators in these parts. A hunter tried to kill him with an elephant gun one time and just blew out an eye of Louie's. He is as wide as our car and when he crawls through the sand he leaves a track like a tank. Those that have seen him say his hide is green with age and has oysters growing on it. No bullet made could ever get through that hide—must be as thick as battleship armor. Nobody hereabouts tries to catch One-Eyed Louie any more."

I hunted Louie with a borrowed twenty-two, but luckily never found him; only later did I decide it was lucky for me.

Gramp told me some local gossip: "Not all just hunting and fishing here. Barratry in the last hundred years was done here."

"What's that?" I asked.

"Barratry is an evil-sounding word that covers a loose kind of criminal action; it means "desert" or "sink a ship for gain," usually by its officers and crew. A lot of hulks rot in the damn dark bayous' bottoms, and only the oleanders and the oaks on the shore line know where and when they were done in."

I could believe it and did. Low, stunted, and harassed by salt and tide, by flood and vine, the twisted oaks still managed to remain. Moss grew on them and twisted in the wind, a lacy beauty all its own. And I saw a man strip this moss into his little paper-thin boat and sing his little song and come home to a dinner (supper, pardon me) of duck and a gumbo, thick and healthy, to stay on a man's·ribs.

Mamma worried me. But then she got better. Her fever left her, and she sat on the porch and at meals she ate a lot and drank the local wine. Soon she said, "I'm ready to go on."

Gramp said, "We could go right home. Sell the car and take a train."

Mamma shook her head. "No, let's go on."

I said, "Maybe we better go home, Mamma."

"Don't you and Gramp want to go fishing in Florida?"

Gramp didn't say anything, and Mamma asked him about his gout and what he was using for catfish fat. That cheered everyone up, and first they laughed over it and then they scolded each other. So it was as it had always been.

The next day we were on our way, heading for the Florida fishing coast. Mamma was wedged in comfortable in the back of the car, wearing a veil, and Gramp drove with care the rutted roads. I was beside him, waving to the redneck and the mudsill kids at the crossroads, and looking up at the live oaks with their loads of trailing moss. We passed shack boats and barges, went through leaning towns about to drop into gullies, and fought the sand fleas and the gnats and the local cooking. Mamma enjoyed it all and said, "It's g.d. good to be alive." And Gramp proved his religion by saying very loud, "Amen!"

JUDGE OTIS FRY

*A man may fish with the worm
that hath eat of a king, and eat of
the fish that hath fed of that
worm. . . .*

—SHAKESPEARE
(From Gramp's notebooks)

WHITE SUNLIGHT

OUR CAR WAS PATCHED AND REPAIRED, AND BORE ON ITS
windshield the stickers of many cities, symbols, like that of a
marble knight lying in full stone armor with his feet crossed to
show he had been butchering in the Holy Land. Gramp drove
in one of his good moods that fought off the inherent disappoint-
ment of existence, those low periods when he didn't shave, and
would recite:

*But we like Sentries are oblig'd to stand
In Starless Nights, and wait th' appointed Hour . . ."*

For Gramp was aware of the changing world. He had seen
the nation turn itself from a country of farmers into cityfolk
and makers of machines, and he had seen the machines bring

in the robber barons. And the resulting prosperity of the barons make a great middle class, whom he blamed for the debasement of taste, as all forms of art and entertainment were made over for them. He had seen the rise of the revolters and the class wars, the left-wing and the horn-rimmed intellectuals; and these too he did not care for.

As he grew very old he became aware that his good fat world had really ended in 1914, that the Golden Age for him had been from the end of the Civil War to World War I, and that the rest of us had missed the best and were struggling in the sediment of an obsession his own early times had lacked.

I shall never forget our ride down the west coast of Florida. Gramp had made up his mind he was going gulf fishing. Mamma gave in because Gramp had bought her a hammered silver wristband and had let her go to some very fancy balls where Southern gentlemen had taken her out on the porch and shown her the Southern moon. ("A respectable woman," Mamma wrote home, "can always trust a gentleman here, and anyway, in New Orleans they talk too much about soft-shell turtle stew with brandy, rather than life, death, and love.")

As for myself, I was growing up fast. It was rough going in those days for the roaring, but ill-slung car, along the sand roads, the swamp bottoms and under the moss-hung Spanish oaks. We crawled and bounced through Wakulla and Taylor and Citrus counties, past the groves of Hernando and Pasco and Manatee. Life was simple in those days: the great Florida land boom and bubble was still five years away. Most of the natives had come from the Middle West to die in the sun and suck oranges while they compared their grandchildren's pictures. It was a neat, lazy, and rather boring life. We used to fill our water bottle in their wells, eat their damn fried chicken, and wonder when Gramp would find a place to catch deep-sea fish.

Below Tampa (from which my Uncle Willie sailed for Cuba with Teddy Roosevelt and his Roughriders and came home

with a limp and a habit of living off innocent bridge players),
below the bay, the points jut out into the gulf, and below Passage Key Inlet and Anna Maria Key, the long lean spits of sand
go out a long way, and here we found Sarasota Key.

Mamma, leaning on a slender sunshade, looked over the sand
and the sky and the heavy sea birds coming landward after a
day's fishing, and she said, "I don't like it."

Gramp was putting up our tent with the aid of driftwood
timbers, and he said, "Hell and high water, Sari, this is living."

"I don't even call it existing."

I was collecting King crabs and I said, "Are they all good to
eat?"

Mamma said, "You two have made a god of your stomachs.
I'm going to Sarasota and to the hotel. You'll find me there."

Gramp sat down on the sand and lit a fresh Cuba stogie,
which had been smuggled in and sold to him by the pound.
"How you getting to the mainland? Man-eating 'gators, wild
natives . . . Indian country here about; I can smell it."

Mamma poured sand from her tiny shoes and said, "If I
don't get any hotel life, you don't go fishing."

Gramp looked worried. "How do you figure that, Sari?"

"I'll run screaming down the beach shouting I've been kidnaped. By the time you explain yourself, the story will be in
every newspaper in America *and* the family will call in Doctor
Magershack."

Gramp stood up and waved his stogie overhead and said,
"—— —— —— we shall stay in town and fish during the day!"

The family, with the exception of Mamma, still felt that
Gramp was a very rich old man. And when he got into trouble,
the sons and the daughters-in-law would hold meetings at the
bank and say that "for the estate's sake, it would be a good
thing perhaps, that if, *maybe*, Gramp were declared not of
sound mind to take care of his business." Mamma and Papa
always voted against it. But Doctor Magershack, the first of
the followers of Freud and the newer methods of head-feelers,

was kept on the pay roll by the family to watch Gramp's habits and ideas. Gramp hated Doctor Magershack and said he was "going to die the way I was born, without anyone looking inside my head!"

Mamma's mention of Doctor Magershack did it. She knew when she had won, but she always rubbed Gramp's face in it, lightly, to show she meant business. "Doctor Magershack is visiting the Mizners, at Palm Beach. *Such* a clever man."

Gramp looked at me and said, "Stevie, I can teach you all about life, but you're going to make all my mistakes. Well, I hear the food is very good at the hotel."

The second night we found a Greek sponge diver's eating place run by a one-eyed Greek with a huge stomach who fell in love with Mamma and made us egg and lemon soup himself, and brought it to the table, his face shining with olive oil and love.

The one-eyed Greek, his full name Captain Demetrius Iambros Mitsotakis (that's how he signed a love poem he wrote to Mamma and which I still have), was a powerful man and a great liar (I hope) about his adventures. Gramp called him Gus, and Mamma called him Over Ardent, but he did cook very good food. And he got for Gramp, by hire, a large blue sailboat and a crew of two Greek boys named Panos and Argiros.

One morning—it was still dark—I was punched awake, and there was Gramp dressed in beachcomber outfit and carrying stinking cuttlefish bait.

"Get up, you lazy little scut! The snappers are running with the tide." I dressed, yawned, and followed Gramp to the dock. The blue boat, stinking of long-dead sponges, was there, and the two Greek boys that Gramp called Hans and Fritz (for no reason at all) were rigging fishing gear. We went aboard and the sail was lifted. The Greek boys crossed themselves, touched their holy medals, and got out the beer bottles. We sailed and Gramp steered and drank beer and I stuck bait on hooks.

Gramp said to Hans (who had a scar on his left cheek made

by a boat hook), using his deep-sea voice, "I want plenty of fish."

Gramp took a rod and line and looked at the bait and added a fresh warm clam. He threw the line into the sea and sat waiting. We all sat fishing. It grew warmer. Noon passed. Gramp made a strike and stood up and shouted, "I've got a hell of a big one!"

He bit his stogie in half, grew red in the face, and began slowly to reel in the rod, bent almost in half. A great silver fish cut the sea to one side, came up, and went down in a half circle. Spume and spindrift took him back. The line smoked out. The sea grew calm, then wilder and wilder as the fish leaped again. I felt the agony of his heartbreaking leap. Gramp reeled in again, cursing. The boat drifted; the gawk of a sea gull floated overhead. Far off a cloud set high in the blue sky, and I felt the wonder of the moment and gripped the sides of the boat and watched. The white sun blinded me as the fish leaped again. He was weaker now and Hans got out the hand net. Gramp fell, recovered, and banged against the side of the boat. Suddenly he fell back, and rod, reel, and a section of tangled line fell in over him. The fish was free. Hans looked over the side and pointed. I made out a blue sliver of life descending in circles. The fish became part of the sea and all I saw were wrinkles of water rippling in a rising wind; I sensed the muscles of the waves and felt them slap the bottom of the boat as she heeled over. My face tasted salty, the wind bit me.

Gramp stood up and untangled himself. "I tripped," he said. "Biggest fish I ever saw, eh, boys?"

"Marlin," said Hans.

"——," said Gramp. "I was just butterfingers."

The boys got the sail up and we went before the wind and around a key past the slimy ribs of a long-sunk boat. The iron was rusted on her, and the wood was riddled to lace with snails and sea slugs. When the wind let up, we fished again and we all caught snappers and some long dark fish whose name I now forget. But the big fish seemed angry at us and stayed away. As Hans said after a fresh bottle of beer, "They tell each other you missed one of the best. How many beers we have left?"

We took our catch to the one-eyed Greek. Gus was full of gloom, chopping at his meat block with a great knife, an un-happy-looking man.

"The lady will *not* be here for dinner."

"Where is she?" asked Gramp.

"She is at the Ringling house. You are to join her there for dinner. And I made for her the best rice wrapped in grape leaves. I made for her the finest lamb on a sword over a charcoal fire. I even bring up my best goat cheese from cellar. I make such a fine crab bisque. I have steak from a steer fed in the Everglades on molasses. I one lousy sad Greek."

Gramp patted his shoulder and offered him a stogie. "I think we better go see what Sari is up to."

We went to the hotel and Gramp bathed me and scrubbed me but said I still smelled like herring salad. We got dressed and took a taxi out to the Ringling palace. It still stands, the home of the Ringlings, the owners of the famous circus—and the circus still spends its winters there. But the old place is a museum now, where rotting old masters covered with mildew prove you can't keep art in the tropics. Mamma had met one of the Ringlings at the hotel porch, and he had invited her and us out for dinner.

The dining room was huge. A dark Rubens rape of a goddess filled one wall, and what may have been a real El Greco watched us eat. The Ringling at the head of the table was highly amused by Mamma's story of our travels. He said to Gramp, "You have a wonderful granddaughter."

Gramp said, "She isn't related to me. My son found her under a raccoon coat at a Yale-Harvard game."

Mamma said, in her little girl voice, "Oh, you sweet old man," and Gramp and I knew we were in trouble.

The Ringling man said, "It's a wonderful idea of hers to ride some of our horses, don't you think? They need exercise."

Gramp was eying Mamma. "Now, Sari, what have you been telling this man?"

Mamma said, "Only that I took three blue ribbons at the last Long Island horse show for my jumping."

"The horse helped," said Gramp. "You can't ride circus horses."

"Gramp, I'm of age to make up my own mind."

Mamma, in her life, had tried to be many things, and I think if she had been permitted, might have become very famous. But the family kept Mamma polite and harmless. She was a fine rider and had a way with horses. But I could see Gramp didn't like the idea. He took a balloon of brandy from a tray and said, "If anything happened, the family would skin me."

Mamma winked at Ringling and said, "Isn't he a wonderful old man, for his age?"

"You're not riding," Gramp said.

I don't remember much more because I was sleepy, but I do remember getting to the hotel and Mamma and Gramp undressing me and talking very loud and with gestures at each other. I slept what seemed a long time, and when I woke up it was morning. Gramp hadn't undressed. There were several dead cigars on the hotel desk. He sat, a defeated old man, very tired, when I went up to him and said, "Mamma rides very well; you don't have to worry about her taking an asser off a horse."

Gramp patted my head and said, "I'm getting old, Stevie. Real old. I'm beginning to think of family manners and morals. I'm beginning to worry over the nest."

"I don't understand."

"When you feel there isn't much to wake up to any more, you feel maybe you can make people see the trouble foolish life can bring. Sari is a wonderful woman and she has you, and a good simple husband, my son, who doesn't really deserve her. But there it is. I've got to bring her back home, safe, unharmed."

I nodded, understanding very little then. Gramp looked at me and said, "I've had a full life, but I wonder if it isn't better to die young, in war, quickly, in love, but unsated. Yes, the first big punch of dawning love and life and strength, and have it over with before it gets drab and too dull to recapture."

"Blood sugar," I said, digging in Gramp's baggage for a square of chocolate. Gramp was low in blood sugar, his doctor said, and he wasn't himself in the morning unless he ate something to level off his blood sugar. Anyway, Gramp *did* change when he ate something in the morning. He nibbled on the chocolate, and I could see his shoulders lift and his face smile again and the gloomy ideas seep away.

When Mamma came in to wish us good morning and ask me about my digestive habits, Gramp was busy writing a letter. He looked up and said, "Morning, Sari, great day, isn't it? Honey in the horn, and every feather on every bird full of life, eh?"

Mamma frowned and looked over Gramp's shoulder. "*Whom* are you writing to?"

"Sari, I hear the fishing is better off the east coast. Off Palm Beach. I'm writing to Doctor Magershack we'll be there any day now. I think we *both* need a little going over."

Mamma folded her arms and tapped her small foot against the hotel rug. She bit her lower lip and said softly in her best high-school French, "*Touché.*"

Gramp looked up. "You don't think I'd tell tales out of school, Sari?"

"The *h* I don't, you old devil! You know it would look crazy to him and his friends for me to want to ride circus horses. You *clever* devil, you!"

Mamma always knew when she was beaten. She never sulked. She just turned on her heel and walked out, saying over her shoulder, "I haven't a thing to wear in Palm Beach. It's going to be fun to go shopping there."

Gramp shut his heavy gold fountain pen, tore the letter slowly into shreds, and said, "Oh, to be seventy again, Stevie. I'd have joined her in a riding act."

So we started for Palm Beach, and the one-eyed Greek saw

us off and gave Mamma a kiss on the hand (and a rum pecan pie which I ate all the way across Florida).

As we left, the car snorting and smoking, Mamma leaned against Gramp, and he drove with one arm hugging her to him. His voice was low and sad. "I know, Sari, I know. But they've trapped us, trapped us and tamed us both. Maybe Stevie will get away."

We broke a car spring in a mudhole at Cooter Springs, and while they repaired it we all sat on the hot, sunny porch of Judge Otis Fry, the local powerhouse, while the men talked about politics, and Mamma fanned flies. The Judge was fat, wise, and bald as a sucking egg. Gramp had brought up the fact that the South, like the rest of the country, didn't send its best men to Washington.

"How the hell are we going to keep the country healthy when you send those mental cripples and hungry mouths to Washington, Judge?"

"Politically, General," said the Judge, accepting a cigar, "if yo' show any signs of bein' one grade beyond a jibbering idiot, you can't run for office. Many a high-class moron, one who could not cross a street unaided, has been rejected by the voters as being too smart for office. Yo' have to he devoid of normal ideas to run for office here.

"Why do we send hillbilly apes and broken-down bartenders and droolin' boys to public office? Hell, yo' ought to know. Yo' been down here. Out here we all grew up to admire the man who could break a wild horse, hit a dime at a hundred feet, make love all night (pardon me, Madame).

"Ah keep thinkin' of our kids inheritin' all this. So much of it, of this land, and the early business of hangin' strangers to a tree seems to have left a lot of it still empty. Million head of cattle live here, grow big, grow wild, are branded, shipped, butchered, and leave behind them the juice for future beefsteaks in new red calves.

"Irrigation ditches are bringin' water to earth so long dry, so long sterile, that even its clods shriek with surprise when the wetness reaches 'em. General, it's been a great day. And Ah've said so. Now Ah'll shut mah face. Ah've had mah say. Ah feel right good sucking this good cigar."

The blacksmith came around to tell us he'd have to heat and shape a new spring leaf for our car and that would take time and we better stay over a few days.

The Judge spread his hands and said, "All Ah can offer yo' is mah humble home. No plantation out of *Uncle Tom's Cabin,* but Ah want yo' to stay with us."

Mamma said, "We can stay in a hotel in town."

"Yo' sho' could, Honey Chile, only the hotel it burned down some time ago. Boys were making 'shine in the cellar, put a run of buck through the still fast, she blew up and now some turp camp riffraff live in the ruins with their shoat. You'll like mah farm."

We did. It was a fine white house surrounded by fields planted neatly. The Judge's grown son Charlie showed me over the place. The Judge was a widower, but "courtin' " down the road, and several Negroes, called *nigrahs* by the family, cooked, cleaned, and served. They didn't work hard, and the Judge said they "toted," which meant, he explained, they took leftovers home. He was paying them fifty cents a week each and he lamented the servant problem. "Help gettin' fancy ideas."

I thought it was a wonderful farm, halfway between the gulf and sea, far inland. The Judge knew what he wanted and had built it because he had a bride who wanted a new house. She—now long dead—had planted the garden's herbaceous borders.

The road came in from the right—a road of broken stone—and it connected five miles on with a highway. And on a hot, windy day you could smell the Big Scrub where no one lived.

The best part of the farm, to me, was the color of the place—the age of the rocks, the lack of garish tones on the old wood fences, the silver gray of stone walls and the apple-green and sage-green corn. Charlie was hoeing up the young bean seedlings, and setting out the poles, and telling me how tall the pecan trees would grow.

The green of corn was impressive to me, and so was Charlie, driving the horses between the rows of corn plants and then disappearing into the tall corn as the sun grew hotter. And the hay and oats were already chrome yellow.

I remembered how Charlie used to wait for the rain, and how he looked at the sky and his eyes were that slit of worry, that narrow look farmers have when they watch the clouds and almost want to leap up and hunt water in the sky.

That's how he comes back to me—waiting for the rain, and the corn leaves crackling and getting crinkly edges, and the silk of the ears drying out and turning dark, and the heavy corn, the big ears of it, splitting open, the cows suffering and blowing their wet black noses in the water pailed out to them, and the hens scratching themselves until their rumps were obscenely bare of feathers and their beaks were always open. Once in a while a hen would go mad and think she was an eagle and try to fly over the milk shed under live oak and moss, and Charlie would go out and sadly twist her neck.

The night was very warm, and Charlie and I went down to the stream and lay in the water, clinging close to the clay bottom, and the frogs worried and barked and we soaked it all up. And even there we could feel the blind, insatiate heat.

Then in the morning it rained and rained, and the corn steamed and seemed to leap up a foot overnight, and then later the sky was yellow and damp. Charlie was busy and I helped, and the farm tools clicked.

The oranges and lettuce came off pretty well, and the weeds went wild. No one cared any more about fighting them, and the crows and blackbirds had a time in the corn until Charlie and I went out with shotguns. It took a week to make a new car spring.

LUCY BOOLEY

No man differs much from an-
other man, but at certain times he
does from himself. . . .
—PASCAL
(From Gramp's notebooks)

LAY MY BURDEN DOWN

MAMMA HAD ALREADY BEEN ILL ON THE TRIP, GRAMP
had suffered several times from gout, the car had been bent
and banged on and repaired; only I had so far escaped from
disaster. Now crossing Florida for the east coast it was my turn
to go into dry dock. We were wandering in the Big Scrub, that
wild country of black inlets and tangled growths, among the
wild oranges, when I developed boils. On my buttocks. It was
not dangerous, but it was painful. And rather indecent, I felt.
It was certainly not a series of heroic wounds.

I could not sit. And riding in the jolting car was painful,
very painful. Mamma shook her head. "We'll just have to wait
the boils out."

Gramp scowled. "He may be another Job, having whole
stables of boils. Let's keep going."

"It hurts to ride sitting down," I said. "Can I stand on the running board?"

Mamma shook her head. "We've got to find a place in the wilderness, and rest up Stevie's boils. It's the food in New Orleans and Tampa. Too much acid in the orange juice."

Gramp said, "Whisky cures everything, we learned that in the Civil War, but he's too young for it I suppose, Sari?"

Mamma said, "Look out for a nice clean place that takes in tourists."

So we found Ira and Lucy Booley, who were poor but clean and lived on the edge of the Big Scrub on an inky inlet and had a sign out reading: *Tourists Taken* (which was *"naïf,"* said Mamma, "but interesting"). We all moved into a new pine house built near their own log cabin (on stilts over the water) and we waited for my boils to cure. I didn't sit much, but I got around. Gramp went fox-hunting with Ira, walking the hounds in the white mist of morning. Mamma learned to knit.

Ira was born Jeremiah Ira Beauregard Booley. Lucy claimed he was once quality and gentry and related to the Hamptons, Stuarts, and of course the Beauregards. But Ira didn't really believe a word of it. He said his grandfather came out of Kentucky trailing his long squirrel rifle and followed by two glass-eyed Catahoula hounds, leopard-spotted dogs that are pretty good for chasing a fox on foot. Why he came to the Scrub, in Florida, Ira didn't know and never found out. He died in some battle near Five Forks, in the War between the States, and when Ira was old enough to crawl shirtless across the cabin set up on Choctaw logs over the inlet up the west coast bay, his father was a mean man who distilled moon in the cypress swamps and tangled palmetto thickets.

Ira said, "He used to come home once a week, smelling of mash (overfermented), malt, and brewer's yeast. He used to beat my mother till she whimpered for mercy; then he'd whistle to his hound dog and go off to Tampa to sell his ten gallons of moon. Everybody in my family that I ever met made 'shine and sold it cheaply in the towns. My father used to spend a lot of time up at the Walls [as they called the state prison]. He died when I was six, falling dead drunk into a boiling tub of corn-meal mash. My mother kept the wreath of *immortelles* tied with a red chenille ribbon from his funeral, and a stalactite he had once brought her lettered: *From Mammoth Cave, Ky.*"

We all liked Ira and Lucy Booley.

When my boils got better I used to take an old skiff out into the bay, with the hound Chester, who was very old and given to fleas, to keep my feet dry on his back. I fished for sunnies and buffalo, and dreamed. Afternoons over the bay a scud of black clouds would come up and all the purple and yellow sky would boil out of the inlet, and I'd spider-crawl for home, pulling the oars like mad. The first big berry drops of rain would hit me like bullets, and the *geek geek* of the sea gulls would die out as the bay water humped itself into little gray waves with hard muscles under them. I would tie up the skiff under the house and watch the rain and wind beat the water, and Chester would shake his mangy old hide—my, how that dog did smell—and try to lick my face. I ran barefooted with the young boys after the fox-hunters, following their braying hounds on foot. "To hunt the local yellow fox on horseback," Gramp said, "is worse than to have fought on the Northern side."

A battered carnival came into the town below the inlet in red, paint-peeling old Ford trucks, with a lot of wide women with bleached silver and yellow hair, and mean-looking men. The spin and toss games were all crooked, and the whirling rides so worn out they were dangerous. I used to get sick on sugar candy and earn a dime running for quart fruit bottles of moon for the crap-shooters. I even poured beer over the yellow head of the high tank diver, while she washed her long hair in the stuff, claiming it gave it "body."

Mamma said I still wasn't well enough to travel.

Ira had troubles. There had been a change of party in power in Washington and he had lost his job on the dredge, and we all used to sit on the porch of his house and fish, listening to the barking of foxes as hunters went after them on frosty nights. Sometimes the eyes of raccoons burned in the night, and giant fireflies, such as I've never seen since, would come suspended in space, all green and a lovely pale blue and a very hot crimson. Lucy would have the kerosene lamp, and she would put a tarpaulin around her shoulders and go slopping out to see how her China hogs were doing on a mound of dirt behind the house. She raised little white porkers but she never got much for them in the market, and because of the 'gators it hardly seemed worth picking up fish heads and corncobs and other truck for them.

Just when my boils seemed all cured, I met some poison ivy, and that laid me up for some time; and when I healed, I couldn't sit again. Ira invited us to the local parties and the dances, and Mamma said, "Mighty nice of you. I like dancing."

Gramp said, "It's not society dancing, Sari."

Mamma said, "It doesn't matter. It's dancing."

"Lots of fights," said Ira.

"I'll risk it," said Mamma, "and we'll take Stevie so he doesn't fall into any more ivy."

"I sat in it. I didn't fall," I said.

I enjoyed it all as much as Mamma, and Gramp got to like drinking the local 'shine. I was young, a "bit rabbity," as the natives said, and I liked the outdoor life. I did not mind the rednecks singing:

> *Ten-cent cotton and forty-cent meat*
> *How in Hell kin a pore man eat?*

I worked shares on a seine net and did some illegal fishing in the bayous and lakes, lived on grits, red bugs, and mosquitoes, heard the sweet-throated hoot owl, and drank the local coffee-and-chicory. I ate the cold gray cornbread, b'iled white bacon and collop greens, and slept on a husk pallet covered with crocus sacks stuffed in part with black tree moss. Mamma too grew fond of the sweet bays and magnolia, drinking sulphurous

well water, walking home across the hummocks and the piny
woods. She liked to dance, and we went to the square-calls
dancing "Shoot the Coon" and "Bird in the Cage" and me not
worrying when the young bucks swung Mamma too hard. I
still remember those dances—the odor of old hound dog, mule
musk, plug tobacco, and the gamy old women dipping snuff on
a stick and rubbing their gums with it. The callers would clap
and sing it out as Mamma stomped and backed.

> *Bird in, buzzard in*
> *Pretty good bird*
> *Fer the shape he's in!*

We all sashayed under the sooty kerosene lamps, the palmetto rustled over the cedar chip shingles, and the bellow of the
bull bat kept time with the cigar-box fiddle. They didn't know
any better life. They were all neighbors and all poor, and even
the store men and the game warden and the local judge who
badgered them were poor men. The Negroes walked in dread
of them, but all were no better off than they were; all hoe hands,
fishers, and turp pine slashers, living with their scrambly-
scrawny girls on a split log floor, digging sand spurs and dog
fennel from their naked toes, and getting malaria from the
brackish river. Gramp mellowed and gained weight. I healed
slowly.

It says in the books I've read since that there isn't any
malaria left and that ignorance and real poverty is pretty much
a thing of the past; but then no one came in to the Big Scrub
to see if it were so.

I liked the suck of the tidal waters, the color of the geraniums
Lucy grew in old cans, the pies of blue cedar berries, her shoat
fattening under the cabin floor on oak acorn. Lucy had chip-
munk-colored eyes and I loved her too; she was lonely when
Ira was out in the boat and the game warden hunted him. She
could cook water-ground meal, make clabber milk, and bake a
possum. Ira had a neat set of fighting cocks the year we were
there. One of his best, with bronze-green feathers, was Little

Eddie. A fat old Hoot Nanny named Gates had a blue cock, Dark Mike, and Gramp bet a hundred dollars on Little Eddie. Ira had raised him on soft food and hard crushed corn. He had plucked out his tail feathers so he looked obscene and naked, and clipped his comb down to a nub with a razor. Ira filed off his own spurs and fitted him with steel needle gaffs. It was a great day on the inlet when they met in an old barn, with Gramp as the judge shouting, "Bill yo' cocks." And after they had touched bills, he said, "Pit yo' cocks."

It was a great fight and Little Eddie was doing fine, springing up in the air like an explosion of feathers and coming in spurs first like a charging cactus plant. But the Blue outweighed him and was lucky, very lucky. Little Eddie got a gaff full in his brain and he died, beak and mouth open, a drop of blood on the end of his horny beak, trying to crawl over to Ira, who wrung his neck tenderly.

Ira was broke. He sang sad songs:

> *Jacob's ladder steep and tall*
> *When I lay my burden down.*
> *If yo' try to climb up*
> *Yo' bound to fall*
> *When I lay my burden down.*

The chinaberry tree grew over the cabin place, and the sour orange marmalade was all gone to the ants in the mason jar. We were getting ideas of leaving. Lucy sang:

> *Five cents in my pocket*
> *Ten cents in my bill*
> *If it don't get no better*
> *I'm bound for Sugar Hill.*

Ira was getting no place and knew it. A toad-strangler of a storm wrecked Ira's boat. We lived on cooter stew and eggs; the big land turtle has a lot of pink and white meat and the eggs were good eating even if the whites never boiled hard. Ira bought some traps and caught varmint: muskrat and possum fat on pinders and persimmons, the gray fox, and others. The piny woods smell remained, the roar of a bull 'gator, the sight of floating tussocks, the islands of pines, and Ira even planted some skinny acres of goobers and chaufas.

Gramp paid our board bill. No relative of Ira's had ever seen that much money in one spot, let alone owned it. Ira bought sweet feed for the two mules, a guitar for Lucy, and a new shotgun with which he knocked tillie hawks right out of the sky. He was some biggety man and started traipsin' around setting up drinks, and he replaced their shoestring latch with a store-bought knob. He bought new biddies of Dominick hens and bred himself some new fighting cocks. His little cockfighting roosters lived better than most people. He bred Roundheads crossed with Carolina Blues and White Hackles.

Ira and Lucy in their new mail-order clothes saw us off the morning we left, I sitting again with ease, Mamma having finished knitting a sweater for Gramp, and Gramp behind the wheel of the car, his cigar burning bright in the morning mist.

" 'By," said Ira. "Hope yo' ain't goin' cause you're bait of us."

"Going," said Gramp, "because we have to. 'By, Ira. 'By, Lucy. We'll write."

Lucy nodded and smiled. "We'll git us Ira's Cozin Artie to write for us. He been to the Walls for makin' 'shine. He writes powerful good."

There was waving, I think a tear or two, a bark from the old hound, and we were off. We drove in silence, the car alone making any noise. Then Gramp threw away his cigar. "Damn it, leaving people you like is hard."

Mamma said, "I've got to remember to send Lucy some store soap and some new pails."

"Buckets," said Gramp. "Pails are what lard is kept in."

I said, "I think a bee bit me on the leg. It throbs."

Gramp said, "Come hell, high water, and you even get bitten by tigers, we're going to Palm Beach. Scratch, but *don't* ask me to stop."

MIAMI IN THE TWENTIES

18

Society is now one polish'd horde,
Form'd of two mighty tribes,
The bores and the bored. . . .
—BYRON
(From Gramp's notebooks)

THE BEST PEOPLE

THERE WAS SUPPOSED TO BE A ROAD ACROSS THE SWAMPS skirting Lake Okeechobee, and past the cypress trees. But even the Indians couldn't tell us where it was. We ran into a Seminole Indian family: mom, baby, pet 'gator, pappy, and long lout of a son. Gramp brought our steaming car to a halt and looked over the swamplands. "Heap lost, damn heap lost. Which way Palm Beach?"

The Indian father, smoking a rank cigar, spit and thought a while and said, "Listen, mister, you no get by here. No bottom here, *no* bottom. You sink in, you never get out, by Joe, never."

Mamma watched the flies play on the Indian baby's dirty face and said, "Gramp, we better try farther north."

"By Joe, you better. Got any chewing gum?"

Gramp gave the Indians a tube of toothpaste and we left them eating it, grunting in pleasure, even the pet 'gator taking a mouthful. Farther north it seemed no better. Once we started to sink in the quicksand, but a turpentine-camp crew got us out with mules. At night the gnats ate us, in the day the sun broiled us. But at last we got past Seminole County and down the coast to Vero Beach, where we found a hotel, unpacked and took stock of ourselves and the car. Mamma was not very happy with the bathtub. "Little fish swim in it."

"Shows it's fresh, Sari."

"They bite."

I said, "They just tickle."

We did meet a Negro conjurer in the hotel garden who told Mamma's fortune. ("Many times, many things will happen—one dollar, please.")

We had been living on sandwiches, rancid fruit, and canned fish. But now we dressed and Gramp shaved, letting me hold the newspaper on which he wiped his huge razor, swinging it in the air with such fury that I was afraid he would cut an ear or nose off.

"Stevie, once we get to Palm Beach, Sari will be as lively as a flea in a fiddler's ear. Women have secret powers when they scent social life. They shout and rant when you're roughing it and often grow faint on you. But show them a dinner jacket and an English butler and they'll go through a social season that would soften a lumberjack's winter socks. Damn! I've cut myself!"

We put some tissue paper from Mamma's glove box over the cut, and Gramp slapped his jug-shaped chin with a lotion and lit a cigar. "Is this the face that launched a thousand heartbeats in ladies long since dead? Is this the face that burned up several fortunes? I spoil a good line in a great play, Stevie, but I don't think I look so bad in the morning, do I?"

"You look fine. How's your gout?"

Gramp wriggled his big toes in his red socks and knocked on wood. "It's red flannel that keeps it away. Me and Bernard Shaw have no use for doctors. Red flannel can cure anything *if* you just give nature a chance to heal itself. Now you take that Doctor Magershack and his talk about Herr Doktor Sigmund Freud. Anybody that has any use for that kind of a doctor should have his head examined." (I know people think Sam Goldwyn's press agent is supposed to have said this, but Gramp said it years ago.)

The wonderful thing about Gramp in hunger was that he could find decent food in any town—if there was decent food. At Vero Beach he found a small inn in a brackish salt-water cove where the smart sportsmen came to eat. We had baked crab and fresh garden greens and a big bowl of steamed clams which Gramp showed us how to eat. "You grab 'em by this little black nose and dip them in this melted butter. Then you bite off the nose and chew the rest. Good?"

Mamma always felt that Gramp ordered too much food, but I noticed that we left pretty empty plates. "The trick in eating," Gramp explained, "is to cut out the nonsense. The breads, cakes, ice cream—the junk that fills you up and builds fat and has no flavor. Eat only the main dishes and send back what doesn't come out right. Never eat because you have to pay for it; never eat because it might hurt someone if you didn't. The true sacred vessel of love and emotions is the stomach. Nero and the old Romans knew that. The heart is only a pump."

"Watch yours, Gramp," said Mamma.

Refreshed, fed, and "feeling no pain," we had the strength to take the road down to Palm Beach. The roads were not what they are today. We blew two tires at Fort Pierce, had spring trouble at Stuart, but when we crossed over to Palm Beach we were feeling the sun and wind. The palm trees and very white sand and very blue sea excited us.

Palm Beach was already trying to look like the south of France. The villas and the palaces were only slightly in bad taste, and many of them were very impressive. Gramp knew many of the owners, and as we passed the walled villas he would describe, like a guide, full of irony:

"Now that million-dollar shack, it was built by a railroad king. He got a million dollars a mile on level ground from the U.S. Mint, six million dollars a mile when he hit the Rocky Mountains. Well, he had his own maps printed and moved the Rocky Mountains fifty miles east; collected mountain scale on level ground. That red house belongs to Old Eagle Beak, oldest oilman in the world. Burned down all the oil wells of rival companies and is learning golf. That wide green place—fat old Kansas countess I knew in Nice. Married a Cherokee Indian who had silver mines under his tepee, millions of dollars of it, and then married a title. And that little blue place, biggest art collector alive, invented steamships with paper bottoms and insured them to the limit. Sank his way into a fortune. . . ."

Mamma said, "Really not *nice* people."

Gramp shook his head. "Well, Sari, I don't know. They built the railroads, the big dams, the ships and the tall buildings, the mills and the factories. And when they die they leave it all behind, the money too. No, they'll do a lot of good, even if they don't want to. If you can't steal immortality, stealing isn't worth while."

Mamma wet a finger, pushed her eyebrows into place, and snapped open her sunshade: "There is our hotel."

Gramp tossed out his cigar. "I'll try to drive up like I'm your hired hand, Sari. Alexander Dumas was so dark and kinky he used to ride in back of his own carriage to give people the idea he had a Negro footman."

Mamma said crisply, "No tomfoolery, Gramp."

Gramp nodded and winked at me. The hotel was fine, flashing in the sun, its red-rose tiles very artistic (I had already read: "A rose-red city half as old as time"), and its lobby very

Spanish and gloomy. There were iron staircases that went no place, balconies that couldn't be reached, heavy scarred church furniture, and big clay pots that had been looted from Europe and brought here to dissolve in the too-healthy sunlight.

A man came in from the gardens, saw us, and smiled. He was bald but proud-looking; a mustache stood out from his face as if it were starched, and he was smoking a Russian cigarette in a jade holder. As he drew nearer, one eye gleamed and I saw he was wearing a monocle. He bowed and kissed Mamma's hand. I heard his heels click together as he said, "*Ach, kennst du das Land wo die Zitronen blühen? I kiss* your hand, Frau Longstrasser."

Mamma said, "This is my son, Stevie, and you know his grandfather."

Gramp withdrew his hand as if worried it would be kissed, and he said, "Doctor, you don't look so well. Let me see your tongue."

"Always the jokes, Herr Longstrasser."

Mamma said, "That's no way to talk to Doctor Magershack."

"Your eyeballs are bloodshot," Gramp said, "and your hand shakes. You better see a good old-fashioned bellyache doctor."

Doctor Magershack bowed and laughed. "Oh, this *Amerikaner* humor, it is so good, so *wunderbar*."

"How is Palm Beach?" Mamma asked. "How is everyone, Herr Doktor?"

The doctor patted me on the head with his gloved hand. "I have here my biggest success. I have invented a new, fashionable disease. Before me, they were still having colitis. Think how tiresome that is. Now, here I have told them repressions of the flesh are the worst thing. And so now I am treating them for their guilt fixations. Today they all talk about their love for their father and how they hated to be put on the potty chair as babies."

Gramp said, "Well, you'll be too busy to see us, I'm sure."

The doctor shook his head. "For old family friends, I make time. Said not the great Goethe: *'Kein kluger Streiter halt Feind gering'*? Such thoughts keep my mind strong."

Gramp said softly to me, "I've seen better heads on a glass of beer."

Doctor Magershack kissed Mamma's hand again. "*Ach*, this native humor. I must learn to understanding it fuller."

When we were settled in our rooms, Gramp shook his head, opened the connecting door, and said to Mamma, who was relaxing in her corset, "I've a deal for you, partner."

"Not if you go into Western talk. Stevie, find my button-hook."

Gramp said, "I'll protect you from the Herr Doktor, if you will protect me."

Mamma nodded and got out her high-heeled shoes. "I see your point, Gramp."

"He's just a dirty Hun spy for the family, that's what he is. He'll report us back home—between wisecracks from Schiller and Goethe."

"Can I button them?" I asked as Mamma pulled on the tiny shoes. She nodded, and very carefully, with the steel button-hook, I dragged the little mother-of-pearl buttons through the proper openings. The toes of the shoes were patent leather, the rest gray deerskin trimmed with yellow edging. Mamma always said, "Vulgar people always trim their shoes in red. I like a plain shoe with sixteen mother-of-pearl buttons." Mamma was a good dresser. "A bit flashy but *never* crude," Gramp explained. "Like a Frenchman's Hamlet, funny without being vulgar."

The next few days we did the town, Gramp pointing out the Gulf Stream, very blue three miles out, and the place where a shipwreck had left a cargo of coconuts which had taken root and become tall, wonderful palms. We were staying at the Royal Poinciana Hotel. Every day at around two o'clock a large fat man would appear, fanning himself with a big fan and often wearing Chinese silk sleeping outfits. He and Gramp used to gather in a few men and play poker till late at night, and Mamma would go out to visit some second-string millionaire into whom Doctor Magershack was building a guilt feeling. The doctor was Mamma's escort, and a kind of armed truce existed between him and Gramp.

I chipped a front tooth showing a bellboy at the hotel how Gramp used to, in the early Wild West, open beer bottles with his teeth. All in all, I remember Palm Beach with great liking, but even then I sensed it was a way of life dying out. The gambling clubs were still open, the old society queens still fought for the biggest guests, and the scandals were polite but sinister, and often very amusing.

A few days later, Doctor Magershack left town in a hurry. He came to see us before he left and he looked pale and worried. He kissed Mamma's hand and made a feeble heel click. "*Kein Rauch ohne Feuer*. I have to leave at once. I come to say my good-bys."

"Good-by," said Gramp. "I hear you got into some gambling trouble at the Yacht Club."

"*Keine Gedänke*. It is an odd place. I must go, and I say again, good-by."

Mamma asked, "Who said, 'Parting is such sweet sorrow'?"

"Goethe, of course, but this local *Kaffeeklatsch* is too much for me."

The family up North in New York City always wondered why they never heard from the doctor again. "His leaving America," Gramp always said, "set the progress of psycho-analysis forward ten years."

We hadn't intended to go down to Miami Beach, but Gramp wanted to trade some of his Butte copper stock to a man living there, and we drove down for a few days. The man lived on a man-made island inside the bay, and he didn't trade for Gramp's copper stock, but instead tried to sell Gramp some scheme to make filled-in land by pumping sand from the bay. Of course Gramp laughed at the idea (which made millions for others). Gramp in his old age suspected all schemes suggested by other people. Mamma said he had "enough bad ideas of his own to go around."

I swam every day in the deep blue ocean. Miami was already going vulgar but had not yet hit its full zany stride. It was beautiful to see, wonderful in sunlight, and I liked to sit on the white beach and dream those romantic daydreams of childhood, most of which I can no longer remember. Mamma usually sat under a big straw hat and read James Branch Cabell, an author who seems to have had a vogue in those days. Gramp played poker in various hotel rooms until he saw he wasn't going to trade off any of his copper stock. Gramp saw Miami as the well-heeled man's Coney Island, and just about as much fun. Along the shore road the rubber swells and auto masters and small-parts tycoons had built up stucco palaces and filled them with wine and servants and pools and sun umbrellas, and lower down there was Lincoln Road, not yet a sort of Technicolor Fifth Avenue. It was only nine blocks long, running from Biscayne Bay to the Atlantic Ocean, part Fifth Avenue, part Michigan Boulevard, part the Rue de la Paix and Bond Street, "and a lot like Flatbush and Church Avenue in Brooklyn," one visitor told me, "during an evening at Loew's King's Theater."

The shops were open in the sun and each night they glowed with hidden lights, and natives of Iowa and the Bronx and Salt Lake City and Boston and Detroit walked the moonlit street and stood in front of shopwindows, and their clean middle-class souls brightened up with pride at this nation of theirs, where there were people who could afford all this neat, nice, lovely, expensive trash. They were usually here on a twelve-day tour with every penny put where it would do the most good, and so they just window-shopped and felt now they could go back home and die. They wrote honest cards home; they had been to Florida and they had seen the rich and seen their toys and had sunburned their noses and bathed in the finest salt-water sea in the whole world—so clear, so blue beyond the sands. . . .

On the piers the great swordfish and barracuda were dying in a glaze of color, as tourists stood with rod and reel and got their pictures taken with fish the captain caught. And blossoming almonds of seventeen walked on good legs in fine hotel lobbies. Already fat mammas, in imitation Paris hats and Hollywood slacks and fox capes, strolled over for a morning orange juice and a fat seeded roll and coffee, and then they stood on the scale and lamented their blubber. Show girls passed in white bathing suits and fox capes ("You just ain't nobody if you got no fox"), and later the few men woke up and sent down for a bromo and a racing sheet and paid the bellboy a half dollar for the errand.

Mamma said the curse of the tropics was not enough men. *Any* kind of men. Thousands of young wives in endless perspective sat on the sands and watched the baby make sand castles. Hundreds of ladies of leisure strutted their stuff at the better-class speak-easies and swimming pools, and men looked them over, very hard to please, "as if sex were an abomination, like war, only more horrible," to quote from one of Mamma's letters.

Gramp sensed it was time to get Mamma home—and one fine day we started north again in our car.

19

UNCLE PAUL'S HOBBY

The fathers have eaten a sour grape, and the children's teeth are set on edge. . . .

—JEREMIAH
(From Gramp's notebooks)

HAWKS IN THE SKY

COMING NORTH FROM FLORIDA, GRAMP FOUND A TOPIC to mull over and talk about: his digestive system was in protest. It was a subject on which he could raise up a temperature and never come to the end of it. A healthy man most of the time, he resented any part of himself that protested.

"Chittlings, hog jowl, catfish cheek, turnip greens, hoe cakes, and Brunswick stew!" shouted Gramp when the driving got hard in the red clay of Georgia. "Chittling, ham fat, buttered beans, corn pones, and parched corn! Chittling, baked possum, fried squirrel, mudfish, and pig's flank! Chittling! No wonder I don't feel well!"

Mamma would yawn and bury herself deeper into the fur robes and blankets on the back seat and say, "Now, Gramp, you ate very well at the last place."

"Sari, don't tempt me to curse our daily hot bread and fried meats, but, damn it, how do the hookworms keep alive in their hosts on this diet?"

Mamma said, "Where we are right now is more important."

" 'Gator steaks, rattlesnake meats fried in batter, spring chickens, turtle eggs, wop salad, garden greens in vinegar, pot likker, chittlings, chittlings, and pig's cheek!"

Mamma said in her voice that demanded an answer, "*Where are we?*"

"Lily bulbs, skunk cabbage, raccoon cutlets, jackassburgers, fox stew, and Southern-fried wildcat!"

By this time I knew Gramp was inventing some new Southern-fried food; at least I never remembered having eaten anything in his last list. Mamma sat up, dropping her blankets, and Gramp saw he had better stick to the subject on hand. He stopped the car on a ridge and waved his cigar at the brass-colored horizon. "I don't know where we are. Like the old Jews in the Wilderness, I had better ask for guiding help from the great big filling station in the sky for this lost tribe."

Mamma, who felt God was too respectable to be mocked like this, said, "Never mind showing off your freethinking. Are we anyplace near Tarheel Bend?"

"I hope so," said Gramp. We were hunting up one branch of the delta of the Savannah for my Uncle Paul's plantation. My Uncle Paul was the lazy one in the family who had made a place for himself in the world by marrying rich women. He made no effort. He just used to comb down his red curly hair, sit around, and, a month or so later, we'd hear he had married some cola heiress or turpentine countess or lumber queen. Or had run off with the wife of some Dixieland banker or New England cotton converter. "He was a respectable man and always married them, if he could. He was very kind to his wives and spent their money for their own good. He was always very sorry when the money was all spent. And he always left them with good, adoring regrets. They loved his memory as

long as they lived." At least that is the family legend. I have
never bothered to look up the number of his marriages, and
most likely he gained or lost a few virgins or plump young
matrons as the myth grew. I met only two of his wives. Both
adored him but could not afford to keep him long. Uncle Paul
had hobbies that cost a lot of money. Making sweet drinking
water from the salt ocean was one. I remember a car he built to
run on charcoal, a typewriter that didn't need a ribbon, hybrid
turkeys that came in all pastel colors. Oddly enough, most of his
hobbies have been perfected by other men. I had no idea what
his hobby was at the moment we were lost looking for Tarheel
Plantation. (It was named for a kind of black tobacco he was
growing that had all its nicotine in the lower discarded leaves,
and he was planning to put a safe cigarette on the market. It
is to be recorded that he did succeed in making the nicotine-free
tobacco—but the stuff was so vile-tasting no one could smoke
it with pleasure.)

Mamma was getting tired, and I was getting cold, and Gramp
was running out of Southern food to curse. It grew dark and
we ran out of gasoline. In 1920 there were few service stations,
and we sat by the side of the road until two Negroes came
along with a brace of mules. Gramp shouted, "You there,
where is Tarheel Plantation?"

"Sure 'nuff," said one of the mule drivers.

"Where is it?"

"Most likely still thar. Sure 'nuff."

Gramp spun a silver dollar through space, and one of the
mule drivers caught it and nodded. "That lil ole Tarheel place
'bout two ridges past the old gum tree by the chinaberry bush,
by the crick."

The other mule driver nodded and slapped his bare feet in
the roadside dust as he turned and pointed. " 'Pears like you
all jus' keep rollin' and you hits it right smack down the
pike."

"Sure 'nuff."

Gramp juggled a fistful of silver dollars and said, "Now you boys just hitch them jennies to the front of this car and pull us a bit, and I'll see you get plenty of cash."

"Mules tired pullin' stumps all day."

"This car don't weigh so much," said Gramp, making musical sounds with the silver.

"Sure 'nuff. Spencer, you go tie them jack rabbits to the auter, like the man says."

So in five minutes we were riding behind two mules along the clay road. By this time we were used to it. In our trip across the nation and back we had ridden behind hay wagons and muck carts and had once even been pulled by a shrimp boat out of a bog. In those days the roads were the kind that needed help. The cloverleaf grade crossing, the six-lane highways, the freeways, and heavy concrete roads were still undreamed-of, and unneeded.

"Git along, you Tom-mules . . . git along."

Gramp, a cold cigar in his mouth, was steering and was cursing under his breath. But as Mamma was leaning forward, he was cursing in his new private code. "Pecan pie, pork chops, pickled melon rind, and chittlings. Yams, corn on the cob, and apple butter. Rhubarb, stewed and jellied, fish pies, and chittlings!"

"Yo' say somethin', Judge?"

"No, just keep the jackasses moving."

"And steering," said Mamma, who was getting cold and angry and tired. In a half hour we turned down a road drenched in night-blooming flowers, past a mock orange tree and a white rail fence, beyond which a row of hickory trees led up to a Currier and Ives print of a white plantation house. Hound dogs, as usual, came out to sniff at us and the mules, and we passed grooms currying horses under a brick shed. It was all a mixture of *Gone with the Wind* and a novel by Henry James. Iron statues of colored boys painted in bright red stood with hitching posts by the wide porch, and a man came walking across the polished floor, a hooded hawk asleep on one wrist. I rubbed my eyes; you don't see many hooded hawks any more.

I was too young to sense the whole façade of a past that was being relived here. I was unaware that my Uncle Paul was trying to hold back time and vulgarity and change. I was young and sleepy, and too dumb to see around me something that had died fifty years before and died hard on the battlefields at Gettysburg and at Five Forks and Cold Harbor. And had gone down to ruin and glory with Robert E. "Massa" Lee and Jeff Davis and the bad romantic novels of Robert Chambers, Thomas Dixon, and Nelson Page.

I whimpered with cold and stiff limbs, and Mamma hugged me tight. The man with the hooded hawk on his wrist came closer and smiled. It was my Uncle Paul, older, but still thin, the red hair retreating into a handsome baldness, a small beard on his chin. The hawk on his wrist stirred, and he said sternly, "Easy, Warlock. Hello, Sari, Uncle, and who's the boy?"

"I'm Stevie," I said. "Is that an eagle?"

"No, a young kestrel. Happy to have you at Tarheel."

"Still playing at games?" Gramp asked of his nephew.

"Hawking, Uncle, is being revived in the South. I'm president of the Southern Hawking Society."

"I bet that cost a pretty penny. Damn it, Paul, get us some food and some fire."

Gramp paid off the mule drivers and they left in the gathering dark, the long ears of their mules wavering in the dusk as they retreated down the lane. We got inside the house. It was very big and very shiny and overpolished. There were old family pictures, crystal lighting fixtures, and acres of waxed floor. Even I had a feeling this was an expensive, re-enacted stage-set, a façade for a long-dead way of life, but I didn't push the idea. I was hungry.

A small scared-looking young woman came forward dressed in fluffy organdy and wearing heavy cameos at her throat. She held out a thin white arm in which the blue veins showed and said, "Welcome to Tarheel."

Her name was Ginny, and she was Uncle Paul's newest wife.

Tarheel was her place, and those were her family looking down at us from the oil paintings on the wall. I don't want to give the impression that Uncle Paul had married into the cream of the Southern families. Ginny was the granddaughter of a half-Indian, half-Yankee carpetbagger who had stolen most of the state, after Lincoln had been shot, and had married the daughter of a ruined family from Peachtree Street in Atlanta. Tarheel was not an old family place but a hog farm, a run-down plantation, when Ginny's father bought it. He rebuilt it and bought good furniture cheaply, getting a lot of stuff at foreclosure sales. When Ginny was left an orphan, she found she was rich, unhappy, and shy. Uncle Paul found her in a Charleston department store one afternoon trying to tell a clerk she wanted a compote pot not a *chamber* pot. Two days later they were married. Ginny made him a very good wife, and she had so much money that he would maybe never run through it all; and so it looked as if this would be his last marriage. (I was wrong.) Anyway, he tore down the place and rebuilt it again.

I have given the full background of Tarheel, not because as a boy I admired it (I did), but because we stayed there a month, and because Tarheel was such a rich background for two rather odd people, neither of whom were what they were trying to be, real ol' Southern family from away back thar.

I don't remember much of that first night, but I do remember three hawks on a stand behind Uncle Paul's chair and him feeding them raw chunks of meat that a Negro servant brought in on a silver tray. And Gramp filling his glass and Mamma asking about the hot water, was there enough for a bath?

Gramp was feeling better because my Uncle Paul's butler was an expert on making Sazerac cocktails: bourbon, a dash of absinthe (against the law), and Italian vermouth. This, shaken up through cracked ice and served with a cherry, would cause Gramp and Uncle Paul to toast the South and its hero, General Sazerac, in glowing words, although neither was a native-born Southerner.

But the thing that was really my Uncle Paul's reason on

earth in those days was his hawks. By apple trees, in a clearing away from the house, were his hawk cotes. He would take me out there in his heavy falconer's costume, wearing leather gloves, pick up a hooded hawk, ruffle its feathers, and explain its blood lines to me.

"Now, Stevie, there are all kinds of hawks and in the old days a man wasn't permitted to carry a hawk that didn't belong to his station in life. The king always carried an eagle; ordinary people had a kestrel. I have here long-winged falcons, pere-grines, sakers, and lannerets. Here, hold this."

I was wearing an old pair of gloves, and he set on my wrist a heavy yellow bird with shining yellow eyes. "That's Nero, my best saker."

"Can they catch things?" I asked as the hawk glared at me and dug his claws into my wrist.

"For rabbits and wild birds I use short-winged hawks. Gos-hawks, sparrow hawks; and they're good enough for a serge of heron, a spring of teak, a walk of snipe. . . ."

I didn't know what Uncle Paul was talking about. But I wrote it all down in my sketchbook that night and that's why I can put it down here now. Years later, reading Chaucer, I found out that each hunted animal and its groups had a special name: ducks ran in mobs called badelynge, and a charm of goldfinches meant a flock.

Uncle Paul was very serious about all this, and he took a small gray hawk out of a hutch and pulled off its leather hood. We walked across a beautiful meadow. And when Uncle Paul was sure he saw rabbits in a tangle of tall grass, he said, "Now watch, Stevie. These small hawks are called, not lured. Which means they don't swoop down, but are tossed toward the game from the hand. There. Go on, darling!"

He had tossed the hawk, and the bird went away like a flash and hit hard toward the ground. A rabbit screamed (they do, I found out) and the hawk rose with the struggling rabbit in its claws. Uncle Paul whistled and the hawk flew toward us, then into a tree, and began to eat the rabbit.

My Uncle Paul shouted, "That's what comes of not using

jesses, leather lines, and I've got to bell them. Hawks grow lazy too fast if you are kind to them. Come down, Rufus."

Rufus nibbled on his prey and paid us no attention. I got a little flushed because I knew Uncle Paul's dislike of anything that wasn't good breeding and social procedure. But we couldn't get Rufus down until he had finished the rabbit, the best parts, and sharpened his beak on the tree trunk. Then he came down, proudly, lordly, ruffling his feathers, his cruel eyes gleaming. Uncle Paul put on his turfed leather hood, and the hawk rested on his wrist, happy in the hunt. Uncle Paul was *not* happy.

That night he read Gramp and me a poem he had clipped from someplace, and he gave me the clipping, and I give it here. It was by a poet called Yeats, and I had never heard it before, but I think it gives a pretty good idea of what Uncle Paul, and Gramp, thought of the condition of the world.

> *Turning and turning in the widening gyre*
> *The falcon cannot hear the falconer;*
> *Things fall apart; the center cannot hold;*
> *Mere anarchy is loosed upon the world,*
> *The blood-dimmed tide is loosed and everywhere*
> *The ceremony of innocence is drowned;*
> *The best lack all conviction while the worst*
> *Are full of passionate intensity.*

I sometimes wonder if the poet ever had a falcon stuck in a tree. . . .

Life at Uncle Paul's was out of this world in the original meaning of those words. I felt, even at my age, cut off from the outer world, living in a blocked-off place and time that had no connection with the rest of the people busy someplace, making history and misery for themselves. It was pleasant and yet full of fantasy, and I have had only two or three periods like it in my life.

Mamma was resting up, "storing up juices," she said, "for the trip home." She and my aunt sat on the porch drinking

Mrs. Hatcher's Dry White Wine with soda water, a wine made of Thompson seedless grapes. I don't know what they talked of, for I didn't listen. But Gramp and Uncle Paul and I would find them there, dressed in white, the sun slanting away in the silent afternoon, the blue shadows printed on the ground, and little gray moths heralding the soon-falling dusk. We would talk of the day in crisp voices, laughing low among ourselves; then we would go slowly in to prepare carefully for dinner. The black butler would light the candles of scented beeswax, flavored with musk, in the silver holders, and Uncle Paul, all shirt front, would sit at the head of the table pulling the long ears of a sleepy hound dog edged between his legs. It all seems so far away, and I can only recapture it when I reread a page of Proust, or smell the faint odor of the old bundle of Mamma's letters.

The night before we left Uncle Paul's he gave us a dinner party with the local hawking society. Behind each male guest's chair stood a servant holding a hooded hawk; and when the toast was drunk, the owner took his bird and pulled off the hood, and the diamond-hard eyes of the hawks blinked in the firelight. I had a feeling the birds were thinking, "What is all this nonsense out of the past? There is a world outside making flivvers and bootleg gin, and the machine gun and the gangster rule of the night streets." Or maybe hawks are snobs and throwbacks too.

Gramp, with a hawk on loan (I think he did suggest a Hawk-of-the-Month Club to Uncle Paul, years later, and got properly snubbed), gave a few well-put toasts. I do remember a huge hawk cut from ice, filled with ice cream (I dreamed about it that night, and he carried me off, far off . . .).

As the live hawks stirred and the ice bird melted, I looked over the chestnut paneled walls, the Chippendale and Hepplewhite furniture, the Copley and Stuart paintings on the wall, the hickory logs falling together in sparks in the marble Adams fireplace, and I was aware of this house, this room, as being part of all the houses and places of my childhood.

I must explain the setting of the world I lived in as a boy and a young man, a world pretty much gone, just a few years later—all the rooms, halls, houses that have been by-passed or destroyed for the modern crates and the functional patter of the bright young men.

I grew up in well-built old houses, houses with lofty cool rooms, great sprawling porches, the graciousness not always of an abundant economy, but the ideas that a house had to be more than a machine to live in.

The curve existed, the magic of age to blend detail, much ornate detail, into a home where one could be comfortable and feel part of recorded history. I lived in crowded rooms, with too much well-loved furniture. Chairs were large and high, and one did not have to crouch on aching bones like savages low to the ground. The walls were never bare, the lighting never hidden. A house was not stripped down, no more than we sat around nude.

Gramp had been an engineer, a builder, so he knew the world of Horatio Greenough, of Louis Sullivan, and of Frank Lloyd Wright. He understood a great deal of what was happening and he hoped it would not become just sterile and fashionable. "Architecture is not the history of art," he used to say. "It's a nest you drag your things to and feel cozy in." Gramp had been one of the people who saw *art nouveau* born, at the Paris Exposition of 1900. The fluted, too delicate columns of cast iron, the steel flowers and tin weeds, buffets out of William Morris, and tentacles of unworldly tin orchids by Edgar Allan Poe, beat out by blacksmiths. Some writhing chairs of that period survived into my boyhood. Gramp knew Van de Velde, the inventor of *art nouveau*, and had told him it was a mistake. But the word *Modern* was in the air. The old houses could not evolve into new things; not in a hurry.

Mission furniture crept into our lives, I remember, from California. Big, square, ugly, held together with pegs, it was of golden oak varnished to a high gloss and had smelly leather pillows. With it went fake Spanish rafters, old rusting iron grilles, and wood art burned with hot needles to make picture frames and ash trays and tie holders. I had an aunt who was an artiste in this smoldering fire art and spent her entire life spoiling good wood with badly traced heads of Gibson girls, Indian maidens, and pine trees.

I can remember during our California visit the houses built up till 1914 along Japanese lines by Charles and Henry Greene. The Greene brothers built their modern houses of good, honest native wood, with overhanging roofs. Many still stand. (I spent a summer in one once rewriting a bad play with an insane collaborator. The house alone retains any charm in my memory.)

In a few years Gramp and I were to see the first *art moderne* at the Internationale des Arts Décoratifs, in Paris, during 1925. I was going to be a painter, and Gramp was pointing out the places in Paris where the artists herded together. *Art moderne* was rare hardwoods, inlaid with gold and mother-of-pearl. It was rich, heavy, square, the first attack of primitive cubism of the home. Paintings by Dupras, Marie Laurencin, futuristic lighting, zigzag skyscraper bookcases—and soon every Hollywood movie and nightclub in America was using *art moderne*. In bad taste, most of it, but the history of the past was now on the run. And the Germans were to take it and invent the piano-box house, the bent pipe chair, all the stark Germanic hate of comfort and beauty. "Modernism," it was called.

"From it came Bauhaus, the most dismal of all architecture," Gramp said, "the hiding of modern man in a series of dull colored boxes, the idea that owning rich good things was a sin." The German hatred of living certainly was in Bauhaus. Gramp used to rave at it and beat about with his cane in the houses of his friends where the *avant-garde* collected. All through my boyhood I tried to be loyal to Gramp's world *and* the new shapes that were already exciting me.

THE HAWK AND THE DRAKE

20

*Painting is the art of protecting
flat surfaces from the weather and
exposing them to the critic. . . .*
—AMBROSE BIERCE
(From Gramp's notebooks)

TOWARD THE NORTH STAR

JUST BEFORE WE LEFT UNCLE PAUL'S PLANTATION, Gramp and Mamma and I had to visit for the last time his collection of hunting birds. The golden and fawn-colored birds stared coldly, their cruel, jeweled eyes reflecting us so tiny and unimportant in the live mirrors set in their heads. I did a little water color of the birds for my aunt.

"Hawks," said Uncle Paul (off on his hobbyhorse), "have many troubles and many diseases. Megrims, casting their gorge, worms, gout, breaking the pounce. Oh, that's a bad one."

"I can guess," said Gramp, who had no more idea of what a hawk pounce was than I did. Uncle Paul went on, "Stone, gaping, foundering, cramp, and eating their own feet. But these birds I have kept in good health."

Mamma said, "They'd look good on a hat. Do they ever use hawk feathers on hats?"

"Only at Newport," said Uncle Paul. "But they don't know better."

Mamma said, "I don't trust a hawk."

Uncle Paul took a small, beautiful hawk from its perch and put it on my gloved wrist. I had by that time learned how to handle a hawk, and the wonderful creature balanced on my wrist and looked at me with contempt, as all hawks do on the human race.

Uncle Paul said, "That's a fine lanneret; I like it even better than a saker or peregrine hawk. I call it Moses. Stevie, I want you to have Moses as a parting gift."

Mamma said, "He already has a canary back home."

I said, "Oh, Uncle Paul, do you think I can raise a hawk?"

"I've written you out full directions. You'll learn a lot from this hawk. His manners, his habits, are different from that of tamed herd animals. Maybe he'll make something fine out of your life."

Gramp said, "Now, Paul, don't get overrating this; you prefer these damn feather dusters to people. Don't expect Stevie to retreat into the past. You keep wine in the past, not people."

I always remembered that remark of Gramp's. I think it kept me from resigning from time to time from the human race. For I did own a real hunting hawk named Moses.

He was resting on my wrist, hooded for travel, when we pulled away from Tarheel Plantation, uncle and aunt standing on their wide white porch watching us depart. I can still see them there, and I suppose they went indoors to dress for dinner later, but I can't get out of my mind the picture of them standing there, among the treasures of a just-gone past, retired from the modern scene, in retreat from a world they never made. And so they faded out of memory, out of family history. I don't really know to this day just what happened to them. Uncle Paul, some ten years later, had a new wife, a ranch house, and new fortune, and perhaps a new hobby; but I hope he still kept a few hawks.

We were heading north, and Gramp and Mamma were in a good mood. Gramp was very old, and Mamma was accepting— for the moment—the idea of burying herself in Papa's adoring of her. Papa, I fear, was a dull man by Mamma's and Gramp's standards, and I don't think she was a very happy woman when I was growing up. But on that ride north, released from the museumed past of Uncle Paul, they were both gay and looking forward to the journey home through flowering dogwood blossoms and the smell of wood-smoke cooking dinners in small cabin clearings.

Gramp was driving us in the general direction of Charleston, driving quickly over the mud bottoms of the Carolinas, trapping himself in the arms of Port Royal Sound. We crossed so many ferries that Mamma said she expected to see "the coast of Ireland any minute." But then Mamma was never very strong in the matter of maps. It amazed me to find there were two Edisto rivers, even if the natives swore it was the same stream. We seemed to recross it every ten miles. Anyway, we found ourselves on Edisto Island, and Gramp gave up and said, "Let's rest, eat, sleep."

I have not much memory of a town also called Edisto, except for a small shop that sold smoked eels and deviled crabs and served a very hard sea biscuit. I still remember the fine nutty taste of the biscuit. It was no tourist shelter, but a fishermen's depot, where the fish were prepared and iced and packed to be shipped north.

There was a smoking soup of cods' tongues. A fisherman came over to us and said, "You them folk what got that car?"

"That's right," said Gramp. "Touring."

"Damn funny place to tour."

Mamma smiled. "We're lost."

"Heading whereabouts?"

"Charleston," I said, feeding my hawk Moses some fish scraps.

"Just keep headin' north and you'll hit it. That's some eagle, boy."

"That's no eagle; it's a hunting hawk."

"Law against catching eagles," said the fisherman. "Yankees call it the national bird. Personally I'd rather have a sea gull. But you know Yankees."

"We're Yankees," said Mamma.

The fisherman nodded. "Not real Yankees; they don't come here. They go to the fancy places and spoil the hired help. If that's a hawk, sonny, somebody goin' to kill it fer you."

"Why?" said Gramp.

"Well, there is a bounty on hawks. They eat some mighty fine chicks hereabouts and they are varmints that go after small game. Guess the state pays two dollars a head bounty on a hawk."

I said, "But this isn't a wild hawk. It's been home-raised."

The fisherman was joined by another fisherman. "Let's hear it talk."

I said, "It can't talk."

"House birds all talk."

Gramp said, "Only parrots talk, not hawks."

The two fishermen looked at each other, and Mamma said, "I'm sure two real Southern gentlemen like you-all two wouldn't turn in a little boy's pet birdie, would you now?"

"Well now, Ma'am, that ain't the Southern way to do things, you knows that. It's just that there are folk around, strangers, moved in from up North, Baltimore, that might do anything fer a dollar."

"Strangers?" said Gramp.

"Yep, come here 'bout forty, fifty years ago. We still ain't sure of them. They might take a shine to the bounty for that there hawk."

"Thank you," said Gramp. "I'd like to buy you both a drink."

"Bourbon and branch water will do fine, thank you."

So we didn't stay the night, but Gramp drove us miles up the coast, and we put Moses into a cardboard carton. Mamma lettered on it: *New Chicks. Do Not Open and Expose to Cold Air.* It was very fine of Gramp and Mamma to do this for me; they were tired and the roads were bad and they didn't really care for Moses. My hawk snapped at everyone's fingers, and his bite was mean.

It was way past midnight when we came into Charleston. I was asleep holding the big carton on my lap, and Moses had given up tapping out code messages on it with his beak. I remember a dimly lit hotel lobby, the smell of harbor water, and the red, worn rugging, a high hanging brass light fixture, the buzz of night flies, and a picture of Robert E. Lee. Then I was asleep, and when I woke up the sun was shining. Moses was perched on top of the headboard, catching the last moth of the night. There was a note for me from Gramp:

"Don't move. Have gone to scout out the land. If anyone asks, Moses is a young molting turkey from up North. Sari says wash behind the ears and change your underwear. Back before noon. Gramp."

From the hotel window I could see the blooming azaleas and the japonicas. There was a regatta at the Carolina Yacht Club, and a Negro was driving up and down the street with a watering cart laying the dust, followed by barefooted coffee-colored kids splashing after the watering cart. I felt lonely and forgotten, and Moses bit me when I tried to pat him.

We were staying at the Planters Hotel. (Not the new Planters Hotel, which was rebuilt in 1937, but the original one started in 1810.) Planters' Punch was invented here. I wondered if Gramp and Mamma had forgotten me and were trying the local product.

Around noon they were back with a tall handsome man whom Mamma introduced as Mr. St. Julian Ravenel, and Gramp explained he was a grandson, or something, of the original Dr. Ravenel who had invented the rebel torpedo boat *Little*

David in the Civil War. I could see that Gramp had been fighting the war over again. Mr. Ravenel went up to Moses and said, "That's a mighty fine bird. So that's the hawk you're scared someone will take away from you?"

"That's right," I said, "his name is———"

Gramp said suddenly, "Jeff Davis, just plain Jeff Davis, nothing fancy as to name, but a good one, eh, Colonel Ravenel?"

Mamma pushed me as I was going to correct Gramp, and Mr. Ravenel said, "Mighty fine bird. Don't you fear, young man. Your critter is safe. The General here and I, we're going to a cockfight out on my farm near the Citadel, but we'll all have dinner tonight."

"You're too kind," said Mamma, batting her eyelashes, "*much* too kind."

"Nothin', Mrs. Longstreet, nothin'. And I've arranged for a guest card for you all at the Charleston Country Club."

Mamma and I spent the afternoon taking a sea ride out to Fort Sumter in the harbor. There was a boat at the foot of King Street that made the trip, and Mamma felt that I should learn history by being on the spot.

"She wouldn't," Gramp said, "follow tourists even to see the Garden of Eden with the original cast and costumes."

The boat captain got a pillow for Mamma to sit on and said, "My grandfather rowed General Beauregard over to the fort when the Yankees dropped their flag, to take their surrender."

"The flag was shot away," said Mamma. "They didn't lower it."

"That's *their* story, ma'am."

The island was impressive to me. I had grown up on Gramp's ten-volume set of *The Photographic History of the Civil War*. And in my boyhood I could recite all the battles, name all the uniforms, and outline every try at taking Richmond. Before I could walk I was already opening a volume of the great work and turning the pages to look at the hundreds of magnificent photographs.

The next day, Mamma and I went to the Cypress Gardens to see the flowering bulbs and be impressed by the deadly looking cypress swamp. The little old lady who sold postal cards there said sweetly to us, "My family hid their silver here when the Yankee looters passed. Never did find my aunt's silver coffee set."

"Not *all* Union soldiers were looters," said Mamma, folding her arms.

"No, I guess not; they had half-wits too, I reckon."

I took Mamma's arm and shook my head.

Back at the hotel, Mamma said, "I'm not going to see another place. There must be some people here who don't still want to fight the g.d. war over again."

I was feeding Moses raw meat and the ends of my fingers. I said, "What's happened to Gramp? More cockfights?"

Mamma was trying on a hat and looking at herself in the mirror. "He promised to be back by four."

Gramp was back at five, a little unsteady on his feet because of the work in the hot sun watching the cocks fight.

He said, with an accent, as he dressed for dinner, "Nice country hereabouts. Yankees never really understood it. I say they all sho' got a raw deal hereabouts. Yo' take rough soldiers and——"

Mamma turned around slowly and said in her frozen voice, crisply, "I would just like to remind you, Captain Longstreet, that *you* led a company of Union horsemen on raids not very far from here. And I think I'll amuse the dinner guests tonight with the story you always tell of wrecking that big plantation house one night and pouring coal oil and flour into the pianos and stabling *your* horses in the French living room."

I added, "And the time you said you horsewhipped two gentlemen who wouldn't take their hats off to the flag, and you tied them on mules backward, bare-assed, and rode them home."

Gramp stared, then sat down on the bed and wiped his face slowly, "Lord, love a hoe handle, you ghouls want to get me tarred and feathered and ridden out of Charleston on a fence rail!"

Mamma showed no mercy. "And that Southern lady who wrote something against Lincoln on a wall and you made her get down on her hands and knees with soap and water and scrub it off until her lily white hands bled."

Gramp held up his arms. "I'm waving the white flag, Sari. What have I done?"

Mamma said, "I don't want to hear the word Yankee out of you, and not one word about the Civil War tonight. Not even a small one, like "Grant," or "rifle." And no accent—Southern or otherwise."

Gramp sighed and said, "I promise. Hell hath no fury like a woman defending her young or her homeland. How is Moses feeding, Stevie?"

"Pretty good; he took a real nip out of the bellboy today. How about matching him with one of Colonel Ravenel's fighting cocks?"

Gramp looked at Mamma and shook his head. "No, you young people are much too bloodthirsty. Sari, I don't know what we're going to do with the younger generation."

Mamma said, "Change your socks, Stevie, and button me up in the back."

We were dining in a famous private club that night. I wish I could remember its name. It was near Battery Park and had iron scroll railings and marble pineapple posts, which were a sign of welcome.

Everyone was dressed for dinner, and the pictures of Generals Francis Marion, Washington, and Lee looked down on us. Gramp didn't write down many details about the event; maybe Mamma had hurt his feelings that day. He did list some drinks special to the South, but I'm not sure he wrote them down in Charleston: Soufriere Lime Punch, made with Persian limes, honey and rum, Ramos Gin Fizz, imported from New Orleans.

Everyone slept late the next day, and I came awake near noon to find Charleston still outside the window, and the bell-boy shaking me.

"Yo' molting turkey is loose in the garden and it's fightin' with a duck."

I came fully awake, and as Gramp and Mamma were still sleeping I got into my clothes and went down to the gardens. Moses was in a tree and he was swooping down from time to time over a big drake. The drake seemed to think Moses was a new kind of lady duck, and every time he arched his neck amorously, Moses raked him with his claws and tried to lift him. But the drake was too big to carry into the tree.

The drake gave up suffering for love and I shooed him away. I said to Moses, "Come on, boy, fight in your own class."

Moses looked at me and got his feathers in order. I held out my wrist. A small crowd gathered around me. The hawk spread his wings, sailed down, and landed on my wrist. He looked around him at the mob. Calmly he nipped the nearest person, then put his head under a golden wing and went to sleep. I went back to our rooms through the lobby, the beautiful hawk on my wrist, everyone staring. For the first time, I suddenly understood what Gramp had meant when he said, "Stevie, you don't have to be like everybody else, or anybody else. Not if you don't want to."

I knew I wanted to be like the hawk, my hawk, the hawk I would never really own, the bird who was a living symbol of the dignity of life. I saw that Uncle Paul had been right in giving me a hawk to learn something from. Back in the room I fed the cruel and handsome bird; somehow I was aware he would never bite me too hard again.

THE DECK BAND

A man first quarrels with his father about three-quarters of a year before he is born. It is then he insists on setting up a separate establishment.

—SAMUEL BUTLER
(From Gramp's notebooks)

JOURNEY BY SEA

OUR CAR WAS CHUGGING ITS WAY HOME, GOING NORTH between green fields; it was plain "as the nose on a drunkard's face," said Gramp, "the old car is dying under us." It was true. The car was battered, repaired by hammers, bound with baling wire, soldered, bolted, and patched by a half a hundred blacksmiths, garagemen, and anyone handy or not with a wrench.

It still ran, but it had strange diseases now; it moaned crossing sand roads, it balked and belched blue smoke on damp mornings, it locked wheels crossing railroad tracks, and the steering wheel froze in trolley rails. Gramp had to go out and kick the wheels free when she wouldn't steer. But the car ran. With every rattle we expected it to break down into a few hun-

dred pounds of old junk. But it didn't. We were in Virginia, going by Norfolk and Princess Anne, stabbing for Chesapeake
Bay, where Gramp was going to spare the car by having all of us
get onto a boat and ride up to Point Centerville. We were trying
for Yorktown, where I knew Cornwallis had been holed up by
General Washington, but by this time I was sure he was already gone. Gramp wanted to pick up the oyster boat *Harry R.*
there, but somehow Yorktown kept evading us. There were
many rivers, too many streams, and every farmer had set up a
ferry and held out his hand for a dollar. Mamma gave up at
Williamsburg.

"Don't bother," she said. "Let me die here on another riverbank. There is no Yorktown, no boat called *Harry R.* I don't
even know what my name is."

"Sari," I said, wedging in my hawk's box.

Gramp got down out of the car and went over to a post and
tried to make out a tattered poster.

" 'County Fair,' " he read. " 'Sulky Racing, Plowing Con-
tests, Prize Cattle, Washington Post Road Band.' "

"Any other clues?" I asked.

Gramp read on, " 'At Tappenhannock, June fifth, 1896.' "

"Too late," said Mamma, sinking back on the buffalo robe.

Gramp got back into the car and started it with a kick, and
we went on down a red clay road. The car died suddenly, and
hot steam came pouring up over us from the hood. We knew we
would have to have a gallon of water at once. The car was getting a little bit like Old Faithful at Yellowstone, going off like
this every few hours. Mamma put up her silk sunshade and sat
there expressionless. She knew it was no use being scared, female, or acting panicky. It had happened too often. She said,
"Scald us alive, old man. Lose us, get us eaten by insects. But
don't say Yorktown *again.*"

Gramp said something else. And I, being practical, said,
"There's people down the road at the crossroads church."
There was, and Gramp peered at it and nodded.

"Seems to be an old-fashioned church picnic. Sari, I feel a return to faith and the godhead. There is water there, and cider, and food. Come on."

Mamma brushed herself and shook her skirts, Gramp curled back his mustache, and we started off down the road, only a few hundred feet. A neat white church stood back from the road, resting among the dead under plain marble gravestones. On a broad lawn, shaded by century-old elms, benches and tables had been put out and baskets of food were being opened. A long yellow paper sign had been put up and it read:

THREE RIVERS CHURCH SOCIAL
50¢
All You Want to Eat for the Church Organ

A prancing oldster, stroking a small white beard, came over to us and shook Gramp's hand. "Welcome, brother," he said. "Welcome to the food and God. The name is Fauves. John K. Fauves. Hardware. Have my card."

We all shook the hand, and a small butterball of a man with a very pink face came over and said in a mountain twang, "The Reverend Sutter. Welcome to the social."

Gramp put some paper money in his hand. "A mighty fine church and a good cause. I hope your organ is in good condition."

"It's new," said Reverend Sutter, "but not paid for yet."

"But in active use," said Gramp.

Mamma stuck Gramp with her sunshade. Gramp nodded and looked at the loaded tables and pointed out to Mamma and myself where we should sit. A fat old lady clicking china store teeth made room for us. "Sister Lee is my name. Run the town linen shop. Here is my card. My, doesn't that food look good?"

It seemed a foolish question to us. We sat down and ate, Mamma smiling and acting dainty, but managing to pack it away properly for such a tiny lady.

Fed, rested, and with Gramp putting a twenty-dollar gold coin toward the minister's new organ, we drove off, contented and digesting. We had even been set on the right road for York-town.

Gramp licked his lips and sighed. "That's the way to do the Lord's work: with knife and fork. Tastier than beating an old dogma with a new stick."

Mamma said, "I wish I had a bigger stomach."

Gramp nodded. "A well-fed Christian is not going to convert his neighbors or burn down old gods with brand and fire. The lean fanatic really needs food, not a mission."

"Yorktown," I said, pointing to a sign saying the same thing. And soon we were rolling down a red-brick-paved street under the grandfathers of all trees. Even the *Harry R.* was at her dock, a dirty old ash-white wreck of a once-great river boat with her old-fashioned smokestacks and some still-remaining shreds of gingerbread decoration. "Like the few remaining teeth in a once beautiful woman," Gramp said sadly. She had big paddle wheels, and we drove right on board.

Mamma said, "She's an old boat."

Gramp agreed. "They don't make 'em like this any more."

Mamma said, "Has it a safety valve?"

Steam was hissing and moaning in the vents and whistles, and steam leaked here and there from many rusty pipes. Gramp nodded. "Don't worry. They know how to work it. They sit a small Nigger, not too hefty, on the safety valve, and if the pressure builds up too fast, why it shoots that darkie up so high they know they better stop feeding the engines pitch pine. Makes nice black smoke, doesn't it?" (Gramp treated Negroes like full members of the human race—no better—but he spoke Civil War English.)

I agreed and let my pet hawk Moses sit on my wrist and enjoy the bay breeze. We cast off, and the heavy strokes of the engine beams shook the scarred deck; the paddle wheels began to hurry around and beat up the green water into foam. Barrels of oysters stood around. Two big turtles lay on their backs sighing, and bins of ice held dying deep-sea fish. I was impressed by the eatable treasures of the sea around us and unaware of what a hack they had made of a once-proud river queen. I still remember the turtles sighing and actually weeping real tears. They made fine stew.

A few years later the *Harry R.* blew up with a great shower of red hot iron and fancy woodwork. She died game, in a fury.

It was a clear warm day, the boat rocked slowly, but was no bother, and the inlets and shores passed "like Corots," Gramp said, and the little shanty boat with a barefoot native trying out his guitar, the fishline tied to his nude toe; dogs and kids splashing bare-bottomed in the shallows, and old colored men, with woolly heads white as cotton, pulling up flat mudfish or raking oysters with the slowest of slow motion, stopping to spit or relight their hand-whittled corncob pipes. It was a world not in a hurry. Sometimes, far off, a freighter hooted, and often a sea gull, cruel, glassy-eyed, came down to stare at Moses resting on my wrist, making hawk sounds in his crop as he digested the raw beef I had fed him.

On the shore roads bordering the bay, men worked fields with a bull-tongued plow, pulled usually by a pair of oxen, heavy and slow. Wood smoke was scribbled in soft lead on the horizons, and from below came the smell of pitch pine burning, and hot brass and boiler iron, and the herd of sheep in the hold, and the gumbo cooking in the cook's galley. A perfect robin's-egg-blue day.

Gramp and I stood at the top rail near the fancy wheelhouse and the six-foot steering wheel and looked over the dancing waters flecked with sun. Gramp, who was out of cigars, chewed on a bit of clean pine wood.

Mamma came up on deck a little pale but freshly dressed and walking high on her heels. Gramp sidled up to her and tossed away his bit of wood.

"Sari, I'd like to bring something fine home. For the house. What do you think of milk glass? Beaded milk glass."

"It's very pretty," Mamma said. She didn't really give a damn about running a house. "Very pretty."

"They make it in Dover, over in Delaware. I want you to pick out a barrel of it for the house."

Mamma said, "Be glad to, Gramp. How much longer are we on this seagoing fish crate?"

"Oh, a hundred and seventy miles from Yorktown to Centerville, guessing a bit. We'll be in by morning. I've gotten you a stateroom with a berth. Stevie and I will rough it in the grand salon."

"Saloon?" I said.

Gramp shook his head. "Saloons are gone."

The bell rang for dinner. There was pan-fried veal, piping hot, a huge shrimp and crab gumbo, and what the mate called fried "chicken" rabbit.

After this dinner, Gramp managed to get a cigar from a man named Josh Cohen, who was "traveling in cotton gray goods from Baltimore." Gramp gave me the cigar band, and he smoked and talked to Mr. Cohen while I aired my hawk, who brooded and couldn't get used to the roll of the sea.

I went down and kissed Mamma good night in her narrow berth. Gramp and I went into the salon and took off our shoes and got comfortable on some huge leather sofas. The hawk slept on the horns of a deer's head on the wall, and Gramp nursed the last inch of cigar with care. A dim light came from a wavering oil lamp turned low in the ceiling. The big paddle wheels beat the sea to fragments with the sound of hissing foam. We floated on water, suspended, I felt, over the solid earth like a magic act.

Gramp looked up at the ceiling. "Always go to sea when things trouble you, Stevie. Always get away, far away from things that make you mean and jumpy. And a sea trip is a great cure. I feel I'm running down like a dollar clock. It's not going to be easy for Sari and Henry after I'm gone. And the world, hell, I've seen better worlds next door on a starry night. But this is the only world you'll have, Stevie, so enjoy it, live it. The world took a wrong turn someplace, I'm not professor enough to figure out just where, but it isn't going to be easy to take for a few hundred years. I've had all the best of it. Yes, sir. But face it, boy, and come toss a flower on an old man resting in all the earth a man needs; old Tolstoy had it right: six feet."

I knew when Gramp was talking like this he needed to, what he called, "wet his whistle." The hawk stirred, opened wide his great wing span, and roughly fanned the air. He dug his claws into the deer horn and then settled down to dream red dreams (I was sure) of tearing muscles and hearing the small sad cries of cornered animals.

A large colored man from the deck band, shiny as a horse's saddle at a horse show, came in and stood at Gramp's elbow. "Con'nel, the Cap'n he says maybe you would like some forty-rod. I'se got me a uncle what makes it prime up a crick, pure mash and buck and run it twice through a quill point. Cap'n drink it all the time."

Gramp held up some bills and said, "Don't sell it, deliver it."

"Mighty potent, Con'nel. Yaller as a beginner brown, and jist as full of rock an' roll. Heh! Heh!"

Gramp took the flat bottle from the colored man and sat up and poured himself a shot glass full. He looked at it with care and said, "It's got the beads and the body."

"Con'nel, I don't handle no catpee trash. I leaves that to the pore white no-account scum. I cater to gentry only, like the Cap'n."

He went out and I watched Gramp sip it slowly. The sadness left his face, he beat his chest and swallowed hard, and he made a mouth gesture, puckering and relaxing. He lay down again at my side, creaking his great bone joints with pleasure.

"Man came out of the sea, boy. He floats on it, but he never licks it. It carries us on the skin of winds." He took a pull on the cigar and a swallow of the brew. "Don't get too old, Stevie. It's best to go in one's prime: unsated, still with illusions, a tang in the air. Make it a fast coming into life, a fast going out. All is vanity, all is vanity, the great Jews shouted in the Wilderness, and they are right. But in vanity we are above the beasts. Boy, put something under my feet."

I got up and put a leather pillow under his feet. I took away the cigar and put it out in a brass tray. I took the glass from his big knobby hands. I sniffed at the delightful odor from the bottle and corked it. The hawk heard me. I made a small lip noise, a secret sound between us. The bird came down in a swoop and landed on my wrist, guided by my lipping call, for the oil lamp had gone out in a reek of burning wick. I went up on deck. It was moonlit, the shore passing, the waters heavy with dark patches. I let the hawk loose to fly and he floated in the wake of the churning paddle wheels as if using their air currents. Then he wheeled off toward shore. He darted down into darkness, and I watched. He flew back carrying something small and furry in his claws. He came down on the top of the pilothouse, by the brass eagle there. I turned to look at our trailing, spinning wake. So much beauty I felt—so much of cruel things, beautiful and dreadful as a feeding hawk. An old man reliving his life, and my mother floating in her sleep three feet over the water. I swallowed it all without understanding too much.

COLLECTING MILK GLASS

Matthew, Mark, Luke and
John . . .
Went to bed with their trousers
on.
(In my handwriting in Gramp's
notebooks)

THE LONG WAY HOME

WE GOT TO DOVER, DELAWARE. IN THE MAIN I REMEMBER
it as being like almost every American town between California
and New Jersey; it was a style that was first to irk me, then
amaze me, and later to impress on my mind the gradual drift of
the nation into a pattern of conforming, accepting, and living.
The same motion pictures, magazines, the uniform shape of
hats, color of ties, size of doughnuts, and sound of slang lived in
Broken Wheel, Oklahoma, West Lung, Texas, East Neck, Long
Island, and Scatterville, Vermont. In Texas the boots would be
high-heeled, in Ohio the hat brims narrower, in Boston the
beans drier, and in Florida frying chicken a little too often. But
in the main when you had seen one American town, you had
seen them all.

We were let into the Dover House late at night and I at once fell asleep after tying my hawk's leash to the brass bed rail. I came awake at morning to find the hawk making his crop noises and shifting from leg to leg. Gramp had gone off on some business relating to his copper company incorporated in Delaware ("for simple reasons"), having a meeting of stockholders. Mamma too had gone, having left early to see about buying milk-glass vases and lamp bases and plates to take back home to the relatives. I don't know if they make milk glass any more, but in my boyhood it was a white opaque glass that you could hardly see through, and usually it was covered with small white bumps. In the form of a shade for a bronze or brass student lamp it gave off a glowing pleasant light, and when filled with water, if it were a vase, the roses and their long stems had an added charm in milk glass. It had some value in those days; today good examples of it are rare and cost a great deal of money. I hate to think how much of it Gramp broke. At home he used to start talking on some subject: "Just expressing myself, damn it, but you'd think people would learn to leave my canes alone." He would pick up a milk-glass vase and bang it down on the dining-room table, to make his point. "It isn't as if there aren't enough hockey sticks and baseball bats around, some wet-nosed little bastard has been using my best blackwood cane, a gift from Sam Clemens ("Mark Twain," Mamma used to whisper to me), to knock tin cans around in the street. Which one of you whelps did it?" And Gramp would attract the attention of all the grandchildren (and they were a mob) by banging a steak knife hard against a milk-glass lamp.

It was the rare glass item that could take more than three or four of Gramp's angry bangs before shattering. And as I had been among the group who had batted tin cans with Gramp's canes, I would just look at the ceiling and wait for the sound of breaking glass and Gramp's howl of rage at the sight.

But in Dover, when Mamma was collecting the glassware, none of us knew its real value, or its dismal fate-to-be. I went down to breakfast, brought back a section of raw meat for my hawk, and fed it to him with wary cunning, having learned to pull back my fingers with speed and skill from his sharp beak. I was always under the impression that I lost a finger to him, but I have reached adulthood and find I have all the ten fingers I was born with.

At noon the phone rang in our room; it hung on the wall, was of fumed oak and black rubber, and I had to stand very close to hear. It was Gramp.

"High noon, boy, high noon. Rise and shine."

"I've been up for hours."

"Stop bragging. You hungry?"

"I could eat."

"A growing boy should always be hungry. Sari around?"

"She left early to buy milk glass."

"Well, you meet me at the Three Sisters for lunch. Bring my big cigar case in my tweed jacket. You get a hired car and tell him to bring you to the Three Sisters Inn. And don't forget the cigars."

I quoted, " 'A woman is only a woman, but a good cigar is a smoke.' "

I heard Gramp laugh his high bourbon laugh at the other end. "You better go back to reading Poe and the rest of them. Did you know that Byron and Shelley were Keats together?" He laughed again and hung up with a bang. I figured out the mint juleps had been passed out at the stockholders' meeting.

I got the cigar case and went down and ordered a taxi, and while it went toward the Inn of the Three Sisters, I dreamed what I would do with the shares of Gramp's copper millions that I would inherit. I decided I would marry a redheaded actress with very small feet, like on the colored pictures they once gave out with cigarettes. I would raise long-eared hound dogs, I would invent a shower that flowed just warm, not cold or scalding, and I would go to Yale and wear a turtle-neck sweater, smoke a bent pipe like Sherlock Holmes, keep a bull-dog, and grow a mustache that could be twisted into curling loops. All this hardly seemed to dent the millions I would get someday, and I gave up thinking of spending and decided I was hungry.

The Three Sisters were really three sisters, Spanish-looking girls, the daughters, Gramp told me, "of a shipwrecked sailor who had drifted ashore, married, spawned, and then moved on," leaving the three dark beauties, who had been taught cooking by their father. ("Proving," said Gramp, "that all great chefs are men." "Proving," said Mamma, "that give a fool a white cap and a big spoon and he'll act like Napoleon among the cold cuts.") The Three Sisters Inn did not look impressive, but it had charm, and under the big elm tree at a snow-white tablecloth sat Gramp, twisting his mustache back and inspecting with pleasure the silver mint-julep mug in his fist. ("Never crush the mint leaves, Stevie, *just* bruise them. And always drink it from a silver mug. The man that would drink juleps out of glass would present *The Boston Cooking School Cook Book* to Oscar at the Ritz.")

Gramp looked at me. "You hungry?"

"Yes."

"Pull up a chair. Things went well at the stockholders' meeting. Diverting the debentures and getting the nonvoting stock divided. Things are a bit below par, but when we get a real floating of new issues and divide the old three for one . . . You follow me?"

"No. Are we going to be rich?"

He looked at me closely and frowned. "Does it matter?"

I thought. "I was thinking it over in the cab. No. Not very much. There aren't enough things I want to buy."

He slapped me on the back. "That's my lad. Understands the futility of desire, the hollowness of material things. Let's eat!"

The sisters were busy inside, and two of them came out with trays and the third one stood in the doorway, holding her roasting fork like a marshal's baton. Gramp bowed to them and introduced me and we fell to. It was a fine lunch. There was baked rockfish cooked with wild rice. ("A grass, Stevie, not at all a true rice. Indians go out in the swamps with their dugout boats, drift among the wild grass, and beat the heads off it with their paddles. What falls into the dugouts they call wild rice. They wash it and cook it, but the Indians didn't wash it in the old days.")

The three sisters watched us eat with pleasure, and Gramp then presented each a good cigar, and being a sailor's daughters, and Spanish—at least in part—they all lit up and smoked.

When we got back to the hotel Mamma was there with lots of milk glass in the shape of vases and plates and other brittle domestic forms.

Mamma said, "I spent a lot of money."

Gramp nodded and tested a bit of glass with a finger, tapping it sharply and listening as it rang out. "Nice clear sound."

"What does it mean," I asked, "when it rings?"

"Nothing," said Mamma, pulling off her long gloves. "The only thing you tap and get an answer from is a melon. If it's ripe it echoes."

"Cut glass," said Gramp. "You can tell the lead content of cut glass by tapping it."

Mamma made a low *hmmmm* sound in her throat. "Cut glass, really, Gramp, cut glass isn't anything but something you get for free by cutting out soap wrappers."

"Damn!" said Gramp, who had a huge collection of cut glass and was well aware that the better people concluded it was vulgar. I liked the feel of it, the running of my fingers over its facets, but I too thought it vulgar, and what was worse, ugly. But no one except Mamma ever told Gramp his cut glass wasn't fashionable any more.

Mamma said, "There's an old farm below town, people named Rodgers own it, used to be very important but have come down in the world. They are selling their milk glass and also some ruby glass. We'll drive out tomorrow."

Gramp looked over the milk glass spread around the room and said, "Haven't we enough?"

"You have a lot of daughters-in-law, Gramp. They'll all want a few bits."

Gramp gave in and went away muttering something about prime cut glass.

The next morning we started north. In the back of the car the milk glass, packed in straw and crated, rested on our luggage. In front the three of us cheerfully looked forward to getting home. We crossed Delaware Bay to Cape May, and we tried to get through to the New York house by phone. One of the maids answered and said the family had gone to the summer place in Pittsfield, "up in the Massachusetts." Gramp frowned and shook his head. "We'll never make it. The car is wearing out."

"Let's try," said Mamma. "She can't let us down."

"Sari, a machine has no soul. You can't appeal to its emotions."

"Maybe if we lightened the load?"

Gramp nodded. "We'll ship the glass and most of the luggage express to Pittsfield. Maybe we'll make it."

So we got rid of most of our luggage and shipped it north by express. Then we went back to the local hotel to get Mamma. The hotel clerk said she had gone picking dogwood blossoms down by the crick (the natives never say creek, only *crick*).

Mamma was certainly there, under the flowering dogwoods, and as she saw us she waved her red sunshade at us. Somebody had left a black four-year-old bull down there, near the creek, and he saw Mamma wave the sunshade too and started for her. Gramp yelled and picked up a two-by-four fragment of lumber and I followed. Mamma saw the bull, turned, looked around her, and very bravely stood her ground. It would have been foolish to run on the boggy soil. As the bull came near, she ducked behind a tree. The bull skidded, braked, and turned, only to face Gramp swinging the two-by-four timber. It hit that bull on the nose, and the creature bellowed and backed. Gramp stepped forward and banged again, and the bull, outraged, went off to stick his sore nose in the cooling mud. I've never been much impressed by bullfighters since.

The encounter cheered everyone up, and we drove up and over the sand roads north, singing "Old MacDonald Had a Farm." Mamma admitted she had been afraid. "But the thing that worried me most was the fear he would disfigure my face, and that I would look a horror in my coffin. Somehow I don't fear death, Gramp, but it's dying I find a problem."

Gramp looked proudly at Mamma and said the best thing he could think of offhand. "Sari, what a man you would have made."

GRAMP'S FARM

23.

*Yet meet we shall, and part, and
meet again
When dead men meet, on lips of
living men.*
(From Gramp's notebooks)

GOOD-BY

THE WOMEN OF MAMMA'S WORLD DRESSED WELL, OR-
nate by our modern stripped-down standards which have discarded decoration, also hips, breasts, and a full head of hair.
Mamma's best years for fashion were from 1900 to 1920, a
period that has been vulgarized by inaccurate movies and
plays.

Her coiffure was often elaborate, her titian-colored hair, later
shading to bronze, was worn puffed up at the sides, helped by
pads, and often ornamented by amber, tortoise-shell, and be-
jeweled combs. Waves and curls came natural to her, but she
helped them by fingering and pressing and combing into place.
She washed her hair in wine-colored soap, and she dressed it
before a huge cheval glass. Women used a lot of arm and body
powder, but face painting was frowned upon. Mamma touched
up a little here and there.

We were going to visit some family friends in Boston before

going on to Pittsfield, and Mamma kept talking about clothes
and Gramp couldn't stand it. "I like a well-turned-out woman,
Stevie. Hell, I collect windy days. If I get two or three good
windy days a month I feel I'm living. Just standing there
watching the women pass and indexing their clothes while the
wind blows."

"Gramp!" Mamma said in her cold voice, meaning he wasn't
to talk that way to me.

"I tell you, Stevie, the more you like women the more you
wish they were better. As Shakespeare says, 'I know that a
woman is a dish for the gods, if the devil dress her not. But,
truly, these same *dash-dash* [I knew he was skipping a naughty
word or so] devils do the gods great harm in their women, for in
every ten that they make, the devils mar five.' That's from
Antony and Cleopatra, so it can't be vulgar."

"Fudge," said Mamma, her mind on what she would wear in
Boston.

Mamma dressed, in her time, with a dash rare in this country
outside a few big cities, but very common in Europe. She
smoked Abdullas then, wore shoes by Raynes when she could
afford them, and there are photographs of her in her high-
waisted *Directoire* dresses that fell with grace right to the floor.
Some had bead fringes, some sequin embroidery, but Mamma
wore them with a skill and charm that overlooked detail. In
black chiffon or velvet she was, Gramp said, "a gasper." She
used coral lipstick and had a peaches-and-cream complexion
that she touched up with a rabbit foot dipped in pale powder.
Harem skirts or the hobble skirts, very tight and with a slit up
one side, became her, with wide, wide hats feathered with para-
dise, osprey, and egret. Long after it was against the law to trap
such birds, Mamma still wore her hats, then somewhat out of
fashion. She favored a low *décolletage;* and in white, pink, or
gray chiffon, she lived in fluted columns of cloth, mixed with
severe tailoring of broadcloth, the tight-fitting toque on her
head trimmed with uncurled heron feathers, *and* wearing spats!

This may sound odd, but the result, as a photograph shows, was something remarkable. Mamma liked to walk into a party wearing her crimson velvet turban sprouting a tall egret. Her world changed: she went into velvet tam-o-shanters, carried lace umbrellas, and wore wide straw brims with ribbons and roses and sheaves of golden and silver wheat.

Later, after the war of 1914–1918, she took to low-hipped tube dresses, tight-fitting felt head helmets, shingled her hair in the fashionable bob, showed her legs, her wonderful slim legs, in sheer silk under short skirts. But she felt grace and beauty were passing out of women's clothes. She never wore riding breeches in town, but stuck to the boots and riding skirt. In the end, after twenty years of dressing well and in fashion, hard times came. My father failed in many ventures, and she wore what she had, or could get. She remained neat and trim, she never put on weight; but after 1920 the full glow was out of her and her clothes.

I remember Boston on that visit, where we stayed with someone Gramp called Spike, as a city of glazed cupolas and polite minds. Spike's grandfather had entertained Ivan Sergyee-vich Turgenev, his father had known Emerson, and one of his cousins had been shot at the personal order of Villa himself. Spike was Boston—that part of Boston that liked the occult and mystic branches of polite arts or translations of bearded writers.

The thing about Boston I remember is the pride they all had, in the right part of the town, in having had a great-grandfather. Gramp would say, dead-pan, "So few of us have, and almost none of us have him painted in oils and hanging next to a per-sonal letter from Lowell asking if the fall apples had all been picked yet. How proud a leathery nonagenarian can be of a letter like that, the ink fading away."

And family heirlooms—what had we in our house but the kewpie doll my uncle won at Coney Island pitching rings in 1917, just before he left for France to get his head blown off, and pictures of my mother as a Gibson girl, very tiny, very beautiful, by John Singer Sargent? Boston had a lot of things. Gramp explained to me its merchants once ruled the land, and its clipper ships went to China for tea and broke records, and its best families took shares in blackbirding, growing rich on black-slave stealing (and later these same shareholders, of course, said you can't keep slaves—in Virginia). "And today about all the old families do is sit among the trustees of the old Boston Library and think everyone a damn poltroon who hasn't old tea-pots with a crest."

Spike told Gramp, "Henry and Edith have written some novels with such a delicate pen-prick, with such a neat irony. But I see little of their dainty ghost world of frumps. Boston is more real, more full of pride, rotting family trees and poor old ladies dreaming of lovers that never come. It's fine to write of moldy traditions, but there must also be a little of the honest love, the great kindness for people."

We were crossing Park Street near Bullfinch's State House, and near the Union Club, Spike pointed to a modern firm.

"They have replaced Ticknor and Fields, who first published Emerson and Thoreau."

"And Mark Twain and Stephen Crane and Frank Norris and Melville?" Gramp asked.

"No. They had to go to New York."

I liked Pinckney Street, which looked down Beacon Hill to the Charles River for mercy, and I didn't care much for Louisburg Square, where the last aristocratic members of stale great names crept behind lowered curtains and wondered how much of the world actually wasn't part of Boston. Even as a boy I felt this.

Gramp took us into one of these houses. It smelled of drains, old *Harper's Weeklies,* and disheveled potted plants "that hadn't seen a garden since Longfellow dropped in for tea." There was a picture of a yard of yellow lilies and green-berried sumac and honeysuckles, and also the shapes of old ladies who still used lilac powder and lavender-scented pillowcases and dressed in watered silk and read old copies of books published, Gramp said, "when Henry James was knocking them dead in a polite way with his prose and his ideas, and indigo and cedar birds and jugs of blackstrap still were seen on hayfields near Boston."

I sat and observed. Everything was black walnut—Victorian Boston in period—and the landscape paintings were in heavy gilt frames, and there were moths in the chairs and most of the good family pictures had been sold for thin slices of bread and butter and weak tea without lemon, served with a blue milk, most likely from well-bred cows, I suspected, with the proper-colored blood in their veins.

It was good to get out again and cross the Common and then walk to State Street, where the polite Boston banker in bowler hat and furled umbrella passed or stood at an old desk smoking a good cigar, remembering, Gramp said, "the killings in rail-road bonds and the good things in steel when copper paid twenty per cent and a gentleman could live on his clippings and think of the sweet bucolic landscapes and woodchucks of his prep-school days."

Gramp seemed bitter about Boston. Visits with Mamma were not much more fun. Brookline was dead as Egypt and the early mansions were an American Gothic, and of course built by earn-ings in black slaves brought across the sea packed like matches in a Boston ship and sold to cotton planters. But the old energy was gone from Boston's past just as the goldfinches eating thistle seeds, the lichens on old stones, are gone.

"They lack something," said Gramp when I asked about these people. "They lack any energy except when they come out of their coma now and again to snub someone who doesn't speak like a Harvard man. Let them rest, these people, in their scent of fennel and sweet cicely. They are tired, Stevie, and the Irish have them well in hand. Rome really rules here, and only the houses and pictures and books are American. Politically, it's all Church and lodges of reactionary politicos—with the gandy-dancers and priests calling the turns. Once this was a race that looked as enduring as an aqueduct. Now it's the outskirts of Dublin."

"Oh, no," I said. "Boston is a good American city."

"Let's have that Turkish bath," Gramp said.

It was my first Turkish bath. Happy, steamy, not too busy— very warm. Fat men with scars of belts on their naked, hairy bellies stood around on their toes smoking cigars. Two cinnamon-colored men called *Griks* hammered at a little man and then flogged him with wet leaves; then they stood him up in a corner and turned ice water on him, and when he fell over they stood him up again and began to throw a large basketball into his stomach.

Wearing a towel, I fell asleep in the steam and dreamed I was in an oven being roasted as a turkey.

The next day we left for Pittsfield. It would only be proper and dramatic if I could say that we ended our great trip across and back over the United States the way we started it, by car. But that was not to be so. We were headed for the Pittsfield farm where the family had taken over Gramp's big white house overlooking one of the Indian-named lakes. But the truth is the car died in Concord in the middle of the main street. One moment we were riding along, then suddenly there was a clatter of iron, a scream of tormented metal; something broke, smashed, and ground itself up under us, and the car no longer lived. We got out, steam and sparks coming from the car.

Gramp swore. "What a place to give up its mangy gasoline soul!"

"The shot fired round the world happened here," I said.

Mamma said, "Stevie, stay away, it's going to blow up!"

It looked as if it would, but it didn't. It was pushed down a Concord side street, and a soiled garageman came over and said, after looking, feeling, and testing with his wrench, "She's dead as a doornail."

"What happened?" asked Gramp.

"Well, I think first off the main bearings froze, then the driving shaft broke and kicked back and chewed up the driving gears; also it may have cracked the engine block. Whatever it was started it, you got a mighty mess of junk, that's all."

"Can you repair it before morning?" Gramp asked.

"Repair it! Mister, you got one good headlight left. *If* I was to jack *that* up and shove a car under it, you could have it by morning."

Gramp was not a man to waste time on small talk. Like Napoleon he believed in direct action. "What's she worth to you as junk, steel, copper, and brass?"

The man looked at the wreck, kicked at a tire, which at once hissed out air and went flat. "Well, now, ten dollars would be generous."

Gramp said softly, "Twenty dollars and you can show us the way to the railroad station."

"I'm a darn fool," said the man, digging in his pocket for his wallet.

So we came home from the great trip by train, came home tired, dusty, carrying our small luggage. The station at Pittsfield was, as I remember it, red brick. And waiting there in the depot (as Joel, the farm's hired hand called it) was Joel himself, collarless as usual, sucking on a corncob pipe. Papa looked dandy in summer linen and a flat straw hat, and an assortment of family, young and old, was standing on the platform as the train pulled in and scattered coal dust over them like a Papal blessing.

Mamma kissed Papa, and Papa shook my hand, as if I were a banker, and said, "My, how brown you all are."

Gramp waved his cane and pushed back a few wet-nosed grandchildren. "There seems to be a lot more kids! How is everyone? Damn it, Joel, stop puffing the horse-leavings you smoke in my face and grab the bags!"

But I could see Gramp was pushing back a tear, and Mamma was weeping into her lace handkerchief, while Papa handed her down to the curb as if she were made of glass. The kids all came

to see my pet hawk Moses sit on my wrist, and I spit skillfully
from between my front teeth, the way I had learned on the
trip. I could see I was impressing the small fry. Everyone said
I was taller and would soon need a shave. We all got into the
carryall, a big fancy carriage Gramp kept on the farm, and the
overflow followed by car.

I was a very young child when I first saw the sugar maples of
New England burn red upon the horizon, the summer I first
came to Pittsfield.

Pittsfield, Gramp explained to me once, was settled in 1743.
It was named after a man of peace, William Pitt, "whose life
was spent mostly in making wars to protect England." Pitt
was popular in New England because he spoke out for the
colonists' rights; his defense of them made him an American
hero.

Gramp's farm was on the edge of town, good rolling acres,
mostly in hay, lots of cows, plenty of soft-lofting hills, and behind us were the dark Berkshire mountains over which summer
storms came running, forks of lightning hanging from their
black mouths.

Several dogs, tails high, ran down to greet us as we drove up,
and the cook came out, and several more sons, daughters-in-
law, and naturally children. Gramp swung his cane at the dogs,
patted a child here and there, and looked over the farm, shading his eyes.

"Looks damn good. Good to be home."

Lunch was served on the sunny porch. And the cook had
"done herself proud," as Gramp expressed it, as he patted her
on the rump and told her of the damned fried chicken of the
South. Mamma and Papa sat together, and Mamma looked
around the table, trapped by family but glad to be back, I
think, and trying not to peer into the future. I had locked
Moses in the springhouse, for he had bitten a few small children, and, while I didn't mind, their mothers objected on the

ground that they didn't raise babies to serve as hawk meat.

I liked Pittsfield best on a Saturday afternoon, when the sun was not too hot, when the great elms were stirring a light breeze, and the whole countryside was being sucked into town by buggy and motorcar, everyone coming to town to shop, get his hair cut, see a movie, enjoy a ball game, drink a few beers, pitch some horseshoes, spark the girls, watch the trains pass to Albany and New York in one direction, or to Boston in the other. The young fry dreamed of eating off white tablecloths and being served fancy food by black men in crisp linen, and then they wandered from the station to drink their pops and dance the same steps they did in Broken Arrow, Ohio, or West Whisper, Texas.

As night fell, the kids, sticky with popcorn, were parked in the wagons or cars, the family dog told to stay put, and the folk went to eat a New England boiled dinner or tried the lobsters and clams brought in by truck from the seaports. Around eleven everyone had gone home, tired, happy, and loaded with packages, except for a few loyal members of the taproom set, who, under old prints of old heroes and battles or the stern features of New Englanders now dead, smoked or had their glass refilled. By midnight one could walk the old streets past the shapes of new glass and wood and pick out here and there the old buildings still standing: *Est. 1817, Built by Amos King and God 1876, Cornerstone Laid 1902,* A.D.

Gramp and I spent a lot of time on the lakes that make Pittsfield almost a small inland harbor. Lake Pontoosuc, named for some Indian now forgotten, can get wild and choppy in a wind. Lake Onota, which means Lake of the White Deer, is calmer, and above it stands Camp Winadu, where I have often awakened at dawn and seen the mist walking the waters and smelled the morning eggs cooking.

Gramp and I would come to Pittsfield in the winter when the blue sky hung like a lead bowl over the freezing world and bare trees, and the roads were packed hard. Breath steamed from faces bundled into wool, and there was a tingle in the crisp air that sledding and skating and skiing only made stronger.

In the spring Gramp's land dripped and drained, the fields turned slowly green, the apple trees put out buds and blossoms, and everything came awake. Calves, colts, and lambs appeared; the young pigs snorted and ate. The farmer plowed and sowed. The tractors walked quickly over the ridges and across the fields. The horses frisked in the meadow and kicked their heels.

Summer was hot, and the lofting distances cleared up. The summer rains and the summer storms came. Lightning scarred the hills, and it was good to sit with Gramp under canvas or a roof and hear the rain bang against timbers or cloth.

Fall came with a roar; the dying leaves turned gold and orange, scarlet and Chinese red. Gramp's fruit fell, the cider mills turned, and there were still a few brave people who tapped the sugar maple and boiled the sap down to the brown lumpy sweetness of maple sugar.

Winter wore white, and in the fury of the wind the blinding walls of snow took over. After a storm the air was crystal clear, the world shod in white. The trees were covered with icy jewels. The snow was packed hard, and the horse was harnessed to Gramp's old sled and went clopping around, passed by cars wearing clanging chains. The apples were stored, the houses made weather-tight, and "punkin" pie was a staple dish.

Pittsfield's factory whistles tooted, and in the hotels I visited with Gramp they served Boston clam chowder in big steaming bowls to put vigor and vitality into a man.

In a way, after our big trip, it was the summer of my boyhood. Gramp wouldn't travel much any more. He was really old and he spent a lot of time in his big oak bed, reading his favorite books, smoking his cigars, getting up at noon if he felt like it, or just resting all day in bed, banging on the floor with his cane for attention. "Damn it, a man could die up here and those waltz fiends downstairs would just go on winding up records and filling their gut with Rhine wine and seltzer. Anybody alive down there? *Any* sign of life below?"

I spent a lot of time with him, and he talked to me of lots of things I didn't understand very well then, and which I no longer remember. I think he wanted to leave something of himself in me, and in the end I think he decided it couldn't be done; that what we can pass on is only the face and features of the tribe, the genes and colors of a clan, but in the end every man makes for himself the fullness and wisdom, or the failure or the nonsense that is his time on earth. So he just read his old classics and grinned at me, the thinning old man in the big wide bed, and I lit his cigars and smuggled in his whisky from the local bootlegger.

In a way he was no longer the Gramp who had been on the trip with us. The energy came back into him for only a little while now; the bones were thrusting sharper through the paling shiny skin. The hand shook when he broke the band on his cigars; the eyes were often half-glazed as he looked from his pillows through the small glass windowpanes out on the summer haying. Perhaps he wondered how much longer he could see his own fields.

Mamma and Papa often sat close together, figuring on bits of paper the future, thinking and planning in real estate their hopes, hopes that would never mature and would leave them very little in the end but themselves.

Gramp's birthday was an event that summer. The cook did herself up brown in much fancy cooking. Gramp came downstairs close-shaved, with wing collar and his best cravat with the good black pearl. And he expressed himself about life, the kids, the family—*the* family—the farm, and the falling off in the flavor of cigars.

There were no candles in the Kentucky Pecan Bourbon Cake, but I had lettered on it in colored icing: *Happy Birthday Gramp,*

Oh You Kid. It seemed clever at the time. I had drawn with the same icing a picture of our car and the three of us in it (it was a ten-pound cake) and added: *Excuse Our Dust!*

Gramp cried like a baby and had to be punched on the back when he choked up on a bit of cake. He had to make everybody the genuine Ramos Gin Fizz he had learned to make in New Orleans with the real orange flower water, the powdered sugar, and the rich cream. Everyone said it was a wonderful birthday and we all guessed at how old Gramp really was. He was cursing again and shaky, and Papa and I took him up and put him to bed. I lit his cigar and he looked at me and wiped his eyes and leaned back on the pillows.

"*Senectus ipsa est morbus,*" he said. "It's been a fine day. Even if age with stealing steps has clawed me. I think I'll rest now."

Papa took away the cigar and I pulled out the extra pillows from under his head, and we left him sleeping, after lowering the shades to make a midday twilight in the room.

I went out, got my hawk Moses from the barn, and went with him to the top of the big green hill behind the farm. The hawk had grown to maturity and was restless. Mormon, the farm tomcat, had tried to get him several times and retreated after each attack with a scarred nose. Mormon would not give up and he watched the hawk on his perch for hours; the cat, his face torn, his fur damaged by the hawk's claws, waited for the moment when the jewel-eyed bird would be off his guard.

The hawk was no longer tame. He had grown to be a heavy golden bird, his eyes brighter, the great wing feathers mottled and powered by steel muscles. He would beat me black and blue with his blows. He sank his claws into whatever gloves I wore. He would let me handle him, but if I made a false move he would punish me and then sit looking at me like something that knew its full proud worth.

In a way the hawk had brought me into a fuller understanding of life, had stripped from me the illusions, the softness, many of the dreams of children. Life was cruel and tearing, he said to me. But in everything there is beauty, in everything there is a vital life force. Much was not worth bothering with, the hawk said; one must ignore, forget, push aside the soft, the easy, and the dull. One waited for the glorious golden moment of striking, of attaining, of creating the perfect gesture, line, style. The hawk also said that in life style was all, one lived a style of dignity and courage; the rest was dust.

I took off Moses' hood. I untied the leash from his leg. I lifted him high in the air and then I flung him hard as I could off into space. He went high, then came down and circled. I waved him off again. Twice more the hawk came close and I waved him off. Then he spread his wings wide. He shot off into space, pumping himself into the sky. When he was a dot under the crayon-blue vault, I knew I would never see Moses again. I walked slowly down to the farm and I knew I would never see my childhood again either. I had hung the child on the hawk and set it free.

PITTSFIELD FIDDLER

ABOUT THE AUTHOR

STEPHEN LONGSTREET'S *widely diversified career as artist, author, critic, and playwright has included writing and drawing for such magazines as* The New Yorker, The Saturday Evening Post, *and* Collier's, *the publication of several novels, among them* The Pedlocks, *already on its way to become a modern classic in its field, and* The Lion at Morning.

He has been active on the editorial staff of Time *and* The Saturday Review *and in the production of plays and motion pictures, and has had a number of one-man shows of his paintings. In 1948 he received the* Billboard *Award for the best play of the year*, High Button Shoes, *and the* Photoplay *Gold Medal Gallup Poll Award for the most popular picture of the year*, The Jolson Story. *He has received, too, many important awards for his paintings.*

Mr. Longstreet is an avid world traveler, and has recorded some of his adventures in a best seller, The World Revisited. *In addition, he acts as a literary critic for the Los Angeles* Free Press.

The Longstreets live in Beverly Hills. His wife is active in politics and conducts the popular television program "Cavalcade of Records," his daughter is at college, and his son is a high-school basketball star. Their cat, Red Prince, is a well-known motion-picture actor.